Suffragettes
of Kent

Suffragettes
of Kent

Jennifer Godfrey

Let your voices be heard !
J. Godfrey
29/9/19.

PEN & SWORD
HISTORY

AN IMPRINT OF PEN & SWORD BOOKS LTD.
YORKSHIRE – PHILADELPHIA

First published in Great Britain in 2019 by
Pen & Sword Military
An imprint of
Pen & Sword Books Ltd
Yorkshire – Philadelphia

Copyright © Jennifer Godfrey, 2019

ISBN 978 1 52672 3 512

The right of Jennifer Godfrey to be identified as Author of this
work has been asserted by her in accordance with the Copyright,
Designs and Patents Act 1988.

A CIP catalogue record for this book is
available from the British Library.

Printed and bound in England by TJ International, Padstow, Cornwall

Pen & Sword Books Limited incorporates the imprints of Atlas, Archaeology,
Aviation, Discovery, Family History, Fiction, History, Maritime, Military,
Military Classics, Politics, Select, Transport, True Crime, Air World,
Frontline Publishing, Leo Cooper, Remember When, Seaforth Publishing,
The Praetorian Press, Wharncliffe Local History, Wharncliffe Transport,
Wharncliffe True Crime and White Owl.

For a complete list of Pen & Sword titles please contact

PEN & SWORD BOOKS LIMITED
47 Church Street, Barnsley, South Yorkshire, S70 2AS, England
E-mail: enquiries@pen-and-sword.co.uk
Website: www.pen-and-sword.co.uk

Or

PEN AND SWORD BOOKS
1950 Lawrence Rd, Havertown, PA 19083, USA
E-mail: Uspen-and-sword@casematepublishers.com
Website: www.penandswordbooks.com

Contents

Preface

In the words of Millicent Garrett Fawcett, speaking at a 1907 Kent meeting, was it just quiet 'spade work'[1] that took place for women's suffrage in the county affectionately referred to as 'the Garden of England'? Or was there more extensive and dramatic

Elliott & Fry.

Mrs. Henry Fawcett, LL.D.
President of the National Union.

Portrait of Millicent Garrett Fawcett.
© LSE Women's Library collection

action within Kent that helped shape the women's suffrage movement and national political landscape?

This book aims to answer these questions and give an overview of and insight into the very many women's suffrage stories from the county of Kent.

Introduction

This book includes details of the involvement of Kentish people in the women's suffrage movement. The research has revealed a vast array of stories, journeys and in some cases mere snippets of information about the campaigning in the county of Kent and by people from Kent. Many warrant a book dedicated to them alone. This book has therefore developed into an introduction to some of the many strands of the campaigning in Kent and by those from Kent. The author has been greatly inspired by the renowned suffrage movement researcher and author Elizabeth Crawford and her words: 'I trust that I have demonstrated that such a lack of material should not preclude any attempt to build up a picture of a life of involvement.'[1]

Likewise, this book cannot have reached all aspects of Kent's contribution to the suffrage movement. It is also hoped that this collection of accounts of journeys will inspire further local and regional studies as there are so many fascinating stories waiting to be discovered, shared and celebrated. The author would love to hear from anyone with further information and insights and can be contacted via email at jgodfrey@btinternet.com

Although mainly in chronological order, this book does begin with a chapter set predominantly in 1912. While researching, the author discovered reference to a Kent woman's arrest in London in 1912 and pursued it further. This led to correspondence and a meeting with some of her descendants, including her granddaughters Eileen Bridge and Tricia Radley; great-granddaughter Sandra Radley; great-niece Margaret Ayres and great-great-niece Gill Rose. They have kindly provided information and family photographs to enhance the telling of what is known of her story. Chapter 1 of the book is therefore dedicated to Ethel Violet Baldock, an as yet uncelebrated Kent suffragette.

Portrait of Ethel Violet Baldock
© Ethel Baldock's family

Glossary

This book is called *Suffragettes of Kent* and so it seems important to discuss the terms 'suffragette' and 'suffragist'. Some have argued that they are interchangeable. However, the research undertaken for this book revealed that there is a difference. It is put rather nicely in this extract from an East Kent newspaper published in July 1913 referring to the Kentish Pilgrimage to London organized by the 'constitutional' National Union of Women's Suffrage Societies (NUWSS):

> There are so many different societies whose object is to secure the vote for women, and there is so much misapprehension on the subject, that it is just as well that the facts should be set out as clearly as possible [referring to NUWSS leaflet used in the Kentish pilgrimage July 1913]. In regard to the term suffragette and suffragist, it is not generally understood that they are quite distinct. I have been surprised to find them regarded, even in otherwise well-informed quarters, as meaning one and the same thing, whereas, of course, the women suffragists are the law-abiding advocates of female enfranchisement, whilst the suffragettes are the militants and law-breakers.[1]

Despite its title, in this book you will find the stories of 'suffragettes' and 'suffragists'. There are also 'vitrifragists'[2] or 'glass-breakers', terms used by a newspaper following the March 1912 window-smashing campaign to describe those women arrested for breaking windows. Then there are the 'female hooligans' and 'shrieking sisterhood'[3] that were described in a local West Kent newspaper, and 'sweet girl graduates'[4] and 'blue stockings'[5] mentioned in an East Kent publication. A phrase that seemingly did not catch on, even in Kent from where it originated, was 'Lympne-pets'.[6] This was used as reference to the three suffragettes that climbed the walls of Lympne Castle in Kent to disturb the dining Prime Minister Mr. Asquith. The Lympne inhabitants were keen to forget about this incident, so it appears that the term did not appear after this first use. Another play on the word 'suffragette' was 'outragette'[7] used in 1913 to describe those militant society members making bombs and committing arson.

The following is an alphabetical list of acronyms/ abbreviations used:

AFL: Actresses' Franchise League
MLWS: Men's League for Women's Suffrage
MPU: Men's Political Union
NCS: National Constitutional Society
NUSEC: National Union of Societies for Equal Citizenship
NUWSS: National Union of Women's Suffrage Societies
WFL: Women's Freedom League
WSPU: Women's Social and Political Union
WTRL: Women's Tax Resistance League

CHAPTER ONE

Ethel Violet Baldock: A 'Vitrifragist' or 'Glass-Breaker' (1893–1939)

Ethel Violet Baldock was arrested in March 1912 for breaking a window of a commercial building in London. She was a 'vitrifragist'[1] or 'glass-breaker', part of the leading militant organization WSPU's campaign at the time. As this account reveals, only parts of Ethel's life and suffragette story are known. Her descendants still have Ethel's christening gown and stories from periods of her life but none specifically of her time as a suffragette. Newspaper reports tell of her involvement in the glass-breaking. Archive material reveals when she was arrested, what she was charged with and where she was imprisoned. The extent of Ethel's involvement with any suffrage activity or organization remains unknown. However, this lack of material has not precluded the inclusion of a 'picture of a life of involvement'.[2]

Ethel was born in Gravesend, Kent in 1893 to Frances Elizabeth and Samuel Baldock. She was their fifth daughter, one of eight children (six girls and two boys). Samuel was a builder, not a labourer. He had standing in the community. Samuel paid a penny a week at St Michael's School in Maidstone for the education of his children. They had slates and were taught to recite poems. He cared deeply for his children and had an older spinster sister that would help him find his daughters their service positions, making sure they were well looked after. He never wanted his children to work in factories.[3]

Despite this oral account provided by Ethel's great-niece about Samuel's occupation, in the 1901 census he is listed as a 'bricklayer'.

Ethel's younger sister, Ellen Harriet, aged 7 years and 10 months, died on 5 January 1899 and her mother, aged only 36, died on 4 May 1899 from meningitis. In the photograph of Ethel at about 8 years old, she is wearing dark mourning clothes on account of these deaths.

Ethel aged about 8 years old, wearing dark mourning clothes on account of the death of her mother and younger sister
© Ethel Baldock's family

Following her mother's death, her father Samuel employed a housekeeper, Martha Nelson, who he then married. Martha Baldock (née Nelson) had a daughter, May C. Nelson, who was about three years older than Ethel. From the account given by Ethel's great-niece, it would seem that Mrs. Martha Baldock was unkind to Samuel's children, treating them harshly and sending them into service at the age of 12.

In 1909, a postcard was sent by Ethel, then aged approximately 16, to her older sister Frances at 43 Mount Pleasant Road in Tunbridge Wells (the home of the sherry manufacturer Mrs. Byass). Frances was in service in the Byass' household at this time. The postcard was postmarked 'Broadstairs Station 9pm De[cember] 24 [19]09 Kent'. It read: 'Dear Fannie, Just a few lines to wish you many happy

Christmas & Bright and Prosperous new year. Pleased to hear I shall soon have my fun. Had a letter from [....] this morning. Love from Ethel.'

Given the late posting time on Christmas Eve, it seems likely that Ethel was in service in Broadstairs and possibly travelling elsewhere for her time off at Christmas.

In the 1911 census, Ethel, then aged 18, is recorded as working as a hotel housemaid and waitress. The name of the hotel is unknown. She lived at 40 Little Mount Sion, Tunbridge Wells with her eldest sister Florence Mabel and Florence's husband, Harry Richard Hollingdale, a butcher. The other two residents were male boarders: a bookmaker and a chauffeur. In 1911 Ethel's sister Emma got married but Ethel did not attend the wedding. This may have been because she was unable to get time off from work as it was usual to only get one day off per month. However, as it was only one year before Ethel was arrested in London, it does sow the seed of curiosity about her absence being linked to her involvement in the suffrage movement and her family's disapproval of it.

Insights into Ethel's character have been obtained from accounts given by her granddaughters from the stories they were told by their father, Ethel's son Donald. Ethel's granddaughters Eileen and Tricia never met their grandmother. Donald had been told that his mother had given birth to a daughter before he was born, but that she was stillborn. Medical advisers apparently told Ethel to give birth to Donald in London and, following his birth, not to have any more children. Ethel was a very heavy smoker and very superstitious. Every new moon, she would turn coins over. She would not allow new shoes on a table and no umbrellas were to be put up inside the

Ethel pre World War One
© Ethel Baldock's family.

house. She frequently disagreed with other people, including her employers. Donald often spoke of how Ethel's disagreements and dismissals from jobs meant that they had to leave their homes quickly (sometimes during the night) to start over somewhere else. Ethel was apparently very proud of her suffrage work and had a certificate on the wall and a pin badge. However, following Ethel's death in 1939 these items were disposed of by her husband, Arthur Hodge.

Archive material reveals that Ethel was arrested in March 1912 for her part in the WSPU campaign to break windows in London, and was held on remand in Holloway for twenty-six days awaiting trial. On Saturday, 2 March 1912, *The Times* reported:

> The militant section of the women's suffrage party embarked yesterday evening on an unprecedented campaign of wanton destruction of property in the West-end of London...some hundreds of women sallied forth carrying large muffs in which hammers were concealed, and at a given moment, according, it is believed, to a preconcerted signal, they went up to the plate-glass windows of various shops and deliberately smashed them with the hammers. The destruction done was immense. Along the Strand, in Cockspur-street, in the Haymarket, and Piccadilly, in Coventry-street, in Regent-street, in part of Oxford-street and in Bond-street, many of the most conspicuous houses of business were attacked in this fashion.

The same newspaper article reported that 121 women had been arrested in connection with this campaign on Friday, 1 March 1912, including Mrs. Pankhurst.

In *The Times* of Wednesday, 6 March 1912 it was reported that a further sixty-five or seventy defendants were arrested for window-breaking on the evening of Monday, 4 March 1912. Those

> charged with committing wilful damage on Monday night were then brought before the magistrate in batches

Anti-suffrage comic card depicts a suffragette wearing a green hat, purple coat and white spats, wielding a hammer and smashing a department store window, printed inscription front: 'The suffragettes get wilder daily & smash shop windows oh! So gaily', 'Reg Carter'
© LSE Women's Library collection

of eight and were remanded until Saturday. They were allowed bail in their own recognisanzes in £200 and two sureties in £100 each, but most of the women expressed their intention of remaining in prison.[4]

A date of arrest for Ethel is not specifically recorded. However, archived material[5] does refer to her being arrested and held on

Photograph, printed, paper, monochrome, a large group of women being controlled by police waiting outside Bow Street Magistrates' Court for women to be released. Printed inscription on reverse 'Copyright. Newspaper Illustrations Limited. 161A Strand' Dated 1908 - 1912 so could have been during window smashing campaign in 1912
© LSE Women's Library collection

remand in Holloway for 26 days. Given this and the fact that Ethel's trial and release from prison took place on 27 March, it seems she was arrested on 1 March 1912. As Ethel was a young 20-year-old lady's maid,[6] the £100 or £200 bail surely would have been out of reach for her or her family. It would seem that Ethel would have been grateful for such a surety as, according to the *Birmingham Daily Gazette* of Monday, 11 March 1912, both Ethel and her co-defendant, Violet Bland, offered to pay the £10 damages but this was refused at the Bow Street Police Courts (on 9 March 1912) and they were committed to trial by the magistrates.

From archived Home Office records[7] a report made by the governor of Holloway Prison, James Scott, on Sunday, 3 March 1912, reveals that 114 of the suffragette prisoners 'were received last night (96 remanded; 10 Committed to the County of London Sessions; and 6 Convicted).' If, as is suspected, Ethel was one of these suffragette prisoners arrested following the disturbances on Friday, 1 March, an account is given in the same report by James Scott of their behaviour and treatment. He wrote:

This morning [Sunday, 3 March 1912], when the remanded prisoners were unlocked for exercise they demanded to see Mrs. Pankhurst. They were informed that she was in another class, being convicted, and would exercise at another time. They refused to go to exercise, or to return to their cells until they saw her. They linked arms, shouted, and made a disturbance. I gave instructions that they should be told that they must cease the disturbance, and return to their cells, or they would be put back forcibly. They refused to go to their cells, so, after allowing them a reasonable time for consideration, I sent female officers to put them back, which they did. Some of the prisoners resisted strongly and got their clothing torn. I have not heard of any injury of consequence either to officers or the [illegible as crossed through]. The matron and I consider that the Officers discharged this disagreeable duty well, and allowed much discretion and forbearance. Mrs. Pankhurst demanded to see me, and told the Matron, 'I gave the Governor a hint yesterday that we should have a talk, and try to come to terms.' As there could be no question about 'coming to terms' with her about Prison rules and discipline, I refused to see her, and did not do so. After the prisoners were put back in their cells, they committed a great deal of damage, and made a great disturbance by knocking on their cell doors, &c. They have threatened a 'hunger-strike', but I cannot speak definitely as to this yet. As a result of the disturbance, the morning Service in the Chapel could not be held. The ordinary prisoners have behaved well. The great majority of them do not appear to be at all in favour of the Suffragettes.

In Holloway at this time, being 'forcibly fed twice daily, as she obstinately refuses to take food'[8] was Emily Wilding Davison. It is unlikely that Ethel would have seen or met with Emily during her short imprisonment. However, it is likely, especially with Mrs. Emmeline Pankhurst there, that word of mouth provided Ethel with some knowledge of high-profile prisoners and of force-feeding, so providing an insight into the world in which she had arrived. For a 20-year-old lady's maid from Tunbridge Wells in Kent with seemingly no prior experience of such matters, this must have made an impact.

Ethel and Violet Bland were arrested for wilful damage. The records at The National Archives[9] confirm that Ethel and Violet were arrested in March 1912 (specific date not provided) for wilful damage and state that they appeared before Bow Street Police Court on Saturday, 9 March 1912 and were committed to trial on 26 March 1912 (although the record of the trial is dated 27 March 1912). *The Times* newspaper report of Monday, 11 March 1912 states that Ethel and Violet were accused of breaking windows at 1 Northumberland Avenue, London. The record of Ethel's and Violet's trial outcome (Wednesday, 27 March 1912) stipulates the particulars of their offence as 'Maliciously damaging one plate glass window, the property of the Commercial Cable Company, to the amount of £10.'[10] On Saturday, 9 March, Magistrate Mr. Curtis Bennett heard 'upwards of fifty cases. Nearly all the women told the magistrate that their conduct was a result of Mr. Hobhouse's speech at Bristol, where he referred to the agitations that led to the burning of Nottingham Castle and pulling down the Hyde Park railings.'[11] At this hearing, Violet 'said she was a law-abiding citizen. She had paid rates and taxes to the tune of nearly £1 a week for 20 years, and had been working for her citizenship for a number of years.' She said that 'she did the act in response to a challenge by a member of the Government.'[12] The member of the government was a Mr. C.E.H. Hobhouse, MP for Bristol and strongly anti-suffrage. He 'was absolutely opposed to votes for women and he declined to answer any questions on the subject'[13] wherever he went. Suffragettes interrupted him regularly in 1911 and 1912 to challenge his views and many were roughly removed from the meeting rooms and buildings. Well-known women's suffrage activist Louisa Garrett Anderson had pleaded guilty to causing window damage (with a stone) to 47 Rutland Gate, the home of Mr. George Fuller. She had believed this was the home of Mr. Hobhouse. She reasoned that

> It was done as a political protest, and in reply largely to a speech made by Mr. Hobhouse some time ago, in which he did not consider that the Suffrage agitation was supported by popular feeling, because women were not doing the damage to property similar to that committed by men in 1832 in the Reform riots.[14]

No record has been found to date of what, if anything, Ethel said at her trial, and her involvement in women's suffrage and motivation to go to London in March 1912 and protest in this way are not clear. However, it may be that she too was

Louisa Garrett Anderson with William and Garrett, c. 1915
© LSE Women's Library collection

motivated by Mr. Hobhouse's speeches. This seems possible as on 24 January 1912, Mr. Hobhouse visited Ethel's home town, Tunbridge Wells, to speak to the League of Young Liberals and 300 women are known to have attended. Ethel may have heard this speech or at least heard about it. It was reported that

> Women were only admitted by ticket and were required to sign pledges not to give them to Suffragettes. One lady who was suspected of being a Suffragette had her ticket inspected seven times and the number of her seat was written upon it by a steward who came to look at her at intervals. Great precautions were taken, and the Hall was searched even to the cellars. On his arrival Mr. Hobhouse was questioned by a WSPU member about the Referendum, and on leaving he hurried to his car amid a chorus of 'No Manhood Suffrage for us', 'Votes for Women', 'Put it in the Bill', 'Down with the Government'. No hostility was shown to the women by the crowd and many departed calling out: 'Wish you luck.'[15]

Challenging this *Votes for Women* account was Frank B. Bending, the Hon. Secretary of the Tunbridge Wells Branch of the League of Young Liberals (of 40 Napier Street, Tunbridge Wells). His letter was published in *Votes for Women* on 16 February 1912 and in it he said that 'Women were admitted by invitation and ticket only, but they are not required to sign any pledge whatever. There were at least 300 women at the meeting.'[16]

Frank B. Bending also refuted the account of the women chanting as Mr. A. Paget Hedges (Member of Parliament for Tonbridge) and Mr. Hobhouse left. He wrote:

> Mr. A.P. Hedges and Mr. Hobhouse left together, and a large crowd waited, and gave them a magnificent 'send off'. As the car moved off four women crept up to the edge of the crowd and presumably said the 'inspiring' and 'damaging' words which one of them must certainly have reported to you, for their nearest neighbour could

not have heard a sound in the tremendous cheering
which was going on, and which continued until the car
was out of sight. A little later I saw three of the ladies
talking together a few yards from the hall and looking
very disconsolate, and well they might for they had
fortunately absolutely failed to 'demonstrate' in their
now well-known manner, either inside or outside the
hall![17]

All reports of the two March evenings of window-breaking
suggest that repairs cost many thousands of pounds. The press
reports of the subsequent hearings and trials told of some
repentant defendants offering to pay for the damage they'd
caused. For example, at the Bow Street Police Court hearing
at which Ethel and Violet appeared (Saturday, 9 March 1912),
an elderly widow was repentant and asked for the magistrate
to impose a fine instead of imprisonment but she, like many,
was sentenced to two months' hard labour. A barrister who
represented three other women charged with breaking two
panes of glass offered by way of defence that 'they had been
carried along by the speeches they had listened to'[18] but all
three women were sentenced to two months' hard labour.
Ethel and Violet were committed to the County of London
Sessions for trial at this hearing. No report is made of any
requests, pleas, comments or reactions that they may have
made to this. They were returned to Holloway Prison for a
further eighteen days.

Meanwhile, and seemingly in line with the tough sentences
being given to suffragette defendants, critics of the attack were
disapproving of the disturbances and there was talk of 'a few
misguided women carried away by an excess of zeal for their
cause'[19] and how this should result in meetings in support of
women's suffrage being postponed. The *Birmingham Gazette &
Express* of Monday, 11 March 1912 reported that Ethel and
Violet had been committed to trial and that Miss Christabel
Pankhurst had not yet been found. In its report, the newspaper
reproduced the wording of a leaflet that had reportedly been

Window Smashing Campaign
© *LSE Women's Library collection*

written by Miss Christabel Pankhurst about the disturbances and distributed on Saturday, 2 March 1912. It read as follows:

Broken Windows

Every step in the militant campaign, including the first, has provoked at the moment when it was made a new outburst of censure. For practical reasons, it is impossible for us to regret this. It is part of the effect of militancy that it shall excite regret and consternation. Our very definite purpose is to create an intolerable situation for the Government, and, if need be, for the public as a whole.

The attack – not indeed a very serious one, but still an attack on private property – is the latest subject of censure. 'Government property,' say the critics, 'you are justified in attacking, but not private property.' Militant suffragists would, of course, be glad if an attack on Government property were sufficient to attain their purpose.

They would have been yet more glad if the eventless militant action of the earlier days had sufficed. But the present policy of the Government proves that these measures are not powerful enough to produce the effect desired. They have produced only a sham concession to our demand. More drastic measures have been proved to be essential to gain the genuine confession that we seek. That is why private property has now been attacked.

The message of the broken pane is that women are determined that the lives of their sisters shall no longer be broken, and that in future those who have to obey this law shall have a voice in saying what that law shall be.[20]

During Ethel's short imprisonment she would have likely not been allowed visitors. Due to the misconduct of the suffragette prisoners, normal privileges were revoked. There is an abundance of archived material about the social normalities and restrictions applied to young women at this time. These would undoubtedly have touched Ethel's life. Such restrictions may well have motivated Ethel to become involved with the leading militant suffrage organization. One example actually relates to a court hearing for two suffragettes charged with involvement in the same disturbances as Ethel. A woman unknown to these two suffragettes attended to provide sureties for their release. Despite being required for the proceedings, namely to justify the bail on behalf of the suffragettes, she was asked to leave the court. It was reported that

The lady obeyed his worship's order, and later, when she re-entered the Court for the purpose of justifying her bail on behalf of the suffragists, Mr. Fordham smilingly observed that he was quite willing to accept bail for the suffragists, as, from what he had heard was going on in the gaol, he believed that they would be better out. Referring to the exclusion of the lady from the Court, his worship said 'You know, some of the details in these cases are not such as a woman should hear.' The Lady: 'But the men are allowed to remain, and we women are interested in social conditions.' Mr. Fordham (rising with a smile): 'We will not enter upon a discussion on the point, if you please.'[21]

Providing a fascinating insight into the likely experiences, thoughts and emotions of women like Ethel, imprisoned in Holloway Gaol for breaking windows, is a collection of poems. These were written by women held in the gaol during March and April 1912. The Glasgow branch of the WSPU published a collection of poems and the foreword to the collection, entitled *Holloway Jingles*, reads as follows:

Comrades, it is the eve of our parting. Those of us who have had the longest sentences to serve have seen many a farewell waved up towards our cell windows from the great prison gate as time after time it opened for release. The jail yard, too, where we exercise, now seems spacious, though at first it was thronged with our fellow-prisoners. Yet not one of them has really left us. Whenever in thought we re-enter that yard, within its high, grim walls we see each as we knew her there: our revered Leader, Mrs. Pankhurst, courageous, serene, smiling; Dr. Ethel Smyth, joyous and terrific, whirling through a game of rounders with as much intentness as if she were conducting a symphony; Dr. L. Garrett Anderson, in whose eyes gaiety and gravity are never far apart – but we cannot name them all, for there are scores whose brave faces made that yard a pleasant place.

The passing of the weeks was punctuated by the flowers that blossomed in those grim surroundings; sturdy crocuses, then daffodils and tulips, and now the lilacs are in bloom. Always, too, we had the sunshine, for the skies were kind.

And within the walls? Ah! there, too, the love that shines through the sun and the skies and can illume even the prison cell, was round us, and worked through us and miracles were wrought. We have each been witness of some wonder worked by that omniscient love which is the very basis of our movement.

At these words other faces will rise up before the mind's eye, bruised, perhaps degraded, crushed, sullen, sorrowful, sometime beautiful, but always endeared to us by the thought that it is for their sakes we get the strength to carry on this struggle.

In service to you, O sad sisters, in your hideous prison garb, we gain the supremacy of our souls. And 'we need not fear that we can lose anything to the progress of the soul.'

Theresa Gough (Karmie M.T. Kranich)
Holloway Jail, 28 April 1912[22]

Madeleine Caron Rock wrote the following poem:

Before I came to Holloway

Before I came to Holloway,
It was not cold nor illness,
Nor harshness that I feared, oh stay!
It was the deathly stillness.

Inside, it's bang with supper, or
It's dinner or 'your apple';
Or 'pass out, please to exercise',
Or 'pass along to chapel'.

'Tis close your door there', 'pass out, please',
It's clattering with the rations,
'Baths', turning locks, and clinking keys,
And 'any applications?'

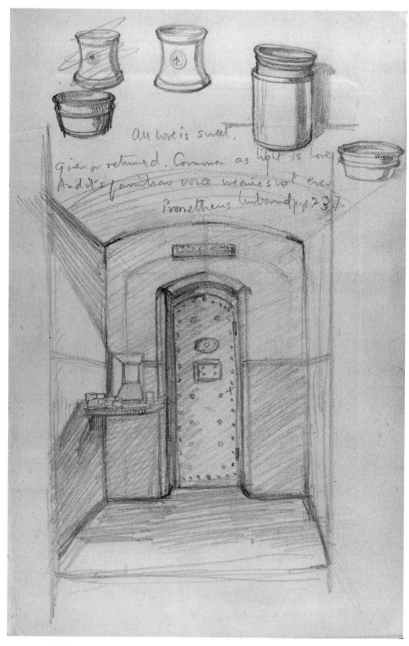

Katie Gliddon's drawing of Holloway cell, March 1912 when Ethel would have been serving time there
© LSE Women's Library collection

All day it's 'have you got those?' Oh,
Bells, banging, people larking;
'You cleaners there', 'Miss So-and-so',
Or 'Are you there, Miss Sharky?'

And if you think you're safely in,
They must have done their caperin',
Then 'governor', 'visiting magistrates',
'The chaplain', 'doctor', 'matron'.

At night, quite late, at nearly six,
'Haven't they finished speaking?'
Your mattress like the whole D x[23]
Is simmering and creaking.

You hear them chopping, stroking too,
And really all the clamour
Breaks up the peace far more than you
Or I, with stone and hammer.

Before I came to Holloway
It was not cold nor illness,
Nor harshness that I feared, oh stay!
It was the deathly stillness.[24]

Katherine M. Richmond wrote the following poem on 6 March 1912 when Ethel was also in the prison:

The beech wood saunters idly to the sea

The beech wood saunters idly to the sea,
Its trunk moss-green and grey, stand clear and bold
From out the blue and dreamy density
Of distance. Chequered here with gold,
And there with primrose stars, the leafy mould
Beneath. Above, the sky's profundity.
In this fair spot that breathes of liberty,
I checked the price at which my own was sold,

The grim walls stand as though they edged away
From the drear yard, but with a dull surprise
Through their barred windows sight the prospect grey,
Reflected from the yearning, human eyes.
'Has God, then, need of prisons?' they would say,
Yet here my soul met freedom in the way,
And saw the heavenly vision in the skies.
If, though we stand alone, in the dark place,
We stay the ladder on its lowest stair;
Then, the dear future daughters of our race
Shall mount, with laughter to the sun and air.
Great God of Freedom, grant to us this grace!
This guerdon of our passion and our prayer![25]

In one of the poems by Kate W. Evans, she refers to suffragettes attending sermons in the 'chapel just to see their friends in F and B and D',[26] confirming that the women were all held in separate blocks of Holloway Gaol. It is unclear in which block Ethel was held.

Another poem refers to the women 'old and young' coming 'From homes both far and near', 'And some from homes where friends beloved no sympathy had shown.' This poem was written by A. Martin and it may be that this was Miss Anna Martin who, the following year (1913), chaired a meeting in Ethel's home town of Tunbridge Wells (see page 186). The poem was untitled and referred to different women from varied backgrounds being 'yet to one cause clung'.[27] As a lady's maid, Ethel was in domestic service and as this poem expresses, would have participated in this WSPU campaign with women of all ages and from many different backgrounds. Violet Bland, with whom Ethel was arrested, was approximately 49 years old[28] at the time of their arrest. She was therefore almost thirty years older than Ethel. Violet was an active WSPU member and had been previously arrested in 1910 on 'Black Friday'[29] but like most at that demonstration, was not imprisoned but discharged. Violet, daughter of William Bland, a labourer, had started her life in Shrewsbury and worked initially as a kitchen maid at Dudmaston Hall. By 1900 she was running a hotel called Henley Grove and a Ladies' College of Domestic Science. At the time of her arrest in 1912, Violet was running a guest house in the West End of London. Another woman from Kent arrested during these March disturbances was Helen MacRae. From Edenbridge, some 13 miles north-west of Tunbridge Wells, Helen had been a member of the NUWSS, but left to join the WSPU and became a member of the East Grinstead (Sussex) Suffrage Society. She had been arrested before and for her part in the breaking of windows she received a four-month prison sentence and was force-fed after going on hunger strike. There is no evidence to suggest that Helen and Ethel knew each other. Helen's signature appears on a handkerchief that was embroidered in Holloway during March 1912. There were more than sixty other women's signatures included, but Ethel's signature is not among them.

Given that Ethel was known for regular disagreements and dismissals from employers, it is not surprising that she didn't receive bail with her employer providing surety. It's also highly

Roll of Honour Suffragette Prisoners 1905 to 1914 front cover
© *LSE Women's Library collection*

Roll of Honour Suffragette Prisoners 1905 to 1914 includes name of 'Ethel Baldock'
© *LSE Women's Library collection*

probable that having missed twenty-six days' work, she would have been dismissed from her employment again. This remains unknown, as does the reaction of her family to any news of her imprisonment.

While Ethel and the other suffragettes remained in prison, there was continued debate about their actions and the whole question of votes for women.

The WFL published a full manifesto about their reasons for refraining from militant action. It referred to the second reading of the Conciliation Bill due on 22 March and called for a truce in militant action. This is an extract from the manifesto:

> When everything depends on the goodwill of the average Member of Parliament and his electors, Suffragists have to be doubly careful that the favourable majority built up by the years of hard work done by the National Union should not be turned into an adverse one. Until it is quite clear that the majority will do nothing for us, our efforts must be directed toward strengthening their hands on our behalf. In the existing circumstances, the Committee of the Freedom League has decided that the truce shall be kept until the events of this Session have shown what are the results of the Prime Minister's pledges, but this in no way commits the Women's Freedom League to abstain from militancy if a new position is created by some changes as yet unforeseen.
>
> Our immediate efforts will be in the direction of securing support for the second reading of the Conciliation Bill on March 22. We are aware that this will be a test division, and we look to every Member of Parliament who believes in Woman Suffrage to be in his place and note for that Bill. We know that the anti-suffragist members of Parliament will vote for broadening amendments designed to wreck the Bill, and we therefore urge every Suffragist inside and outside the House of Commons not to endanger our Cause at this critical moment by insisting on particular amendments.

We would also appeal to all those Suffragists who believe in militancy, but who agree with us that this is not the right time to use it, to give practical help both in money and work to the Women's Freedom League.[30]

In the same edition of *The Vote*, Charlotte Despard makes reference to the lengthy prison sentences ordered to many of the women arrested as a result of the WSPU militant action, including Mrs. Pankhurst (given two months' imprisonment). Mrs. Despard wrote:

Let our readers study the column in *The Vote* entitled 'How Men Protect Women'. Let them compare the sentences passed on men for outrageous offences against women and children with that on Mrs. Pankhurst, and they will, we hope, begin to realise how low we have failed in our man-administered justice, and how deep is the necessity for reform.[31]

A report of questions asked of and answers given by Prime Minister Mr. Asquith in the House of Commons about the WSPU militant action in March 1912 was also published. Mr. Keir Hardie asked why certain privileges of those imprisoned in Holloway had stopped. Mr. McKenna replied that the suffragists recently 'confined in Holloway in consequence of the destruction of property in streets had been guilty of insubordinate conduct in prison'.[32] The prime minister was asked whether

he would take steps to introduce and pass through both Houses of Parliament with all possible speed a Bill giving to the persons or firms who might be damnified by further outrages of these people a right of action against the Women's Social and Political Union or other suffragist bodies to which the delinquents in each case might belong.[33]

The prime minister said that he should like to consult the attorney general first but did say 'I am quite sure the hon. gentlemen is only giving utterance to very widespread opinion when he indicates that these disgraceful proceedings (loud cheers) ought to be brought home not merely to the wretched individuals who are immediately concerned, but to those who are responsible.'[34] His reply was cheered by others in Parliament.

The second hearing of the Conciliation Bill fixed for 22 March 1912 was postponed. The government announced that the strike crisis had compelled them to first consider the Minimum Wage Bill.

At the Wednesday, 27 March 1912 trial hearing in Newington Court, both Ethel and Violet were found guilty of maliciously damaging one plate-glass window at the property of the Commercial Cable Company to the amount of £10. Violet was sentenced to four months' imprisonment at Holloway Gaol, while Ethel was ordered on her 'own Recognition in £5, to appear for judgment if called upon and to keep the peace for 12 months'. Ethel's sentence meant that she was released because she bound herself to pay £5, agreed to return and give evidence at judgements if needed (for further hearings) and promised to keep the peace for twelve months. It is not known if Violet was offered the same sentence but refused it. This is of course possible, given that she was a known active WSPU member. It is understood that the legal system at the time would have required an assessment of Ethel's character in order to grant her the sentence decided upon. This seems therefore to point towards the fact that she was not a known active suffragette, that she did not have previous criminal records or involvement in similar activities (no other documents to this effect have been uncovered) and that she had employment (she was listed in the prisoner records as a 'Lady's maid') and a good standing in the community. Violet, on the other hand, had been arrested before (on 'Black Friday') and as a known active WSPU member may have refused to agree to keep the peace. Indeed, given Mrs. Emmeline Pankhurst's stance, reported in the Press about the huge number of prisoners that the government would need to deal with and the attention that this would bring to the cause, it is possible that Violet Bland wished to continue her part in this.

Violet went to Aylesbury Prison to serve her four months' sentence where she joined the Aylesbury hunger strike and was force-fed. Violet said: 'They pinched and clutched my nose unmercifully, and at the end of the assault, when I did not rise quickly from the chair because of my helpless and breathless condition, they snatched the chair from under me, and flung me on the floor.'[35]

It is unknown if Ethel was ever in contact with Violet again.

During the First World War, Ethel worked delivering post. She went on to marry Arthur Hodge and have a son, Donald, in 1919. She died at the Tonbridge Sanitarium from tuberculosis. She was just 46 years old.

Ethel during World War One, a couple of years after her involvement with women's suffrage and her arrest
© Ethel Baldock's family.

CHAPTER TWO

7 June 1866: The First Mass Votes for Women Petition

Leaving the individual story of Ethel Violet Baldock in 1912, this chapter now focuses on 1866 and the first mass votes for women petition presented in Parliament. It shares information, stories and insights discovered about the Kentish signatories.

In 1866 only males over the age of 21 had the right to vote, provided they met certain property qualifications. This followed the 1832 Reform Act, which increased the male electorate in England and Wales from 435,000 to 652.000[1] by extending the range of men who could vote. Despite extending suffrage for men, the 1832 Reform Act legally excluded women as voters by stipulating 'male persons'. Prior to this Act, the exclusion of women from Parliamentary elections was based on custom and some women may still have voted at the parish-level elections.

On 7 June 1866 the first mass votes for women petition was presented to Parliament by John Stuart Mill MP. The petition read:

> The humble Petition of the Undersigned,
>
> Sheweth,
>
> That it having been expressly laid down by high authorities that the possession of property in this country carries with it the right to vote in the election of representatives in Parliament, it is an evident anomaly that some holders

of property are allowed to use this right, while others, forming no less a constituent part of the nation, and equally qualified by law to hold property, are not able to exercise this privilege.

That the participation of women in the Government is consistent with the principles of the British Constitution, inasmuch as women in these islands have always been held capable of sovereignty, and women are eligible for various public offices.

Your Petitioners therefore humbly pray your honorable[2] House to consider the expediency of providing for the representation of all householders, without distinction of sex, who possess such property or rental qualification as your honorable[3] House may determine.

And your Petitioners will ever pray,

Barbara L.S. Bodichon.

Mentia Taylor.

Emily Davies.

&c. &c. &c.[4]

John Stuart Mill (1806–73) was an MP for Westminster but lived in Blackheath, then part of Kent.[5] He was a friend for more than twenty years and married for seven years to an early campaigner for women's rights, Harriet Taylor (1807–58), and was influenced by her views. After her death, her daughter (and his stepdaughter) Helen Taylor (1831–1907), continued to live with him in Blackheath.

The original petition document presented to Parliament was not

John Stuart Mill, pioneer of Women's Freedom, published by the Women's Freedom League
© *LSE Women's Library collection*

preserved. This was normal practice for such documents at that time. The House of Commons Select Committee on Public Petitions counted but did not list the names of 1,521 signatures. A pamphlet was printed by the petition organizers (the Kensington Society) with 1,499 signatures included. Only two copies of this pamphlet still exist. The signatures have been transcribed and this has been used to identify the Kent signatories. There is no way of knowing who the additional twenty-two signatories counted by the Select Committee were as a record was not kept. However, it is possible from examining the 1,499 signatories recorded by the Kensington Society to identify 55 from the county of Kent (with the county boundaries as they were then).

The Kensington Society boasted of being the first women's debating society in England and was predominantly London-based (the society's name was derived from the residence in Kensington of its president, Mrs. Charlotte Manning), but had strayed beyond this. Country members had been admitted. One of these three country members was Barbara Bodichon (1827–91), née Barbara Leigh Smith, who had a second home called Scalands, near Robertsbridge in Sussex. This is only 13 miles south-east of Kent and meant that Barbara was in an ideal location to be the canvasser of petition signatories from both Kent and Sussex. Helen Taylor, stepdaughter of John Stuart Mill MP, canvassed in the Blackheath area. Helen and Barbara canvassed their areas differently. Barbara had to cover a large rural area and the signatories she obtained were from a mixture of a few middle-class acquaintances, crafts people and shopkeepers. This would have

Barbara Leigh Smith Bodichon influential in Kent canvassing and collecting signatories for the first mass Votes for Women Petition, 1866 © LSE Women's Library collection

required some door-to-door canvassing. In contrast, Helen used local social networks and relatives.

In less than a month, 1,499 signatories had been collected. This is truly impressive when it is remembered that this was long before the age of social media when the women's options were to have a conversation, print bills (advertisements), canvass on foot, write letters and, while doing all this, encourage those they were communicating with to tell others. An appreciation of the magnitude of this task is best understood by reading the following extract of the report of the House of Commons Select Committee on Public Petitions for this 1866 Petition:

'Your Committee have reported the number of names appended to this Petition,[6] but they observe that, with the exception of seven, they are all written on Slips of Paper and pasted on the Petition.'[7]

So that's approximately 1,514 signed slips of paper, from all areas of the country, to be collected and manually pasted on to one document to form the petition. The Parliamentary Archives acknowledge that this collation process took place at Aubrey House on Campden Hill in Kensington, the home of one of the organizers, Clementia ('Mentia') Taylor (1810–1908), wife of Peter Taylor MP. As these petition organizers also recorded the names in order to have them printed and circulated in a pamphlet, they really did have a huge task involving much teamwork and many hours.

Specifically in Kent, it is known that Barbara was influential as 'an innovator and inspirer, not a

Clementia ('Mentia') Taylor wife of Peter Taylor, MP. She was one of the organisers of the first mass petition for votes for women in 1866 and her home, Aubrey House in Kensington, was used to collate the signatories
© *LSE Women's Library collection*

committee woman, and left the seed she had sown to be cultivated by others'.[8] Her opinions on women's issues would have been conveyed during her canvassing. Her views on women's suffrage are clear from her 1854 published pamphlet, *A Brief Summary in Plain Language of the Most Important Law of England Concerning Women*. In her 'Remarks'[9] she had written:

> Having put in a few pages, before our readers, the Laws of England concerning women, I will proceed to consider what are the legal grievances removable by legislation. In my opinion, the most important of all these is the fact that women have no voice, and no influence recognised by the law in the election of the representatives of the people, while they are otherwise acknowledged as responsible citizens, are eligible for many public offices, and required to pay all taxes. It is not as a means of extorting justice from unwilling legislators that the franchise is claimed for women. In so far as the claim is made with any special reference to class interests at all, it is simply on the general ground that under a representative government, any class which is not represented is likely to be neglected. Proverbially, what is out of sight is out of mind; and the theory that women, as such, are bound to keep out of sight, finds its most emphatic expression in the denial of the right to vote.[10]

In a collection of letters to and from Helen Taylor are examples of the approach taken and difficulties encountered with canvassing for signatories, including in parts of Kent. An early version of a letter that Helen Taylor used when canvassing for votes is indicative of the thought given to and care taken over these letters to potential supporters of the petition. Helen Taylor had crossed through words (shown below with strikethrough) in this draft as she made amendments:

> Dear Miss Chadwick,
>
> I do not know whether you ~~will~~ have heard of the enclosed petition and I therefore venture to send it to you

believing that you will ~~probably~~ certainly be interested in it and hoping that you will ~~be willing~~ like to add your signature. May I at the same time ask you to request that of your Mother and if among your friends there are any whom you think likely to ~~agree sympathise~~ agree with the object we should be glad to have their signatures also and with as little delay as possible. Apologising for ~~troubling~~ addressing you on the subject but hoping that a common sympathy will be a sufficient excuse. I am, dear Miss Chadwick yours very truly.[11]

Miss Marion Chadwick, to whom Helen Taylor had sent the letter, signed the petition. However, her mother, Rachel Chadwick, then wrote to Helen Taylor to say:

I have this moment discovered that my daughter cannot legally express an opinion on the subject of the petition you forwarded as she is not yet of age. Would you therefore erase her name from the list of signatures. I do not think she will have shifted from her opinion when she is of age – should the question at that time still need to be urged by a petition.[12]

Refusals to sign were received and below is an example of one sent to Helen Taylor:

Beg to return the petition unsigned well knowing that my daughter's views on the subject of it agree with my own. I had already rec'd from Mrs. P.A. Taylor the petition, and to her I more fully stated my reasons for declining to enter into the movement.[13]

Records demonstrate that signatories were missed off the petition as they were not received in time via the post. An example of this is from a letter written to Helen Taylor from Caroline Lindley in which she wrote:

I kept the petition which you left in my care because only one dear friend had signed it. I have still two unanswered letters but my experience where I hoped the most and failed leads me to forward the one name as it may be of some use, though I fear for the present use it will be too late. It is well for us that dear Mr. Mill will present the petition.[14]

The following section takes the form of an alphabetical list of place names in Kent with details discovered about any signatories:[15]

In **Beckenham**, **Annie J. Harrison** signed the petition. She was the daughter of Daniel and Anna Harrison, born in 1842. In the 1871 census Daniel was a retired tin merchant and they lived at The Avenue Shirley House, Beckenham, Bromley, Kent.

Sarah L. Lambert also signed. In the 1861 census she lived at 5 London Place, St Mary's, Eltham, Kent. She was an officer's widow with three young daughters. No link was found between Sarah and the Lambert family from Tonbridge who also signed the petition.

Jane Panther signed the petition. No further information on her has been found.

Bessie Pepler of Stanmore House signed. No further information has been found for Bessie. However, a 'Joseph Pepler' is recorded in the 1873 to 1884 (inclusive) Electoral Registers as qualifying because of 'occupation of house' with the 'house' being Stanmore House. No further information as to his relationship to Bessie has yet been uncovered.

In **Belvedere**, **Jane Eleanor Wood** of Sylvester Villa signed. She was Mrs. Jane Eleanor Wood (née Ellis, b.1834) daughter of John Ellis (b.1786) of the Home Office. She spent her childhood at Eaton Street, Upper St George, Hanover Square in London. She had three older sisters and one younger one. Jane Eleanor was a governess in Plumstead, Kent in 1851. In 1859, she married John George Wood (1827–89), a clergyman and author of many books about natural history. They lived together in Belvedere and in the 1871 census had five children and four servants. They left Belvedere in 1876 and moved to Upper Norwood.

In **Blackheath**,[16] **Ellen and E.B. Laird** both signed the petition. The petition records that they lived at 22 Woodlands Terrace in Blackheath. It has not been possible to identify the 'Ellen Laird' that signed using the same address as 'E.B. Laird'. It is possible that 'Ellen' is short for 'Eleanor' and that she was 'Mrs. Eleanor H. Laird', mother of 'E.B. Laird' (see below).

'E.B. Laird' is 'Eleanor B. Laird' (b.1839), daughter of Mrs. Eleanor H. Laird and her husband Macgregor Laird, Merchant (General). In the 1851 census they lived at 7 Crooms Hill in Greenwich, Kent. By 1861 Mrs. Eleanor H. Laird is a widow. Eleanor B., her younger sister Agnes and their mother, Eleanor H., are all described as 'Lady' in the 1861 census. In 1871 their address changed to Kinnersley House in St Julian, Shrewsbury, Shropshire and in 1881 to 23 Hyde Street, Winchester in Hampshire. By 1881 their occupation had changed from 'Lady' to 'income from dividends'. In 1891 they are traced back to Kent, this time in Park Road, Tonbridge.

Caroline Lindley signed the petition. She was single and lived at 10 Kidbrooke Terrace, Shooters Hill Road, Blackheath. She was described as a 'fund holder' in the 1871 census and 'Annuitant' in 1881. She lived with her brothers and cared for her young nieces and nephews. She wrote a letter to Helen Taylor regarding late replies when sending her signature (see above[17]) and seems to have been keen to collect signatures on behalf of Helen.

In **Canterbury Mrs. Frances S. Alford**, known as 'Fanny' (b.1812) also signed. She was the cousin and wife of the 'Very Rev. Henry Alford'[18] of The Deanery, Green Court, Canterbury. Originally from Somerset, Mrs. Alford had two daughters with the Dean of Canterbury Cathedral. In a letter from Emily Davies (Kensington Society member), writing in the 1890s about not having much recollection of the petition, she wrote:

> A distinct recollection of a party of friends who met at Miss Garrett's[19] house from day to day and worked it. One of the early signatures that we hailed with special delight was that of Mrs. Alford, the name, the address

The Deanery, Canterbury, being so highly respectable –
and therefore influential.'[20]

In **Greenwich**[21] was **Maria Charlotte Mondy** (b.1843) of 2 Cold
Bath Street ('a very poor working class district of Greenwich'[22])
who signed the petition. Originally from Bristol, Maria was
recorded on the 1871 census as an 'Assistant' and 'Governess' at
Denmark Hill Grammar School.

Emma Roberts of 12 Upton Grove, **Celeste Sinibaldi** of 40
Trinity Square and **Selina Mary Spratt** of 2 South Villas, all in
Greenwich, added their signatures to the petition. No further
information has been found about them.

In **Lee**[23] **Louisa Ellis** (b.1816) of 17 Essex Terrace signed the
petition. According to the 1871 census, she was the sister of
Augusta Drayson (see entry for 'Caroline A. Drayson' of
Northfleet below). Louisa was a widow. By 1881 she had moved
to 40 Clifton Road, Brighton in Sussex and at 65 years old was
an 'Annuitant' like her sisters.

J.E. Lewin of 12 Blessington Road, Lee signed the petition.
It is not known if this was Mrs. Jane Elizabeth Lewin or her
daughter, Miss Jane Elizabeth Lewin (both of the same address).
Interestingly, Mrs. Jane Elizabeth Lewin was a sister-in-law
and Miss Jane Elizabeth Lewin the niece of **Harriet Grote** (née
Lewin, 1791–1875). Harriet would definitely have been involved
in this petition as she was married to George Grote who was
elected to Parliament as a reformer in 1832 and who was one
of the founders of London University. Harriet was also close
friends with John Stuart Mill MP. She established the Society of
Female Artists in 1856 and was a public speaker on the subject
of women's suffrage throughout her life.

In **Margate, Isabella Theakston** (b.1814) of Burleigh House,
Cecil Street, signed. She was the older half-sister to Helen and
Josephine Waude, detailed below. In the 1861 census she lived
with her half-sisters in Margate, and is described as 'unmarried'
and with an occupation of 'Proprietor of Houses'.

Isabella's half-sisters **Josephine Theakston Waude** (b.1830) and **Helen Waude** (b.1834), also of Burleigh House on Cecil Street in Margate, supported the petition and signed it. In the 1861 census they are recorded as 'unmarried school mistresses'. It is known from a local newspaper that the sisters kept 'a boarding school for young ladies'.[24]

In **Northfleet**, **Caroline A. Drayson** (b.1817) of 4 The College signed the petition. She was the daughter of Landed Proprietor William Drayson and his wife, Ann M. They had many daughters. One daughter was Louisa (married name 'Ellis') who also signed the 1866 petition (see 'Ellis' above under 'Lee'). In 1851, Caroline lived with her parents at 20 Prospect Row, Gillingham, Kent. At the time of signing the petition in 1866, Caroline was living at Huggens College: 'Huggens College, described in a contemporary guide book as a handsome college consisting of forty residences and a chapel. Twenty-eight of these residences were occupied by ladies and gentlemen of reduced circumstances who had a weekly allowance of 20 shillings each.'[25] In the 1871 census it is noted that she continues to live at The College with her sister Sarah A. Drayson and niece Laura Coxworthy. In 1881 she is living at 9 The College as head of the household and with her occupation described as 'Annuitant'. Another of her sisters, Augusta Drayton, also single, lived with her. In 1891 they were both still residing at The College and both described as 'Annuitant of Huggens College'.

In **Plumstead**, **M.A. Howard** of 52 Frederick Place, Sandyhill signed. It is likely that this was Mary A. Howard (b.1798), an unmarried woman living in 1871 with her two unmarried sisters, Charlotte and Elizabeth (all annuitants). However, the address of 52 Frederick Place has not been identified with her, but Conduit Road and Hanover Road, both in Plumstead, have. Research shows that Mary A. Howard also paid rates/tax in Westminster between 1859 and 1863.

In **Sevenoaks**, **Eliza Cresy** (b.1798) of Riverhead signed. Mrs. Cresy is known to have sent a letter to the Local Board of Health in 1864, 'expressing her satisfaction at the improvements made by the Board in front of her property at One Bell-row, Lowfield-street.'[26] She was married to architect and Superintendent and Inspector of the Board of Health, Edward Cresy. He was reported to have been the civil engineer, Government Superintending Inspector that in 1850 had commented on the likely costs of installing 'sewers for draining Margate'.[27] However, by the time of the 1866 petition Eliza was a widower, Edward having died in 1865.

Interestingly, also signing this petition (but not with Kent addresses) were Eliza's two daughters-in-law. Mrs. Theodore Grant Cresy, wife of her younger son and medical surgeon working in Suffolk, signed with address included as 'Aldeburgh, Suffolk'. Mrs. Mary Cresy of Alleyne Road, Norwood, wife of Eliza's eldest son, Edward, an architect, also signed the petition. However, neither of Eliza's unmarried daughters, Adelaide and Bertha, added their signatures.

In **Staplehurst**, **Elizabeth Wilmshurst French** and **Eleanor French**, both of Collier Street, also signed. Research has not resulted in any obvious family connection between the two women. The first, Elizabeth (b.1832), was the unmarried daughter of farmer Jessie/Jesse French. In 1851 her occupation was described as 'Employed at Home' and 'Home' was in Chamber Lane, Rolvenden, Tenterden, Kent. By 1861 it is recorded as 'Housekeeper to her father' but they are then living in Porters House, Crow Plain, Yalding, Maidstone. Her father's occupation is detailed as 'farmer of 120 acres employing 6 men and 4 boys'. Elizabeth continues her association with women's suffrage as she is known to have presented the first Kent-specific petition in 1867. According to independent researcher and author Elizabeth Crawford, she 'had tried, unsuccessfully, to find a few other women to add their names'[28] and collected signatories for a later 1868 petition in favour of votes for women. Then on 28 March 1868, Elizabeth wrote to Helen Taylor apologizing for not being able to collect many signatories for a petition:

> The men have the Bible at their tongue's end from Genesis to Paul's epistles and the women are cowed and

silent. I doubt if I ever knew a woman who dared do so much as sign a petition without the approbation of the men, husband or other, who determined the amount of cash she had in her purse and whose temper governed her. Whether women get enfranchisement or not, they need it.[29]

It is likely that this was the May 1868 petition of 21,757 signatories presented to Parliament and reported in a Kent newspaper as 'Rarely has a petition representing so much moral and intellectual thought been laid on the table of the House of Commons.'[30] According to Ann Dingsdale in her thesis,[31] Elizabeth wore trousers and advocated population control.

Eleanor (b.1827) appears to have been married to a farmer by the name of Edward French. They lived on Collier Street, Yalding, Maidstone. In 1851 they had a baby son Richard, and Edward is described as a 'farmer of 142 acres employing 9 men and 2 boys'. By 1861 with four children aged 10 and under, Eleanor is a widow.

In **Tenterden** four members of the Avery family signed, namely Mrs. T. Avery, A. Avery, Miss M.J. Avery and R. Avery.

Living at the Greyhound Inn, 2 The High Street,[32] **Mrs. Thomas Avery** was married to Thomas Avery, a wine and spirit merchant. Their daughter **Miss Ann Avery** (1825–1904) was unmarried when she signed the petition. She went on to marry Edmund Hook (wheelwright and grazier of 54 acres).

A second daughter, **Miss Mary Jane Avery** but known as 'Polly' (1844–1931), was 22 and unmarried when she signed the petition. In the 1881 census she is recorded as married to George Geer Godfrey, a builder eight years her senior, and living at Miriam House, Ashford Road, Tenterden with a 1-year-old daughter Kate. In the 1901 census, Mary Jane or 'Polly' is described as a widow living on her own means in Laurelhurst, Tenterden.

The other signature was that of 'R. Avery' and from the records examined it is difficult to attribute this to another female

Avery family member. The only 'R. Avery' was Richard, Mr. and Mrs. Thomas Avery's son. However, he was married to **Annie** (née Bowyer from Cheshire) who may have been known as **Mrs. R. Avery**. She is likely to have been the fourth Avery signatory. According to the 1861 census, Mr. and Mrs. R. Avery lived in Ashford Road, Tenterden where Richard was a wine merchant. By 1871 they were living with three children in the High Street, Tenterden with Richard then recorded as 'Wine and Spirit Merchant'.

Mrs. Jane Blackmore from Tenterden signed the petition. In the 1861 census Jane was recorded as a widow aged 81 living at West Cross in Tenterden with an occupation of 'Landed Proprietor'. Mrs. Jane Blackmore may have known Mrs. Ann Cloute, another widow, and Jane Ashby, both also living at West Cross in 1861 (see below).

J.A. Briggs (from Tenterden) signed. In the 1864 Electoral Register for Tenterden there was a John Atkinson Briggs listed with qualification being that he had freehold houses, land and mills. His address was recorded as 'The Water Mill'. He was married to **Jane Briggs**. It looks likely that the 'J.A. Briggs' who signed the petition was Mrs. John Atkinson Briggs, first name Jane.

Mrs. Cloute, Tenterden, signed the petition. Three women by the name of 'Mrs. Cloute' were living in Tenterden at this time. **Mrs. Ann Cloute** (b.1794), a widow, was living at West Cross as at the 1861 census. This is the same address as Mrs. Blackmore and Jane Ashby. The second possibility, **Mrs. Sarah Cloute** (b.1803) of the High Street, was married to Thomas Cloute, listed on the 1864 Electoral Register as owning a freehold house on the High Street. They had a son, Thomas Martin Cloute. The third Mrs. Cloute is Thomas Martin Cloute's wife, **Mrs. Eliza G. Cloute** (b.1844). The 1871 census records this married couple living with Mrs. Sarah Cloute (Thomas's mother) at the High Street. Thomas is described as a 'farmer and grazier' and Sarah as having 'independent means'.

E. Comfort, **Louisa Comfort** and **Miss Custers** of Tenterden all signed the petition. No further information has been uncovered about them.

Mrs. Amelia C. Mace (b.1786) and **Mrs. John Ellis Mace**, both of Tenterden, supported the petition. Amelia was a landed proprietor and widow by 1861 when 75 years old. Mrs. John Ellis Mace could be Amelia's daughter Mary, because Mary married a Charles Ellis. However, because of the use of 'John' rather than 'Charles' this is not clear.

Mrs. Mary Ann Mercer (b.1820) signed the petition. She was married to agricultural labourer Joseph. In the 1851 census they are recorded as living in Tenterden and in both the 1871 and 1881 census they live in Dandy House, Tenterden. They had a daughter, Harriet, who according to the 1861 census was the housemaid to Mrs. Amelia Mace (see above).

Mrs. Milsted and Miss A. Milsted both signed the petition. Research suggests that Miss A. Milsted was **Miss Ann Elizabeth Milsted** (b.1845) who lived in Tenterden with her mother, **Elizabeth Milsted** (b.1815), blacksmith father Charles (b.1804) and brothers. Her father was described as a blacksmith employing one man in the 1861 census and she was a schoolmistress (aged just 16). In the 1871 census Miss Ann Elizabeth is recorded as living with her father and brothers but there is no mention of her mother or of her occupation. Miss Ann Elizabeth remains single and in the 1881 census has become the head of her own household in the High Street in Tenterden. She is a 'Fancy Shop Keeper' and has one servant, a woman boarder with independent means. However, in the 1891 census her fortunes appear to have changed as she is now described as a servant and 'Wool Shop Assistant', still in the High Street but working for 'wool shop fancy keeper' Sarah Buckland (b.1822).

Tracking down the 'Mrs. Milsted' is not as straightforward. It could, of course, be Miss Ann Elizabeth Milsted's mother, Elizabeth Milsted (b.1815). However, there are four other Mrs. Milsteds in Tenterden in the period from 1861 to 1871 as follows.

There was **Mrs. Sarah Milsted** (b.1828) married to a blacksmith, Edward, and living in a blacksmith's shop in the High Street.[33] Also cited in the 1861 census was **Mrs. Francis Milsted** (b.1812), married to the High Street tailor, George Milsted. Finally there was **Mrs. Jane Milsted** (b.1823), wife of a shoemaker, or the shoemaker's mother, **Mrs. Sarah Milsted** (b.1789) all living in Stone Cottages, Rolvenden, Tenterden.

Mrs. John Francis Newman signed the petition. Mrs. John Francis Newman, or **Louisiana Newman** (b.1842), was married to John Francis, a master grocer employing one apprentice.[34]

Miss Anna Pay signed. She was born in 1810 in Dover, Kent and lived in the High Street, Tenterden. In the 1851 census she was recorded as servant to 75-year-old 'Fund Holder' Elizabeth Mace (likely to be connected to the Mace family mentioned above, but a relationship has not been identified) and unmarried, aged 41. Anna Pay had a son, John Hunter Pay, aged 7, also living with them. In 1861 the census records that Anna Pay was now head of the household at 'Private House, High Street, Tenterden', unmarried, now 51 years old and a 'Charwoman'. The 1881 census reports that Anna Pay is now a 'Mangles Woman', still living on the High Street.

Miss Roberts, **Mrs. C. Valder** and **Miss Winsas** of Tenterden signed. No further information has been found about them.

Mrs. Wells signed. However, there were too many women of that name in Tenterden at the time to determine who had signed the petition.

In **Tonbridge**, both **Elizabeth Lambert** and **H.E. Lambert** of Barden, Tonbridge, signed the petition. Elizabeth Lambert (b.1817) lived in Barden House in Tonbridge. In 1871 she was 54 years old and married to George Lambert, a farmer of 200 acres. By the 1881 census, she was 63 years old and George was the farmer of 96 acres of agricultural land, employing six men and three boys. The 'H.E. Lambert' signatory seems likely to have been that of their daughter Harriet Elizabeth (b.1845).[35]

The signature of **Catherine Masters** of Tonbridge was included. However, it was spelt 'Tunbridge' and so could have been referring to Tunbridge Wells rather than Tonbridge. These two towns are approximately 4 miles apart. This could therefore be the signatory of Mrs. C. Masters (b.1811), wife to beer shop keeper John Salter Masters, living at the time of the 1851 census at Calverley Road, Tunbridge Wells, Kent.

Emma Tress of Tonbridge signed. She was born in Kent in 1829, so in 1866 was 37. It appears that she had a son called William, born in 1855. She married a retired surgeon, John B. Lindsey, in the same year as the petition and was then living at 93 Upper Grosvenor Road in Tunbridge Wells.

In **Tunbridge Wells**, Jane Ashby from 1 Neville Bank signed. It seems likely that this was Jane Ashby (b.1791), an unmarried 'fund holder'. In 1861 the census lists her as living in West Cross, Tenterden. It seems likely that Jane Ashby knew of Mrs. Blackmore and Mrs. Ann Cloute, who both lived in West Cross.

Three members of the **Ashurst Biggs** family living in Barden Park, Tunbridge Wells, signed the petition. They were Matilda and two of her daughters, Caroline and Elizabeth. **Matilda Ashurst Biggs** (1818–66) was sister to Emilie Venturi (1826–93) and Caroline Ashurst Stanfield (1816–85), both of whom were living in London and both also signed the petition. They were the three daughters of William Ashurst, a solicitor and member of the National Association for the Promoting of the Political and Social Improvement of the People. According to independent researcher and author Elizabeth Crawford, Matilda 'gave a donation to the Society for the Promotion of Employment of Women in 1865, signed the 1866 women's suffrage petition and was a subscriber to the Enfranchisement of Women Committee in 1866.'[36] Matilda married Joseph Biggs, a Unitarian from Leicester, and they had three daughters, two of whom also signed the petition. Together, Joseph and Matilda established a rescue mission for 'fallen women' in Leicester. Matilda died in 1866 and her family then left Kent and moved to London. Both **Elizabeth** and **Caroline** signed the petition. They were both active supporters of women's suffrage and it is known that Caroline Biggs, alongside Mary Anne Apps of the Dover Suffrage Society

Isabella Tod who spoke to an audience of 400 in Dover, East Kent, in December 1876
© *LSE Women's Library collection*

and Helen Blackburn and Isabella Tod, spoke to an audience of 400 in Dover in December 1876.

Susan Sibella Rucker of Mount Ephraim Road, Tunbridge Wells signed the petition. According to the 1861 census Susan lived at Ashford Lodge in Mount Ephraim Road, Tunbridge Wells. She lived with her mother, Ann Rucker (b.1788), with the occupation of 'Fund Holder', older sister, Caroline A. Rucker (b.1818) and servants.

In **Wrotham, Mrs. William E. Hickson** (b.1805) (otherwise known as 'Jane Hickson') of Fairseat signed. She was married to William

E. Hickson, a farmer of 70 acres employing four labourers.[37] They lived in Manor House, Fairseat, Stansted, Malling, Kent. Jane Hickson was clearly a women's suffrage supporter. She was referred to in a letter from Caroline Lindley to Helen Taylor:

> With great surprise and pleasure I see our loved friend Mrs. Hickson not only able to write her name but after so long an indisposition we must rejoice together in the energy and spirits with which she rouses to aid the good cause which we have in hand. Mr. Hickson asks me 'to give the compts.[38] of himself and Mrs. Hickson to you and Mr. Mill and say we both wish success to Miss Taylor's efforts, congratulation her at the same time upon her ability to be useful – a great privilege.'[39]

In **Wye**, **Anna Bach** signed. On the 1861 census there is an 'Anne' (rather than 'Anna') Bach (b.1840) living in Blean, not far from Wye. She was described as a 'domestic servant' and the daughter of Mary Bach, a charwoman. No further information has been uncovered about her.

These Kent signatories are from different backgrounds. There were servants, teachers, farmers' wives and daughters, shopkeepers and merchants, proprietors of land and houses, a wife of a surgeon and annuitants.

Geographically, Tenterden had a high concentration of signatories. This was most certainly due to its proximity to Robertsbridge in Sussex (just 15 miles away), where Barbara Bodichon had her second home.

The Kent signatory of Eliza Cresy from Riverhead in Sevenoaks highlighted the communication between family members in other parts of the country, as both her daughters-in-law also signed the petition. One lived in Suffolk and the other in Norwood, Middlesex.

Kent signatories that are known to have carried on their association with the suffrage movement are Miss Elizabeth French of Staplehurst and Caroline and Elizabeth Ashurst Biggs of Tunbridge Wells. It is known, for example, that Miss Elizabeth

French signed a later petition in 1868. Both Caroline and Elizabeth Biggs remained active women's suffrage campaigners, and Caroline often spoke at Kent meetings.

Some twenty-four years later, in 1890, some of the women that signed this first mass women's suffrage petition drafted and presented a further petition, known as the 'survivors' petition'. Of the seventy-eight signatories, only three are known and these were Barbara Bodichon, Louisa S. Goldsmid and Elizabeth Garrett Anderson. There was a strong Kent connection to this 1890 petition as it was presented to the House of Commons by Edward Watkin, Liberal MP for the constituency of Hythe in Kent.

It is reported[40] that the Kensington Society 'proved a catalyst for the birth of the suffrage movement', and if so, Barbara Bodichon, Helen Taylor and John Stuart Mill enabled Kent to play a part in this initiation. While Barbara Bodichon and others from the south-east involved in this first mass petition seemingly stepped away from continued involvement in formal committees and societies for women's suffrage, others picked up the reins for 'the cause'. The next chapters detail some of those involved in Kent.

CHAPTER THREE

1908: NUWSS 21 June, London Procession

New Prime Minister Mr. Herbert Henry Asquith had challenged the suffragists to prove that their demands were the demands of the majority of their sex.[1] In response to this challenge, a demonstrating march in London was organized by women's suffrage campaigners on 21 June 1908. There was some involvement by Kent inhabitants in this demonstration.

A special train was scheduled from Tunbridge Wells and the Sevenoaks branch of the NUWSS displayed its own banner. The inscription read: 'What concerns all should have the consent of all.'[2] Sadly, this banner is no longer in existence and photographs of it have not been discovered.

Miss Marjorie Crosbie Hill was the Sevenoaks NUWSS branch secretary in 1908, living at 2 South Park. She was born in 1887 to William Samuel James Hill and his wife, Elizabeth Mary Crosbie. William was a Justice of the Peace in Sevenoaks. In 1891 the family of eight – William, Elizabeth and six children – were living at The Red House on the High Street. In 1911, Marjorie lived with her widowed father at the South Park address. Marjorie was only secretary for one year (succeeded by Mrs. Reinold), but continued to be involved in the women's suffrage movement. She is recorded as being heavily involved in organizing the Sevenoaks part of the later 1913 NUWSS Pilgrimage from Kent to London.

A local newspaper published details of the special train leaving from Tunbridge Wells travelling to London's Victoria Station. They were promised a warm welcome:

> At Victoria there will be a welcome party awaiting the travellers; a Station Marshal with Captains in colours and regalia. Outside the station the new arrivals will meet with another welcome. They will find bands playing, and, banners flying, and their special Procession Marshal waiting to conduct them to their places in the march.[3]

Kent readers were told: 'This great demonstration will be a landmark in the history of the progress of women.'[4] Indeed, this demonstration became known as 'Women's Sunday' and saw the largest number of men and women gathering at that time for a political purpose.

It was reported that

> There were three thousand standard bearers and thirty bands, and as most of the processionists were in white or light dresses the colour scheme was most effective. The speakers were drawn from all sorts and conditions of women. Some were mothers of families, others were teachers, mill and factory workers, shop assistants, clerks, journalists, novelists, musicians, a playwright, a bachelor-of-law, a tailoress and a nurse.[5]

The *Kentish Mercury* reported

> it is estimated that the demonstration numbered somewhere about 35,000. Naturally their progress through the streets was watched by thousands of people, whilst in the park itself some 200,000 gathered, in the vain hope as far as the vast majority of them were concerned, of hearing what the advocates of 'Votes for Women' had to say. Thereupon the *Daily News*, characteristically hysterical, only seeing, as is its habit, what it wants to see, tell us that 'all London' gathered in Hyde Park, that

the Suffragists 'saw a city converted, their sex justified, a day of triumph truly.'[6]

This newspaper continued:

> The demonstration of last Sunday is their [the leaders of 'Votes for Women'] answer they say to Mr. Asquith's challenge, but even a demonstration of 30,000 women and 200,000 onlookers, of which obviously large numbers were merely curious, others indifferent and certainly many hostile, is no proof that the franchise is demanded even by a large minority of the women of this country.

Quite boldly, the author of this article proclaimed that it was

> not by any means difficult to get a huge crowd together in such beautiful surroundings as those presented by Hyde Park on a fine Sunday afternoon in summer, when the greater number conceived they had nothing better to do than to watch battalions of women clothed in white – neither mystic nor wonderful – and bearing banners.

An article written 'by one who was there'[7] was included in another Kent newspaper, namely the *Kent and Sussex Courier*. Reportedly, 'Only ten people went up from Tunbridge Wells, though a few others who were staying in London were present.'[8] Mr. Le Lacheur drove Miss Leicester, Miss Sherris and Miss M.M. Le Lacheur 'in his motor car, which was brilliantly decorated for the occasion, with rosettes in green, white and purple, the colours of the NUWSS; a small "Votes for Women" placard was fixed in front of the car, and a large notice advertising the Demonstration hung out at the back.'[9]

Those that went by train had a two-hour journey into Victoria. The author of the report, a demonstrator, referred to being three hours early for the demonstration but added 'we were ready to face much more than that in our anxiety to show our earnest determination to secure the right for women to constitutionally voice their own views.'[10] Upon arrival at Victoria

Embankment where the procession was to start, it was reported that there were crowds of men and women already collecting banners, 'women in white dresses with scarfs, bells and hats in the tricolours were unfurling the banners and placing them in position. This opportunity was not missed by a passing bus driver, who exhorted them with "Now, my duckies, come and hang out the washing."'[11] The author tells of feeling proud to be asked by the 'group marshal' to carry a banner that had black lettering on a white background saying 'Working Women demand the Vote'.

There were many items being sold: badges, handkerchiefs, artificial flowers and programmes.

> Miss Christabel Pankhurst, in academic robes, Mrs. Pethick Lawrence, and Mr. and Mrs. Isaac Zangwill, the leaders of the procession, continually passed up and down, reviewing and arranging their followers; and Mrs. Drummond known as 'General Drummond', who was overseeing all the seven processions, came to visit us before we started. She wore her new general's cap and gold epaulettes.[12]

The author describes it being very difficult and slow to move once at Hyde Park corner due to the large crowds: 'All along the

Emmeline Pethick Lawrence receiving flowers from Jennie Baines. Frederick Pethick Lawerence and Flora Dummond watching, c. 1906 to 1910
© LSE Women's Library collection

Miss Christabel Pankhurst, c.1911, standing in the street, holding a bag and a newspaper, watched by a crowd of women
© LSE Women's Library collection

route, as we marched to the music of our bands, we had crowds to watch us, lining the roads, standing at doors, and leaning out of the windows. We were cheered at times, but heard very few unfavourable or jeering remarks.'[13] The eye-witness also relayed that the police kept good order.

This same account describes hearing 'two women speak, a doctor and a teacher, both of whom were listened to with much interest and very little interruption.' The account continues:

> Of course we wished to hear Miss Christabel, but her great popularity had attracted such huge crowds, that we could not get near enough to hear. She had a number of 'roughs' round her, who made several attempts to rush the platform, and she was forced to speak the whole hour and a half herself, as her supporters were unable to control the hooligan element. Mrs. Pankhurst also we were unable to hear for the same reasons.[14]

Agreeing with this account is the brief reference made in the *Sevenoaks Chronicle and Kentish Advertiser* that

> The crowd that gathered in Hyde Park on Sunday… were all asking one another, 'Which is Mrs. Pankhurst's

Emmeline Pankhurst standing, speaking to a crowd from a horse-drawn carriage. Christabel Pankhurst seated beside her
© *LSE Women's Library collection*

Flora Drummond carrying a travel rug waiting outside court with others, 1908
© *LSE Women's Library collection*

platform?' When they had found it they stayed there, and a great many of them tried their hardest to prevent the women's leader from speaking; but she got her way in the end. The attentions of the crowd were a tribute to the place Mrs. Pankhurst has made for herself in the women's movement.[15]

At five minutes to five the resolution was put to the 20 different crowds, 'That this meeting calls upon the Government to give the vote to women without delay.' The great shout at six o'clock, which was to have been a great feature of the afternoon, was not a success. Where we were the bugle could not be heard owing to the direction of the wind, and the shout was feeble, though the cheering, which followed, showed the enthusiasm of the meeting.[16]

The unknown author describes the crowds demonstrating and stopping the traffic as they streamed out of Hyde Park Corner. The report ends:

I hurried to the garage and found them [friends] waiting there in the car. I was offered, and accepted with pleasure, the third seat in the back. We arrived home just before lighting-up time, very satisfied with our day, and hoping for the sake of all men and women, and especially perhaps for the brave leaders of the movement, that Mr. Asquith's answer to the resolution and demonstration would be satisfactory.[17]

CHAPTER FOUR

1908: WFL Caravan Tour of Kent

Prior to the challenge by Mr. Asquith and the demonstration in London, the WFL had been planning tours of different parts of the country. For Kent this resulted in a lengthy and geographically widespread tour by a horse-drawn van.

At the time, the WFL had only a few hundred members and approximately twelve branches, mostly in London. In comparison,

WFL Caravan on the move
© LSE Women's Library collection

at its peak, the NUWSS had 50,000 members and the WSPU had financial support from the generosity and capacity of 5,000 supporters. The idea of this first tour came about because of the WFL looking to compete with these larger movement societies by gaining support from smaller towns and villages. Kent, like Surrey and Sussex, was an ideal focus area for a travelling van as while it had train lines linking London to its larger towns and cities, many smaller towns and villages were not so well-connected, yet they had ideal public halls where the WFL could arrange to speak.

This first campaign travelled through Surrey, Kent, East Sussex, back through Kent, then returning to Surrey. The 31-year-old Miss Muriel Matters (1877–1969), an Australian actress, and Mrs. Lillian Hicks (1853–1924), aged 55 years at the time and a veteran suffrage campaigner, with WFL president 64-year old Mrs. Despard were the first to start the tour. Mrs. Hicks was the initial van organizer secretary or 'Van. Org. Sec.'[1] and appealed prior to the start of the tour on 16 May 1908 from Mrs. Charlotte Despard's Surrey cottage for names of cyclists who were willing to work during the summer, accompanying the van. She was also one of the speakers at the 'send-off' alongside Mrs. Despard and Mrs. Billington-Greig. Mrs. Billington-Greig was a member of the newly-formed (January 1908) Bromley branch of the WFL. The speeches given at this send-off were reportedly 'full of hope and courage'.[2]

The van was wooden and painted green with white lettering reading 'Women's Freedom League', 'Votes for Women', and 'Women's Suffrage'. Inside there were two beds, a writing table and stove and a small bookshelf. The van was pulled by horses and

> some amusement was caused by the persistent refusal of the Van to go through the gateway of Mrs. Despard's garden. This was attributed to the fact of one of the horses being nicknamed 'Asquith'. So, naturally, he would feel a reluctance to advance the cause of Women's Suffrage. However, the gate was lifted off its hinges, the Van got through, amid enthusiastic cheers, and made

Inside the WFL Caravan whilst on tour in August 1908
© *LSE Women's Library collection*

its first official appearance on King's highway. May we
soon lift off its hinges the gate which bars the progress
of women.[3]

Their first stop was in Leatherhead, Surrey where they needed
police protection and their meeting was shut down early. Mrs.
Despard left the tour at this point.

Within three weeks on the road they had travelled over
90 miles. Having travelled through Surrey, they moved into
Sussex and began to speak at meetings limited to women and
'guaranteed men'. The WFL had recognized that the tour set

them apart from the other societies as its simplicity won them attention. In his biography of Miss Muriel Matters, Robert Wainwright describes the tour as 'a grassroots campaign that won attention by its simplicity: an engaging message delivered from a wooden van in a grassy field or from the plinth of a town hall statue'.[4]

For Kent the first sighting of the van was on Monday, 29 June in Tunbridge Wells. One of the first women to approach the van was Violet Tillard. Muriel Matters recalled that 'As the caravan made its way slowly up the hill to Tunbridge Wells, Violet Tillard came forward with her sister Irene and greeted us. We became friends from that moment, although we did not foresee all that the future would hold for us.'[5]

Violet and Muriel remained lifelong friends, continuing to campaign for women's suffrage. Both were involved on 28 October 1908 in the large demonstration at the Palace of Westminster. Violet and Muriel together with Helen Fox and two male supporters went to the Houses of Parliament. Muriel

Women's Freedom League caravan tour: Muriel Matters seated in the window, in Guildford, Surrey, 1908. She began the tour of Kent shortly after this photograph was taken
© *LSE Women's Library collection*

and Helen chained themselves to a piece of ironwork known as 'the grille' in the Ladies' Gallery that obscured their view of parliamentary proceedings. Violet used string to attempt to lower a WFL proclamation 'Women's Freedom League demand votes for women'[6] to the floor of Parliament, while the two male supporters showered those in the House of Commons with WFL leaflets. All were removed from the House of Commons. Violet and Muriel then joined their comrades protesting outside and were later arrested for trying to break the police lines. Both served a month in Holloway Prison.

Violet's half-sister Irene also continued her involvement with the WFL and was herself arrested, along with Charlotte Despard, in 1909 for picketing outside 10 Downing Street.

Violet was the daughter of army officer George Tillard and his wife Louisa. Violet's mother had died in 1883 and her father remarried and had two further daughters, Irene and Georgina. George and Lillian E. Tillard moved to Westwood in Southborough, some 2 miles outside Tunbridge Wells. It is known that Violet, a nurse, trained at the Poplar and Great Ormond Street hospitals, and had already been involved in the women's suffrage movement at least a year before the caravan arrived.

The tour party, now including the Misses Tillard, arrived in their 'cosy caravan, which was stationed in a field near the Rocks Lane'.[7] The women's intention was to hold evening meetings on the Common. However, at the first meeting there were 'disgraceful'[8] scenes and the ladies were hustled. A huge crowd, estimated at 2,000 or 3,000, gathered near the Lower Cricket Ground. Reportedly a considerable portion of the crowd was made up of lads and youths. However, two or three policemen remained nearby.

For the first half-hour Miss Muriel Matters could be heard:

> As she herself put it, she was 'neither a freak nor a frump', but she certainly was a lady of amiable demeanour and a speaker able to put her points with a great deal of force and forensic skill. She faced her big and ever-growing audience pluckily, and fluently detailed the reasons in

favour of female franchise. The very rare interruptions were met with ready and witty repartee, and the laugh was always against the interruptor. Occasionally a piece of turf or other missile was thrown at the speaker, and once she was struck on the face, but she courageously stuck to her guns. This went on for about thirty minutes, and then the rougher element among the males became impatient, and, perhaps, a little ill-tempered, because there appeared to be little cause for a row. The dense mass of heated and perspiring people became denser still in the neighbourhood of Miss Matters. An ominous swaying to and fro of the crowd was noticeable, and the lady vainly endeavoured to continue her speech.[9]

Miss Muriel Matters who participated in the 1908 WFL caravan tour of Kent and the 1913 NUWSS Pilgrimage from Kent to London
© *LSE Women's Library collection*

On this warm June evening, the scent and image of 2,000 to 3,000 people perspiring as they swayed is imaginable. The newspaper account of this scene describes 'the roughs' as 'distinguished by cigarettes, high collars, straw hats and unintelligent faces'.[10] How terrifying for Muriel, to be surrounded in this way. Undeterred though, despite being knocked from her chair, luckily caught as she fell, Muriel was keen to continue. However, Chief Constable Mr. Prior insisted that for her own safety she accompany him to the police station. Having waited in the police station until the crowd had left, Muriel then stayed at a friend's as she preferred not to return to the caravan.

The following morning, on Tuesday, 30 June, a reporter from the *Kent and Sussex Courier* newspaper interviewed Muriel 'and found her busily engaging in writing notices for a meeting to be held the same evening. She said she was none the worse for her experiences.'[11] The interview, which was subsequently printed in this local Kent newspaper, made an interesting read and is therefore included here:

'Is that your first encounter with hooligans?' she was asked.

'No,' she replied, 'I have been through it before and I am getting hardened to it now. I do not mind their heckling, but their brutality gets on my nerves. One man had his head fractured at one of our meetings.'

'You won't tempt Providence by going to the Commons again, I suppose?'

'Well, I don't know. We may have a farewell meeting on the Wednesday evening. All this sort of thing brings the women on our side and all the decent men. We shall have a meeting to-night for women and "guaranteed" men; that is to say, men who accompany their wives, and so on.'

'What do you think of the rougher section of the crowd?'

'My feeling was that they resembled a herd of buffalo. Once emotion crosses them, it is like a wind at which the animals take fright, and these people are really no higher than the animals. But I saw many intelligent and sympathetic faces in the crowd, and here and there, as one walks to the station, little knots of women cheered us. I think the women were on our side.'

A parting question put to Miss Matters was, 'Have you suffered imprisonment for the cause?'

'No,' she replied, smiling. 'I think I can do more by educating the women, as I am trying to do; but if I thought I could serve any useful purpose by being imprisoned, I would be willing to undergo it.'[12]

On the same Tuesday evening a further meeting was held, but this time at the Town Hall. It was packed with women and the speakers had a good hearing. Muriel presided over this meeting and mentioned that supporters of the cause had been insulted by women in Tunbridge Wells when giving out leaflets. She said that 'She was sorry to find so little mental clarity in Tunbridge Wells.'[13]

The following day an 'At Home' meeting was hosted by Mr. and Mrs. Tattershall Dodd at Grosvenor Lodge. This was organized by the recently-formed women's suffrage local committee. The audience consisted of more than 100 ladies and just 3 men. Miss Corbett presided, saying that she was not a member of any women's suffrage society. Mrs. Hicks then spoke and confirmed that she belonged to three societies and described herself as a 'militant suffragette'. Miss Muriel Matters spoke at some length and a Miss Burnett followed.

That evening, the WFL campaigners also held a further open-air meeting on the Common. This 'proved more successful. The police were more in evidence and order was preserved until twilight set in, when there was some attempts at hustling which the police duly dealt with.'[14]

Despite the initial difficulties, the WFL campaigners' resilience and determination appears to have paid off, for in the WFL's newspaper, a letter was printed from someone in Tunbridge Wells which read 'I must congratulate you on your success.'[15]

On the evening of Friday, 3 July, an open-air meeting was held at Southborough Common. A good attendance was reported, with the two speakers initially being granted a fair hearing. However, it transpired that

> later on the proceedings became noisy, and ended in hustling and disorder. The lady speakers had to have police protection, and were escorted to a friend's house, and ultimately left in a cab by the back way to elude the noisy crowd, who remained outside the house for some time.[16]

Southborough feedback, printed in the WFL newspaper, was that the talks were 'a splendid and lasting lesson'.[17]

Upon leaving Tunbridge Wells, Violet Tillard was now on board and they next travelled 10 miles to Goudhurst. Muriel Matters reported that after their 'exciting campaign at Tunbridge Wells' they 'found Goudhurst very peaceful and comforting'. However, this appears not to be a compliment because she continues that 'lack of opposition generally goes with apathy, and to a great extent this is what we had to confront in the village of Goudhurst'.[18] Muriel speaks of many helpers (named as Mrs. Hicks, Miss Bennett, Miss Cowen and Miss Hicks) stirring things up and then holding three meetings on 3 to 5 July.

In a rather lovely description of the village and her surroundings, Muriel further states that

> We quite understand these country folks' point of view: it is difficult to feel strenuous-minded or militant in the midst of cornfields scarlet with poppies, and hedges of dewy honeysuckle, and sweetbriar surrounding the caravan, and wide horizons showing purple shadows, save where the sunlight makes gold the distant hills.[19]

The caravan arrived in Cranbrook on Monday, 6 July with Muriel and Miss Bennett on board. The account of their time in this village makes interesting reading:

> We took up our stand in the Market Place, beneath the shadow of St. Dunstan's. Our strongest opponents were a sore-headed Liberal and a fat old lady, who clung to the Market Cross and made an impassioned declaration against us and our disreputable behaviour. However we rallied ourselves against the opposing force, and soon the victory was ours. We decorated between fifty and sixty soldiers with the Legion of Honour 'Votes for Women' badges.[20]

Both Tuesday (7 July) and Wednesday (8 July) evenings saw 'victorious' meetings in Tenterden. Muriel reported that 'All the men in Tenterden Town are prepared to lay down their arms and make peace with their women comrades.'[21]

Miss Eustace Smith joined the tour and on Thursday, 9 July the caravan made its way to Wittersham. Here the weather was poor with 'slow-falling rain'. Two meetings were held here: one on Thursday, 9 July and the other on Friday, 10 July.

The caravan then proceeded to Sussex and by the end of July had reached Eastbourne in East Sussex. Following the meeting at this seaside resort, Muriel Matters left the tour and returned to London. Charlotte Despard took the reins of 'Asquith' at Eastbourne on Monday, 3 August[22] and continued the tour. Joining her as van organizer was Miss Alison Neilans, and Miss Lenn from the York branch of the WFL.

Returning to Kent, the caravan visited a small agricultural village near the town of Ashford called Appledore. Mrs. Despard reported via *Women's Franchise*:

> Our first night at Appledore, for instance, was rather unpleasant, and we had almost made up our minds to stay there only two days, but the strength and independence of the women whom we met there, with the far friendlier attitude of the young men, determined us to spend another night in the place, and we were

WFL caravan tour in Kent, 1908. Charlotte Despard and Alison Neilans at the window. Miss Alison Neilans became the van organiser on the Kent tour in July in 1908 when Muriel Matters returned to London
© LSE Women's Library collection

Miss Alison Neilans. She became the van organiser on the Kent tour in July 1908 when Muriel Matters returned to London
© LSE Women's Library collection

rewarded by visits of sympathisers to our van, and a really delightful meeting on the last evening of our stay. One woman said to us emphatically, 'You have brought new life to Appledore. We shall never forget your visit.'[23]

The caravan travelled from Appledore some 8 miles east towards the coast, to New Romney. This was a small, agricultural town on the edge of the Romney Marsh:

> 'Here we fell on our feet,' reported Charlotte Despard, 'for a large, pleasantly-situated field was placed at our disposal by a sympathiser. It is quite close to the High Road of the town, and after Miss Neilans and Miss Henderson had well chalked the pavements, with regard to our intentions, we found shy groups of people clustering together outside our fence; and these, with a little encouragement, were induced to come in, so that presently our van was surrounded by a crowd that increased as the dusk drew on, and that gave us the closest attention. As usual, we had to justify our methods and define our position. We felt, however, that we had the bulk of the audience with us.'[24]

The tour party then travelled to Ashford and on Sunday, 16 August held a meeting which 'was very well received. Indeed the people there begged that we would bring on our caravan later.'[25]

The next day (Monday, 17 August) they 'had a little deeply interested audience on Littlestone Sands, and in the evening [we] held another meeting'[26] from the caravan.

Interestingly, it seems that the role of the van organizer included securing the hire of a horse to pull the caravan because it was reported that 'The van was drawn from place to place by a horse hired in each town or village.'[27] There is likely a historical footprint somewhere of such arrangements which would show further strands of this tour's story.

Continuing with the aim of being heard in rural and remote areas, the tour party arrived at Hythe, 'after travelling through the Marsh and addressing the people of the villages en route'.[28]

This was on either Tuesday, 18 August 1908[29] or Wednesday, 19 August.[30] It seems that the aim was to spend a minimum of a week in the area as 'All these seaside towns are very full of visitors, who, being in holiday mood, are delighted to have something new to talk about. Other visitors are already interested and only want an invitation to join the league and become active workers.'[31]

Mrs. Despard again called upon people to help 'as auxiliaries to the caravan' and said in this same report: 'I am more and more convinced that this is a fine mode of propagandism, and I wish there were twelve instead of only one van upon the road. The life is extremely interesting. Will no one start another van for the Women's Freedom League?'[32]

Charlotte Despard, 1912. Charlotte toured Kent in 1908 with the WFL © LSE Women's Library collection

From an account given by Charlotte Despard, it appears that if it wasn't for the landlord of the Red Lion Hotel, 'whose wife is a sympathizer',[33] they would not have been able to stop in Hythe. Mrs. Despard reported it as 'a difficult place to work'[34] because meetings were not allowed on the beach or in any public place. When challenged, the authorities of Hythe explained that their rules were in place 'to ensure the comfort of visitors'[35] and Charlotte Despard believed them 'to be of the opinion that Suffragettes' speeches might be harmfully exciting to their visitors' nerves'.[36]

However, despite these initial difficulties, Mrs. Despard reported a positive start to their time in Hythe:

The good landlord…came to our assistance, with a pitch for our van in his yard, and a meeting-place on the ground outside his house which, though touching upon the main road, is private property. The corner is a busy

one, as the trams and motor cars in and out of Hythe
stop close by. When dusk came on, and we, with our
table of literature, took up our station, curious groups
gathered round us. These, when Miss Neilans began to
speak, came closer; and we were presently surrounded
by a large crowd of people, who listened to us with close
attention.[37]

While passing through Dymchurch, a village neighbouring Hythe,
a lady, Mrs. Pratt, had run out from a farm 'on the outskirts of
the village',[38] telling them that she had been a suffragist for many
years, and that her daughter and other visitors to the area were
sympathizers. Mrs. Pratt requested a meeting at Dymchurch
but, despite initial enthusiasm to do so, on closer inspection
'It did not seem possible to hold a meeting there. The tide was
high, the sea was singing lustily, and the few grown-up people
were looking after delightful children and babies.'[39] However, it
transpired that later that same day two more sympathizers were
met, Mrs. Griffiths and Mrs. Jephson, who with their families
were spending the summer in Dymchurch. It was agreed that a
meeting would take place on Saturday, 22 August. Mrs. Despard
reported that

> I shall always be glad that it was so ordained, for that
> Saturday night has left an ineffaceable mark upon my
> memory. The day had been stormy, and the out-of-doors
> tea arranged by Mrs. Griffiths had to be taken in the
> cottage parlour. During the tea there was talk of dark
> rumours – rowdyism was on foot – all the eggs in the
> village had been bought for missiles – and one gallant
> young cricketer asserted that he would stand near Mrs.
> Despard and catch the eggs. Good little friend! Probably
> he was disappointed that there was no occasion for this
> gallantry. When we came to the place of meeting –
> beautiful and still it was under the sombre sky, the
> old church in front, large trees behind – we found a
> number of people, villages and visitors, waiting for us.
> They gathered round, many more came pouring in, and

their intelligent interest, the intentness with which they
listened, was delightful. A brisk discussion followed the
speeches: an unusually good collection was given. Many
went with us to the inn, where we took up the motor-car
for Hythe, and I felt so much charmed with the quaint
picturesqueness of the place, so much interested in the
people, that I began planning a summer retreat there,
when the vote is won.[40]

In addition to this meeting in Dymchurch and some good
meetings in Hythe itself, Mrs. Despard spoke at a garden party
in Smeeth,[41] 'a village 4 miles east of the town of Ashford. The
van, meanwhile, will go on to Folkestone, where we have to
arrange for a meeting in the evening.'[42]

The caravan party did move on to Folkestone, where they
'were exceedingly fortunate in enlisting the sympathy and
interest of Mr. Stainer, an old citizen and a J.P.'.[43] They pitched
the caravan in Mr. Stainer's garden and reported being given
'every kind of help and hospitality'[44] by his wife and daughters.

Two large meetings were held in Folkestone, 'the first
was comparatively quiet, the second was more noisy.'[45] At
these meetings Mrs. Despard was described as speaking
'enthusiastically and vigorously'.[46] Apparently what was very
noticeable about Miss Neilans was that she was very quick at
repartee. When there was a lull in questions she said: 'Am I to
take it for granted that you are all in favour of our movement?'[47]
and almost the whole crowd called 'No!' However, when asked
to explain why, no one responded.

In the local East Kent newspaper, a report was included of
the speakers being 'mobbed by a crowd of 500 people, and took
refuge at the house of a tradesman in Tontine Street until the
police arrived'.[48] However, Charlotte Despard maintained that
'As a fact the crowd became packed and rather curious, and but
for the kindness of Mr. Stainer and many of the young men in
the crowd the crushing might have been dangerous. As it was we
reached our caravan calm and unhurt.'[49]

Miss Henderson is reported to have left the tour and been replaced by sisters, the Misses Violet and Irene Tillard.[50]

The van moved from Folkestone to Dover and was parked in Dr. Baird's stables in Winchelsea. On Wednesday, 26 August, the WFL members held a public meeting on the corner of the Market Square outside the museum. Miss Neilans introduced herself and her co-speakers and explained their mission, 'her words being received with loud boos and derisive laughter'.[51] The large number of small boys in the crowd began interrupting her as she spoke of equal voting terms for men and women and 'older people in the crowd joined in, and they were reinforced by a number of people in the upper bar of the Palace music hall, led by a man who styled himself a "humorist".'[52] The newspaper report continued:

> In the brief moments of quietude it could be heard that Miss Neilans was speaking of the militant methods which had been adopted by the Suffragettes. Some people objected to them, while they recognised the legitimacy of their claims, she said. They had tried proper, ladylike, and constitutional methods for 50 years, but found that they attracted no attention. No reform had been gained by men, she said, by gentle methods.[53]

Interrupted by the 'comedian', Miss Neilans then had to stop her speech on women's suffrage to silence him. She tried to continue by stating that 'Nearly 300 women had been to prison to win the vote.'[54] Although interrupted and booed by the crowd, the newspaper report said that the attitude of the crowd was not hostile. However, Mrs. Charlotte Despard described this as an 'attempted meeting' from which they were 'jeered and howled and followed [us] in tumultuous procession to the pier' where they evaded them. She confirmed that 'We heard that some of the mob were in waiting below the pier with stones, but, on leaving, we separated, and so passed through quietly.'[55]

Of this first meeting, Mrs. Despard said:

> We find almost always that the greatest opposition, the
> worst rowdyism, is at the first meeting. Presumably we
> are expected to be very rowdy persons, and like is ready
> to meet like. When, however, we have held two or three
> meetings – when we have met several people – interest takes
> the place of opposition, and the rowdy element is kept in
> check by bodies of serious men and women determined to
> hear what these strange women have to say.[56]

She went on to report that a second meeting on the beach went
well and having left her colleagues, Miss Neilans and the Misses
Tillard, for the weekend she heard that they had become very
popular.

The Dover meetings appeared to show an active distancing of
the WFL from Mrs. Pankhurst and the WSPU. It was reported
that 'An inquiry as to Mrs. Pankhurst's health was answered
by the statement that she was not a member of the speaker's
society.'[57] Also answering questions at another Dover meeting
on Thursday, 27 August, it was stated that 'no member of her
league had ever chained herself to the Prime Minister's railings,
nor did they intend to'[58] and 'They [WFL] had never broken up
a Liberal meeting as the society had done.'[59]

On Tuesday, 1 September, the van arrived in Deal. The Misses
Tillard had gone, replaced by a new organizer, Miss Marguerite
Annie Sidley (b.1886). Miss Mocatta had also joined. Miss
Marguerite Sidley had spent twelve days in Holloway for her part
in the deputation to the House of Commons in March 1907. She
had been a member of the WSPU along with her mother, but in
the summer of 1908 she switched to the WFL. This was the first
of three years that she spent between eight to ten weeks per year
travelling around the country in a WFL caravan.

It seems that at this stage of the tour, those organizing
and speaking had greater experience of militant action. Miss
Mocatta and Miss Alice Neilans, for example, knew each other
and had worked together for the cause. Earlier in 1908, they had

both been arrested and charged with 'wilfully and wantonly disturbing the inhabitants of Mr. Harcourt's house by pulling the bell or knocking at the door'.[60] Mr. Lewis Harcourt was a Cabinet Member, and women including Miss Mocatta and Miss Neilans called at his residence seeking to ask for an interview. When Mr. Harcourt refused an interview, the women protested and some arrests were made. It appears that Miss Mocatta had paid the fine of 40s, while Miss Neilans had opted to go to prison for a month instead. 'Before accepting the month's imprisonment, she [Miss Neilans] said, in reply to the magistrate, that, while women were disenfranchised by their sex, she did not admit the jurisdiction of the Court.'[61]

The pitch eventually secured in Deal was a 'large field, which a young butcher, Mr. Voysy'[62] provided for the travellers. Mrs. Despard left on this Tuesday, 1 September, travelling by motor car to Winchelsea to

"VOTES FOR WOMEN."

MISS MARGUERITE SIDLEY
WOMEN'S FREEDOM LEAGUE, 1, ROBERT STREET, ADELPHI, LONDON. W C

Miss Marguerite Sidley, c. 1910. She was the van organiser for the WFL Kent tour from September 1908. The previous year, Marguerite had spent 12 days in Holloway for her part in the deputation to the House of Commons in March 1907

© *LSE Women's Library collection*

speak at a garden party organized by Mrs. Percy Harris and Mrs. Lambert. The bad weather prevented an open-air meeting, but a hall was found and Mrs. Despard reported that 'The afternoon meeting was delightful – a pretty little hall, well filled with kindly people, many of whom were villagers, whose interest and sympathy made my task of speaking very easy.'[63]

In Deal, the boatmen had promised space on the beach for meetings, and an Irish compatriot of Mrs. Despard, Mrs. Stoker, whose house overlooked the field, helped with auxiliary matters. Mrs. Stoker also stood bravely by these women when difficulties arose in the first meeting. The afternoon meeting on Wednesday, 2 September had been abandoned due to 'heavy sweeping rain'. Charlotte Despard reported that

> In the evening we went out again, to find a large crowd waiting for us. Everything went well at first; we were listened to with only occasional interruptions; but, as the darkness deepened, the crowd grew larger, and there was so much noise that when the time for questions came it was impossible for either question or answer to be heard. At last I thought it wiser to adjourn when we were immediately surrounded by young men and boys, who were, however, as at Dover, more curious than hostile. Mrs. Stoker stood bravely by my side; some strong men cleared the way for us, and we went through the town to her house, followed by a big procession. Whatever else our agitation may be doing, it is certainly giving the country notice that women Suffragists are abroad, and that they do not mean to be silenced.[64]

There was then a daytime meeting (possibly on Thursday, 3 September) at Lower Walmer, a small coastal town with a castle, only 2 miles from Deal and some 6 miles north-east of Dover. The evening meeting in Deal was abandoned due to the torrential rain. The following day the women 'held a small meeting of deeply interested people near one of the shelters on the beach'.[65] The same day, Miss Sidley went on to the small town of Sandwich to make arrangements while Mrs. Despard followed in the van. The following report was included in the Women's Freedom League newspaper:

> The pitch found for us by Miss Sidley, who makes a first-rate organiser, was in a tanner's field, away from the tannery and looking out on the ancient raised footway, above a little stream and overhung with fine trees, that runs across the interesting old-world town. Our place of meeting was to be the cattle market. Miss Sidley had chalked the pavements and made our mission known;

we had also been well advertised by the passage of our van through the narrow streets. When we came out into the town we found we were expected. We were followed by a host of boys, who shouted our battle cry 'Votes for Women', and, in the market, there was already a good audience gathered together. We feared at first that it would be a rowdy meeting. But I spoke a few words to the boys who had ranged themselves on the lorry, and as soon as the meeting began they kept silence, indeed they became presently attentive listeners.[66]

Described as 'ardent friends of the cause and members'[67] of the WFL were Mr. and Mrs. Meeson Coates. They were staying in Sandwich and rallied around them at this first meeting. Mrs. Despard again left for London for the weekend while Miss Mocatta chaired and Miss Sidley spoke at an evening meeting in the cattle market. When Mrs. Despard returned to Sandwich on Monday, 7 September, she described Sandwich being 'alive with sympathy'.[68]

In a later Sandwich meeting, Mrs. Meeson Coates took the chair and a rather poetic account was given of this particular meeting by Charlotte Despard:

> There is a great lamp in the middle of the square, which enabled me to see the faces in the crowd, and their responsiveness, earnestness, and sincerity touched me more than I can express. Also it made speaking easy. A man in the crowd called out, 'Go on; we're beginning to like you, mother!' I said, 'I hope you'll go on liking me,' and there was applause.[69]

There appears to have been great interest in Sandwich because a large collection was taken at that meeting and as a result of the WFL van visit and much canvassing,[70] thirty men's names were sent to the Men's League and there was talk of a WFL branch being established in the town. However, no evidence of this has been found. A Deal and Sandwich committee of the National

Society existed from 1873, but it was 1912 before the NUWSS established a society in the area. This was the Deal and Walmer Society and whether or not this covered Sandwich as well has not been concluded.

Miss Mocatta left the caravan in Sandwich, and Miss Balham of the Hampstead Branch joined the convoy.

On Tuesday, 8 September, the caravan moved 2.5 miles south to Eastry. The weather continued to be challenging, with high winds and heavy rain. The caravan pitched up on the roadside just outside Eastry and the women walked to the little market place as planned. Miss Balham took the chair at this meeting and, according to Mrs. Despard, 'occupied the position well'.[71] The group spent two nights on the roadside pitch in Eastry. Mrs. Despard reported that 'the people were not inspiring' but they felt that 'some sympathy was aroused'.[72] The women spoke of hop-pickers that returned year after year to this area of Kent. A rather interesting account of the meeting with some of the female hop-pickers in a field was given by Charlotte Despard:

> Women of all ages, mothers, grandmothers, young girls, and with them their brown and red babies and small children were gathered together in groups; and the women were so gentle and well-mannered, they listened with so much interest that we enjoyed our visit to them. We went aside while they took their meal. Then some of them clustered round and I talked to them; yes, and they seemed to realise the importance of our subject, for there came a light into their faces. One little woman pressed forward. 'Excuse me,' she said, 'but women have always been more persevering than men. I've noticed it.' How beautiful this new pride in womanhood is![73]

The journey continued to a village called Wingham, approximately 6 miles north-west of Eastry. The women pitched the caravan in a field at Wingham Court Farm, owned by Mr. and Mrs. Robinson. The planned meeting-place was in the square outside the Red Lion Inn where it was reported that the people were intelligent and sympathetic. Again, Mrs. Despard and Miss Balham spent time speaking to hop-pickers, while Miss Sidley travelled ahead to make arrangements in Canterbury.

The party arrived in Canterbury in 'a storm of thunder, lightning, and hail'[74] which meant it was impossible to hold their planned meeting. Mrs. Despard left the caravan at this point to venture north. Mrs. Margaret Wynne Nevinson and Miss Joseph joined the caravan. When signing off her report as she left Canterbury, Mrs. Despard reminded readers that money was already being collected to fund a second van, such was the success of this one. She wrote:

> I hope next year we shall be able to have our vans followed by organisers. The educational value of such a course would be incalculable. Let us remember that it is the country we wish to arouse. Until this is done, there can be but little hope of any definite success.[75]

Mrs. Margaret Wynne Nevinson took the reins, leading and reporting on the tour in Mrs. Despard's absence. Margaret Nevinson (1858–1932) was married with a son and daughter. She was an educated woman who had taught at South Hampstead High School in London. She had been a member of a number of the women's suffrage societies including the WSPU. However, she left the WSPU with Charlotte Despard to found the WFL. Margaret was appointed a JP for the County of London in 1920 and became the first woman to adjudicate at criminal petty sessions. She was therefore a strong character to take over the helm of the tour. In Canterbury the van was pitched outside the County Hotel. Almost immediately, a woman called Mrs. Innes arrived claiming to be the only suffragette in Canterbury. She 'proved a valuable friend and ally, introducing' the party 'to many people, and shedding a halo of respectability on' them 'by her presence on the cart'.[76]

In the local newspaper, a relatively large article titled 'Votes for Women' reported of a meeting in the Canterbury Cattle Market on Saturday evening (12 September): 'There was a large attendance and able addresses were given by the ladies deputed by the league to speak, although they had to face a considerable amount of heckling from the crowd.'[77]

The report said that

> Miss Sidley is an [engaging] young lady, who is gifted with considerable amount of eloquence, which she uses to full advantage, and whatever one's opinion may be on the question of 'votes for women' one could not help admiring her for the way in which she dealt with the many carping hecklers who interrupted her.[78]

The WFL campaigners reported that much kindness was shown to them in Canterbury by Mrs. Innes, Mrs. Walker, Mrs. Williams, Mr. and Mrs. Horsley, and Mr. and Mrs. Phelips. Mr. and Mrs. Phelips organized a drawing-room meeting for the WFL at which four new members were recruited.

On Wednesday, 16 September, Miss Sidley and Miss Joseph moved on to Herne Bay while Margaret Nevinson and Miss Balham stayed behind to clean the caravan.

On the journey with the caravan from Canterbury to Herne Bay, Margaret Nevinson recounted that while travelling through the streets of Canterbury she was 'crocheting ostentatiously at the window' and people were smiling and waving. However, as they approached Herne Bay she described a feeling of a 'hostile aura'.[79] At their first meeting that Wednesday evening in Herne Bay, the women received verbal abuse as well as showers of rotten plums. More concerning, however, was that their 'cart was dragged swiftly and dangerously through the enormous crowd, fortunately causing neither death nor mutilation' and as reported by Margaret Nevinson: 'Hooting masses hustled us through the streets as if we were unpopular malefactors, our one protector, a small but gallant policeman; however, presently a cordon of chivalrous gentlemen of all classes formed up around us, and stood on sentry outside our yard for over an hour.'[80]

The WFL campaigners received apologies from Herne Bay inhabitants and sympathizers the following day. That morning

(Thursday, 17 September) some WFL campaigners travelled 13.5 miles to the more easterly seaside town of Margate to hold a meeting on the beach. However, they were refused permission to hold the meeting. That evening they held a second meeting in Hythe on the outskirts of the town in 'a dark street'. They found a large and respectful audience.

It was reported that Miss Joseph and Miss Balham had made their debut speeches as WFL campaigners on this part of the Kent tour. Margaret Nevinson commented that on Miss Balham 'falls the heaviest burden of domestic duties',[81] but exactly what this burden was is not known.

On Friday, 18 September, with gorgeous weather, the van moved to Whitstable. However, no account of the campaigners' time here has so far been discovered.

It is known that the caravan moved on from Whitstable on Tuesday, 22 September to Faversham. On the evening of this Tuesday, the first of three meetings was held at the entrance to the cattle market. 'There was a large crowd present and the speakers received a very attentive hearing.'[82] Miss Leighfield, believed to be Miss Marian Leighfield[s],[83] spoke first. Miss Leighfield was one of the women arrested in October 1908 for protesting outside the Houses of Parliament while Miss Matters and Miss Tillard were inside the Gallery. Other WFL members that took part in the Kent tour and were arrested that day included Mrs. Emily Duval, Margaret Henderson and Mrs. Billington-Greig.

Miss Sidley spoke next of the laws that acted against women and

VOTES FOR WOMEN.

MRS T. BILLINGTON-GREIG
HON. ORGANISING SEC. WOMEN'S FREEDOM LEAGUE.
1, ROBERT STREET, ADELPHI. LONDON W.C.

Mrs. Billington-Greig, member of Bromley Branch of WFL. She gave a "send off" speech at the WFL Caravan Tour of 1908 alongside Charlotte Despard
© *LSE Women's Library collection*

the need for votes for women to help rectify this. 'She also stated that the League was not going to be crushed by persecution, and they would go on fighting until they got a definite pledge from the Prime Minister that he would enfranchise women before he left office.'[84] Mrs. Emily Duval was the final speaker. She spoke of her personal experience in jail, having been imprisoned for one month. An account of this speech has not been located, but it is known that Emily very much continued her campaigning for women's suffrage after being arrested in 1912 for window-smashing and stating in court: 'I am prepared to die for Votes for Women.'[85] For die she could well have done as it was recorded that she 'had been brutally knocked about and thrown on her back'.[86] Seemingly therefore a tenacious, strong-minded woman, this must have been conveyed at least in part to the Kent audience.

The WFL asked for a show of hands in terms of votes in favour of suffrage and those not, but it was reported that 'few hands went up either way'.[87]

There were apparently two further meetings on the Wednesday (23 September) and Friday (25 September) evenings, but no accounts of these have been uncovered.

Sittingbourne was the next stop for the WFL caravan, arriving there on Friday, 2 October. The women were able to pitch the van in the grounds of a large empty mansion and hold 'two very large orderly meetings in the Cattle Market'.[88] Margaret Nevinson also addressed the Men's Adult School in the Town Hall and reported that 'A great deal of sympathy was aroused in the town, and we have received many promises of help should we ever revisit Sittingbourne.'[89]

Travelling some 12 miles, the tour proceeded to Kent's county town, Maidstone. There the women received 'very rough treatment. Mrs. Despard joined the van here, and Miss Mocatta left it.'[90] There is no mention of Mrs. Nevinson leaving the van, but she is not referred to in any of the accounts found about Maidstone, or the later stops, West Malling and Sevenoaks. There are several accounts of their first night in Maidstone and, pieced together, it appears that the meeting was arranged outside

Sessions House Square in Maidstone. As soon as Mrs. Despard and Miss Sidley arrived, they

> received showers of broken granite and small pebbles. One of these struck Mrs. Despard on the forehead, leaving a nasty cut and bruise. However, she mounted the chair and began to address the crowd, which immediately made a rush for her.[91] Mrs. Despard was knocked from her chair, and, but for the support of a couple of men near the van, must have fallen into the roadway. One man picked the chair up, and was on the point of slashing round with it among the crowd, when his arm was arrested.[92]

The chair was apparently smashed up and, according to Miss Sidley's account, 'things looked indeed very dangerous.'[93] However, there was reportedly a small group of working men that tried to protect the women. This allowed the women the opportunity to climb inside their van to escape the situation. However, 'Amid a terrible upload the van containing the ladies was assailed by the mob, and its tailboard was broken, doors pulled off, and hinges and windows smashed.'[94] Miss Sidley described blocks of heavy stone and granite being used to smash the van, including four windows. She also referred to the 'pretty exterior' of their 'house' being scratched and spoiled. The *Whitstable Times and Herne Bay Herald* newspaper reported the arrival of a police sergeant and five constables which enabled Mrs. Despard to say a few words, including telling the crowd that they had shown the greatest cowardice they could possibly have done. Most perturbing to Marguerite Sidley, however, was that 'hundreds of so-called "gentlemen" stood by looking on, not one attempting to prevent the dastardly attack upon us, many of them smiling with evident satisfaction.'[95]

The local newspaper reported that when interviewed after this violent encounter, Mrs. Despard had said:

> Someone…threw that stone. I don't care who he is, for I don't suppose he meant to do any harm, but I do say

it is a most disgraceful thing that there should be this horseplay in a town like Maidstone. I have come here for the first time to speak and I am surprised at your behaviour. I lived in Kent when I was a little girl, and I thought I was coming into my own county. Those boys here will never make decent men. They don't know how to respect a woman.[96]

This event must have been disconcerting for the women involved and it would have been understandable if they had ended their tour of Kent and returned home. However, clearly made of much sterner stuff, Mrs. Despard and Miss Sidley returned the following evening and spoke to a crowd of approximately 2,000. With the mayor of Maidstone and the chief constable present, the meeting proceeded 'with little interruption. They spoke from a chair, the van having been too much damaged overnight to be used.'[97]

The village of West Malling (approximately 7.5 miles from Maidstone) was the next location for a meeting. Miss Sidley reported that she and Miss Seruya (a key donor of funds for the caravan tour in July and an organizer for the WFL on their London Constituencies Campaign which started later in 1908) and Miss Cowen (a speaker in Surrey on an earlier part of this WFL tour) held a 'perfectly delightful meeting' where 'so much interest was displayed'.[98] The women received so much interest in this small village, taking a good collection and selling a large amount of literature, that they wished they could spend longer there. However, they were scheduled to move on to Sevenoaks next.

Sevenoaks is about 12 miles west of West Malling and they arrived there on Saturday, 3 October. The first meeting was held in the evening on the waste ground below The Vine. The *Courier* reported that there was a large crowd, but that most were there to disrupt and even to throw fireworks. The speakers had trouble being heard. In her account of the first night at Sevenoaks, Marguerite Sidley said:

Our first meeting at Sevenoaks was somewhat noisy –
a number of youths and boys delighted in throwing

fireworks and clods of earth at us, and in occasionally practising pantomime songs. The police do not appear to think it their duty to prevent fireworks or other missiles being thrown at women. However, we must teach our youthful opponents better, and hope that on Monday they will leave more decorously.[99]

The local Sevenoaks newspaper, the *Sevenoaks Chronicle and Kentish Advertiser*, reported that

The deputation of women agitating for the female vote visited Sevenoaks, and held meetings on the waste ground near The Vine, on Saturday and Monday night. There were lively scenes on both occasions, Monday's meeting being somewhat rowdy. Fireworks were thrown at the speakers and it was evident that the vast majority had attended simply for a lark. The women on the van platform were subjected to rude remarks and continual interruptions, and on more than one occasion the police had to interfere. On Monday night two lads were 'run in' for throwing fireworks, but liberated later.[100]

The WFL caravan tour seems to have ended here after more than three months in Kent. However, a record of the finish has not been identified. Given the oncoming autumnal weather, and despite the reported unusually high temperatures of 72 degrees,[101] it seems unlikely that a tour in a caravan could have continued for much longer.

These WFL tours, travelling to the more rural and remote villages and towns in the country, continued and many successes were reported of them. One success of particular significance to this Kent tour was that a Tunbridge Wells branch of the WFL had been formed after the 'recent campaign conducted'.[102]

CHAPTER FIVE

1909–13: Forcible Feeding – Awareness, Kent Women, Kent Prisons

Suffragette prisoners were held as ordinary prisoners, not political prisoners. They were therefore processed and held in the same way and quarters as pick-pockets, paupers, beggars and drunkards.

Hunger strikes became a 'tool' used by suffragette prisoners from 1909 and showed that women's suffrage campaigners were willing to die for their cause or, in the words used at the time, they were 'in earnest'.[1] 'As with all the weapons employed by the WSPU, its first use sprang directly from the decision of a sole protagonist; there was never any suggestion that the hunger strike was used on this first occasion by direction from Clement's Inn.'[2] Scottish-born Marion Wallace Dunlop (1865–1942) was the first suffragette prisoner to go on hunger strike in 1909, fasting for ninety-one hours. According to Home Office records, 'She refused food, but her case was not brought to the attention of the Home Office until she was too ill for the question of forcible feeding to be even considered. She was discharged on the 8th July, 1909.'[3] The same Home Office report stated that in August 1909 when two further suffragette prisoners began hunger strikes in Holloway, despite their physical condition being 'sufficiently good for forcible feeding to be adopted',[4] Prime

Minister 'Mr. Asquith's view was, as matters then stood, against the proposed treatment. The two women[5] were discharged, and Prison Governors were instructed to report to the Home Office as soon as self-starving women reached a point of debility at which risk of severe injury to health arises.'[6]

There then followed cases of suffragette prisoners hunger-striking but being released without forcible feeding when 'their self-imposed starvation became dangerous to life.'[7]

During 1909 there were several cases of forcible feeding of suffragette prisoners. Seven women imprisoned in Winson Green Gaol, Birmingham for disrupting Mr. Asquith's meeting at Bingley Ball in Birmingham were forcibly fed. One of these women was Laura Ainsworth (1885–1958), who in 1911 became the WSPU paid organizer in Maidstone and North Kent and later that year while living in Margate, the organizer for the Isle of Thanet. Prior to this, forcible feeding had only ever been used on 'fasting girls' in asylums who were deemed not to be of sound mind. This was therefore a significant change. Forcible feeding was being used on women considered of sound mind.

In Kent there was definitely awareness and knowledge of the use of hunger-striking by and forcible feeding of suffragette prisoners. Laura was a regular speaker at meetings in North Kent and the Isle of Thanet and was behind the drive to recruit support for the WSPU and increase the readership of their publication *The Vote* in Kent. A record of Laura speaking of her experience of forcible feeding in Kent has not been identified but, given her regular speaking engagements at meetings in the county, it seems likely it would have been mentioned. For those Kent readers of the weekly suffrage paper *Votes for Women*, the 8 October 1909 edition included a detailed account of her experience and an extract appears below:

> For three days after being taken to Winson Green I took no food whatever. Then, on the Saturday morning, I was taken into the matron's room, where there were two doctors and six wardresses, in addition to the matron.

The prison doctor said, 'I have orders that you are not to be released. I have to do everything in my power to feed you. I am going to commit a technical assault, and I take full responsibility for my action.'

He then asked, 'Will you take food or not?'

'No,' I said, emphatically.

Whereupon I was rounded and my pulse felt. Afterwards I was placed in a chair, my head was held back by the wardresses, and one of the doctors opened my mouth by inserting his finger between the teeth at one side. Milk was poured down my throat by means of a feeding-cup.

While this was being done both my mouth and nose were held. I was then put to bed. Afterwards the Governor asked me if I had any complaints to make, and when I complained of this treatment he simply referred me to the visiting justices.

At six o'clock on the Saturday evening the two doctors returned. I again refused to take food out of the cup, and resisted their efforts to make me take it.

Then they tried to force tubes into my nostrils. There seemed to be something sharp at the end of these tubes, and I felt a sharp, pricking sensation.

Owing to an injury received before going into gaol through someone hitting me on the nose with a stone it appeared that the nasal passage was closed. One of the doctors then said, 'It is no good; we have to use the tube.'

I was raised into a sitting position, and a tube about two feet long was produced. My mouth was prised open with what felt like a steel instrument, and then I felt them feeling for the proper passage.

At this time I was held by four or five wardresses. I felt a choking sensation, and what I judged to be a cork gag was placed between my teeth to keep my mouth open. It was a horrible feeling altogether. I experienced great sickness, especially when the tube was being withdrawn.

Twice a day, morning and evening, I was fed in this way. In the middle of the day a small quantity of meat extract was forced through the teeth, a wardress meanwhile holding my mouth and nose.

On Tuesday I was very sick in the morning, but I was fed again in this way in the evening.

After the evening meal the two doctors visited my cell and had a whispered consultation. One of them said to the other, 'Yes, I agree' and I was then told that they were thinking of removing me to another cell.

They actually took me to the hospital, and there I have been until my release.

In the hospital food was administered by means of the feeding-cup. This was also a painful operation. The mouth was forced open, the feeding cup forced through the teeth, and fluid poured into the mouth, the nose and mouth still being held. About half the food in the cup was taken in this way. This operation always produced headache and pain in the throat.

Miss Ainsworth saw none of her fellow-prisoners during her stay in gaol.[8]

Laura's campaign in North Kent and the Isle of Thanet was short (she was in Gillingham in February 1911, then Margate after Easter, leaving Kent altogether in July of the same year to return to Newcastle). However, her weekly articles calling for support in the publication *Votes for Women* and the references to WSPU infiltrating previously untouched Kent areas suggests that her presence had some impact.

Given the criminal proceedings for assault brought by Mary Leigh (the first of the seven women held in Winson Green Gaol to be forcibly fed) and others (including Laura Ainsworth) and a further incident in January 1910 involving Lady Constance Lytton, the Home Office clarified the prison rules in relation to forcible feeding and the following extract from a Home Office memo (HO 220196/658) illustrates this:

> In January 1910, Lady Constance Lytton under the name of Jane Warten was convicted at Liverpool, and although she had been previously discharged from prison as too weak (heart) to endure forcible feeding, her identity was not detected and as she refused to be medically examined she was forcibly fed. An inquiry was held, but afterwards Mr. Churchill gave directions that there should be a formal certificate before forcible feeding; and he also raised the general question of the period before forcible feeding, suggesting 24 hours as minimum of starvation to be allowed. On its being pointed out that forcible feeding could only be justified on a medical necessity and that it must be left to the responsible medical officer to say when it must begin, and that if it was to be treated as a matter of discipline and enforced after 24 hours, a Prison Rule would be necessary in order to legalise it, the Secretary of State agreed to the issue of an order as follows, see 183,256/17.19:-

> The Medical evidence at the Royal Court of Justice in the recent case of Leigh v. Gladstone and others[9] so clearly indicated the advisability of resorting to compulsory feeding in an early stage of voluntary starvation that the Commissioners are advised that as a rule Medical Officers should not allow process of self-starvation to produce any weakness of a serious character, although of course the discretion must rest with the Medical Officer, even 48 hours as a general rule would appear to the Commissioners to be an exceptionally long period and to be a limit which should not be exceeded unless there were good medical reasons for so doing.[10]

In 1912, Olive Walton of Tunbridge Wells, Kent was forcibly fed at Aylesbury Gaol and news of this reached Kent as objections were made about her treatment. Olive had been imprisoned for her part, together with Miss Emma Casey, in the breaking of windows at Messrs Marshall & Snelgrove's at a cost of £240:[11]

> Miss Evelyn Billing, the West Kent organizer of the Women's Social and Political Union, has issued an appeal to the women of Tunbridge Wells urging them to write to the Home Secretary and to the Members of Parliament for the district 'demanding the immediate suspension of the dangerous and barbarous treatment of Miss Olive Walton, of Tunbridge Wells, in Aylesbury Prison'.[12]

In the same April 1912 report it quotes a prisoner, Dr. Ede, released from Aylesbury Prison after enduring forcible feeding. The report reads as follows:

> Until one of the ladies – Dr. Ede – was released owing to the effects on her health, it was not known that the practice of forcible feeding had been resorted to by the prison authorities. Presumably, Miss Olive Walton is among the sufferers, but the only details known are those which Dr. Ede supplies as follows: 'Apparently the hunger strike was not discovered till Tuesday, when, owing to the condition of some of the weaker ones, I informed the governor as to the state of things. Forcible feeding was then [initiated],[13] in most cases by the painful process of a tube through the nostrils, in others by the feeding-cup, and in at least one case that I know of by the tube through the throat. It so happened that I was one of the last to be forcibly fed by means of the nasal tube last Tuesday, and by far the more terrible experience than my personal suffering was to hear the agonising cries from other cells as the prisoners in turn were subjected to the painful treatment. Additional distress was caused for a time by taking away all water

from the cells on Wednesday night and substituting milk. This deprivation of water occurred immediately after the visit of a medical inspector of prisons. The women threw away the milk. On the following day they were allowed free access to the taps, but as I was released on the grounds of health in the afternoon of the same day, I cannot say whether the policy of depriving the prisoners of water was again tried. I may add that after forcible feeding was [initiated],[14] both exercise and chapel was stopped.'[15]

On page 9 of the same newspaper (*Kent and Sussex Courier*, 19 April 1912) was an article titled 'Votes for Women'. In it were reports of WSPU meetings in Five Ways, Tunbridge Wells, where 'The audiences were large and friendly and interested. Many questions were asked and answered.'[16] The speaker, Miss Evelyn Billing, listed here as organizer for North and West Kent, explained that having been arrested at the recent militant protests in London, 'the Suffragettes in Aylesbury Prison had adopted the "Hunger-strike" as a means of protest against Mr. McKenna's[17] action in denying them the special privileges due to political offenders,[18] which privileges were conceded to Suffragettes sentenced to imprisonment for window breaking in November.'

The report of Miss Billing's request continued:

Medical men like Mr. Mansell-Moullin and Sir Victor Horsley have declared forcible feeding to be dangerous and inhuman. The WSPU, therefore, not only in the interests of legal justice, but also in the interests of humanity, are calling upon the general public to petition MPs, and especially Mr. McKenna for the immediate suspension of this barbarous method of torture.

Miss Olive Walton, of Tunbridge Wells, is amongst those who are 'forcibly fed'. Many letters and petitions have already been signed on her behalf and despatched from this town to Mr. McKenna, but the WSPU call upon men and women to bombard Mr. McKenna with demands for Miss Walton's immediate release or, failing that, at any rate the concession to her of her rightful privileges under the law.[19]

Following her release, Miss Olive Walton, together with other prisoners Miss E. Wedgwood, Miss Durham and Miss Marion, attended a Tunbridge Wells branch of the WSPU meeting at the Grand Hotel, held in late July 1912. Miss Walton spoke of her experience:

> On the second day the doctor came round in the afternoon, but in the evening the wardresses came round alone, and six of them tied me into a chair and fed me. When they saw that I would not keep still they began to pummel me as hard as they could all over my stomach and chest, causing me intense agony. I was very sick, very weak, and frantically bruised.[20]

The author of this piece for the newspaper describes the other talks given by released prisoners and the effect it had on those in the Kent audience: 'Other speakers made further allegations as to the torture caused by forcible feeding, and the whole pitiful story made a very painful impression upon the audience.'[21]

In March 1912 it was reported in a Kent newspaper that 'About twenty of the window-smashing suffragettes have been brought to Maidstone Gaol to serve their terms of hard labour.'[22] It was not possible to locate further information about these twenty prisoners. However, it was reported that four of the prisoners were serving a six-month sentence[23] and the Home Office records[24] evidence this and provide further details about the four women. The first table below details the number of window-smashing suffragettes or 'vitrifragists' (glass-breakers) like Ethel Baldock discussed in Chapter 1. It shows in which prison they were held and the number of them released on medical or other grounds.

Prison	Number sentenced for window-smashing	Number released on medical grounds	Number released on other grounds
Aylesbury	28	8	9
Birmingham	25	13	1
Holloway	145	24	12
Maidstone	4	4	-
Reading	1	-	-
Total	**203**	**49**	**22**

The information in this first table demonstrates that Kent's role in the imprisonment of the 1912 vitrifragists was very small, with only Reading Prison holding less prisoners than Maidstone. However, Kent's Maidstone Prison did play a role in forcible feeding as it was recorded that 4 'persons connected with the Suffrage movement convicted of offences against the Law during 1912 [who] were forcibly fed'.[25] The following table shows the numbers of prisoners imprisoned in connection with the Suffrage movement forcibly fed during 1912 in each prison.

Prison	Number of Suffrage movement-connected prisoners forcibly fed during 1912
Holloway	51
Aylesbury North	24
Birmingham	23
Maidstone	4
Total	**102**

While it was recorded that four prisoners were forcibly fed during 1912 at Kent's Maidstone Prison, from examination of more detailed records it appears that only three of the four were. The discovery of these further records has enabled a greater level of detail to be pieced together.

Beginning with their names, it is known that they were Hope Jones, Ethel Lewis, Maud Joachim and Nellie Neave.[26] Below is a table that details their sentences and release dates:[27]

Name	Home Office File No.	Sentence	Probable date of release	Date released on medical grounds
Hope Jones	221964	6 months, 3 days	20.8.1912	23.6.1912
Ethel Lewis	222179	6 months, 3 days	20.8.1912	25.6.1912
Maud Joachim	222057	6 months, 3 days	26.8.1912	25.6.1912
Nellie Neave	222543	6 months, 3 days	26.8.1912	25.6.1912

While Hope, Ethel, Maud and Nellie served their sentences at Maidstone Prison, WSPU organizer Miss Evelyn Billing of 79 Tonbridge Road, Maidstone organized protest meetings in Maidstone and the nearby towns of Rochester and Gillingham. Reports of good meetings in Tonbridge and Tunbridge Wells were made in the 26 April *Votes for Women* journal with the proclamation that 'the general public is beginning to understand the truth about "forcible feeding". Maidstone is now being aroused, because there are Suffragettes serving six months' imprisonment there.'[28]

In May, Miss Evelyn Billing had initiated an 'open-air campaign in connection with the imprisonment of Suffragettes in the prison' in Maidstone and she appealed to all parts of Kent 'for subscriptions for providing hampers for the prisoners'. She also sought out 'introductions to people in Maidstone'.[29] Meetings took place in Maidstone and Chatham. Mrs. Mary Leigh was a speaker at one of these meetings, so Kent inhabitants would have heard from one of the first

Mary Leigh, one of the first WSPU members to be forcibly fed, was a speaker in Maidstone and Chatham, Kent, in 1912
© *LSE Women's Library collection*

WSPU members to be forcibly fed in 1909. Large crowds were reported[30] as attending these open-air meetings.

By the end of May the report was circulated that 'Maidstone prisoners are much cheered by hearing of the good meetings being held in the district. Meetings continue satisfactorily, and the neighbouring townships are now being attacked. Snodland people showed keen sympathy and interest at the three meetings held there. New sympathisers are being found everywhere.'[31]

Early June saw the prisoners being donated jam by Miss Sharman. There were also further open-air meetings in Maidstone and Hollingbourne. Miss Morling and Miss Olive Ibbotson were thanked for their help with these meetings and Mrs. Kessick Bowes and Mrs. Perkin for their financial donations.[32] A week later, a meeting took place outside Maidstone Prison, and funds were still being collected for the prisoners' hampers. Miss Olive Ibbotson was 28 years old and lived in the village of Rotherfield, near Tunbridge Wells. She had been arrested three times and imprisoned instead of being bound over to keep the peace for her part in the 1909 deputation to the prime minister. Her own experience of imprisonment likely fuelled her involvement with these meetings.

Later in June, the WSPU compared the sentence of one of the Maidstone suffragist prisoners with a prisoner in Aberdeen, stating:

> Contrast, for instance, the monstrous sentence of nine months passed on the WSPU Leaders, with the same sentence given in the Central Criminal Court, last Friday, to a young man convicted of the manslaughter of a woman with whom he had been living, and who had kept him! More significant still is a comparison between the sentence of six months in the Second Division, now being undergone by a Suffragist in Maidstone Prison for breaking £3 worth of glass, and the sentence of fifteen days, with the option of a 15s. fine, given to a young fellow in Aberdeen last month, for assaulting a little girl.[33]

Despite the above report by the governor of Holloway Prison that four suffrage prisoners had been forcibly fed at Maidstone

Prison, medical notes state that Hope Jones was not fit to undergo forcible feeding and was released at that time.[34] It seems, therefore, that the number forcibly fed in Maidstone Prison during 1912 was actually three.

Mrs. Hope Jones served three months and four days in Maidstone Prison, released on 23 June 1912 as reportedly 'suffering from palpitation'.[35] Hope was reported[36] to be 43 years old when she participated in the March 1912 window-smashing. However, in the Home Office records she was reportedly 56 years old. The same report states that she had 'general irritability'.[37] She was charged at Bow Street Magistrates Court on Saturday, 9 March, interestingly at the same hearing as that for Ethel Baldock and Violet Bland (see Chapter 1), with damage to the extent of £10 to Parliament Chambers in Westminster. She was arrested and sentenced to six months' imprisonment. Before receiving her sentence, it is reported that Hope said:

> I should like to say that I have accepted Mr. Hobhouse's challenge, and I appeal to you to say that you would have done the same thing. I should like to say to Englishmen that you can give us women hard labour and fill your prisons with our bodies, but the spirit which encourages the women will remain. The light is still burning, and will never be put out by the hand of man.[38]

Many of those women arrested for their part in the March 1912 window-smashing spoke of their conduct being the result of Mr. Hobhouse's speech. Many argued that it incited them to behave in this way. Mr. Hobhouse was MP for Bristol and had unfavourably compared the non-violent methods of the women with previous successful but violent suffrage movements.

This was not, however, the first time that Hope had been arrested. In 1909 she participated in a WSPU deputation to the House of Commons and was arrested. Reportedly, Hope 'welcomed this, her first opportunity of following in the wake of the earnest and self-sacrificing leaders'.[39] There were 114 defendants at Bow Street, all accused of their part in this deputation.

According to *The Globe* newspaper, 'The majority gave some idea of their determination for "the cause" by carrying portmanteaux and kit bags in preparation.'[40] A portmanteaux was a large travelling bag, typically made of stiff leather that opened in two equal parts. With the large number of defendants prepared with their large travelling bags, an image of a busy, packed courtroom is conjured up. Miss Kathleen Streatfield from Chiddingstone in Kent was among those arrested at this 1909 deputation. She served a month's imprisonment in Holloway.[41] Nellie Neave and Maud Joachim were also arrested at this deputation. Three years later they would be imprisoned with Hope in Kent.

In December 1911, Hope appeared again in court for her part in a protest following a demonstration in Parliament Square. She refused to provide her address when asked. It seems that this was a particularly rebellious, riotous deputation, for 'Many of the prisoners broke windows with their elbows while waiting in the charge room, and one woman actually smashed a window with a stone while walking to the station under police escort.'[42] It was also at this deputation that the

> arrest of one of the most notable figures in the suffrage movement – Miss Billinghurst – created more than usual interest. Miss Billinghurst, who is a cripple, uses a hand-propelled cycle. She was arrested about ten o'clock, and, still seated in her quaint cycle, was carried through the thick crowd in Whitehall and Bridge-street by half-a-dozen stalwart policemen.[43]

Maud Joachim and Ethel Lewis were also arrested at this demonstration, as was Olive Walton of Tunbridge Wells, Kent.

Hope's time in Maidstone Prison was cut short as she was released on medical grounds. A report in *Votes for Women* on 28 June 1912 reported: 'At Maidstone, where the Hunger Strike also started last Friday, Miss Hope Jones was released on Sunday. The three remaining prisoners, Miss Nelly [*sic*] Neave, Miss Ethel Lewis, and Miss Joachim, after being forcibly fed two days, were released on Tuesday morning.'[44]

Miss Ethel Lewis (b.1885–86), like Hope Jones, had been arrested prior to her imprisonment in Kent in 1912. After the 1911 WSPU deputation, Ethel appeared in court and, described as a young woman, charged with breaking a window at Charing Cross Post Office, she said: 'I did it to protest against the Government bringing forward a Manhood Suffrage Bill when the only real demand has been votes for women.'[45]

Ethel was forcibly fed in Maidstone Prison. In July 1912 the *Votes for Women* newspaper published statements made by the Home Office about forcible feeding. The Home Office statement was printed and then each was refuted by a member of the women's suffrage movement who had experienced the treatment referred to in the statement. One statement was refuted by Ethel, that made by a Mr. Ellis Griffith: 'It must be borne in mind that feeding by tube is not in itself dangerous or injurious but the danger is caused by the violent resistance of the prisoner, which like any violent action involves risk to a person with a weak heart or poor physique.'[46] In her reply, Ethel said:

> Although I made no resistance, the nasal tube curled up in my mouth and the second day this occurred three times, and they had to use a longer tube. After the third feeding I felt a sharp pain round my waist, and in the afternoon I had an agonising pain round my heart. Some days afterwards the pain became so acute and breathing so difficult that I sent for the doctor. He said it must be muscular rheumatism.[47]

Ethel's continued determination is highlighted by the letter she sent to the *Daily Herald* in February 1913. It read:

> Sir,
>
> Some of your readers suggest that Women Suffragists should begin to be militant in the home. As a Suffragist who is earnest enough about the Vote to destroy property, to face prison, and even the hunger strike, with its attendant horror of forcible feeding, for the sake

of justice, yet to make the Dad (I haven't a husband to practise on) go to work without his dinner, that cannot be done. Besides, what good can it do? What can the men do more than the women, except send messages to Asquith, demanding a suffrage, or vote against the Government at the next election. How would it be, though, if every Suffragist and Suffragette pledged herself to get her men friends to write to the Government, demanding a Government Measure of Votes for Women? And if they sent in shoals of letters, and every one from a voter, would the Government take any notice?[48]

The rather magical image of shoals of letters floating continuously into the Houses of Parliament is created when reading this, as is the clear exasperation expressed by Ethel of the suggestion that women suffragists should begin to be militant in the home.

Also imprisoned and forcibly fed in Maidstone Prison was Maud Amalia Fanny Joachim (1869–1947). Maud was the daughter of a wool merchant and niece of Joseph Joachim, violinist and composer. She was an educated woman, having attended Girton College between 1890 and 1893. She joined the WSPU in 1907.

Arrested in 1908 for her part in the raid on the House of Commons, Maud was sentenced to six weeks in prison. She participated in the deputation from Caxton Hall to the House of Commons on 30 June 1908 and was arrested and imprisoned for three months. In February 1909 she was working in Aberdeen. In October 1909 she was again arrested, this time in Dundee, with four others including Helen Archdale and Adela Pankhurst for their part in the interruption of a meeting being held by local MP Winston Churchill. Maud refused to pay a fine and so served ten days in prison. They all went on hunger strike during this imprisonment; the first time suffrage prisoners had taken this stance in Scotland. They were not force-fed. In November 1909 she was a speaker for the WSPU at the Portsmouth by-election. Maud was arrested for a fourth time at the Black Friday demonstration in November 1910. She was held that day but not charged. Then in December 1911 Maud was arrested at the protest against the dropping of the Conciliation Bill and imprisoned for three weeks.

While participating in window-smashing in March 1912, Maud Joachim was arrested and sentenced to six months' imprisonment. 'She was transferred to Maidstone Prison because, the Home Office reported, "she is a person of some influence with the others and is fomenting trouble at Holloway."'[49]

During one of her open-air meetings near Maidstone Gaol, Miss E. Billing of the WSPU stated: 'If women can break windows conscientiously, cannot they also vote conscientiously?'[50] She spoke of the case of Miss Joachim, a university graduate and daughter[51] of a famous musician, who was serving a sentence in Maidstone Prison for breaking windows at Bow Street. The damage she was alleged to have done amounted to more than £5 so she was committed to Sessions, the magistrate being powerless to deal with the case:

> At the Sessions there was a re-adjustment of the amount of the damage, which was reduced to £3. That being so, Miss Billing proceeded, the case should not have been heard by that Court; yet, on the other hand, it could not be sent back to Bow-street, as in that case, Miss Joachim would have been tried twice at the same Court for the same offence. If the person charged had been a man, the case would have been dismissed; in fact, the Court was really bound to do so, but because the prisoner happened to be a Suffragette, the Sessions Magistrate broke through all traditions of his court, and sentenced Miss Joachim to six months' imprisonment. As many of them were aware, the conviction was appealed against, but without success.[52]

It is recorded that a Mrs. Willock donated 10s for Maud Joachim.[53] It is not clear if there was any relationship between these two women. Her name (and address in Warwick Square) did appear on 'a letter signed by a number of influential women' and 'sent to the Chairman and Committee of the meeting convened by West End tradesmen to protest against recent militant action on the part of women suffragists. The letter, after expressing sympathy with shopkeepers on account of the damage to trade and inconvenience to the public resulting from such demonstration' sought their support in urging the government to 'redress the grievance which lies at the root of the discontent'[54] and give women the vote. It is also believed that that same Mrs. Willock had a home in Tunbridge Wells, called Western House. She had been married (until his death in 1903) to Henry Davis Willock, HM Bengal Civil Service. A mystery remains about any connection there may have been between Mrs. Willock and Miss Maud Joachim. A story to be discovered another time, perhaps.

The fourth prisoner held in Maidstone Prison in 1912 was Nellie Neave. Like the other three Maidstone suffrage prisoners, Nellie had previous convictions for her part in deputations and demonstrations. Nellie participated in the June 1909 disturbances outside the Houses of Parliament. She was also one of 153 arrested in 1910 for the attempted raid on Downing Street. There are many records of Nellie making contributions to women's suffrage movement societies and this fits with the likelihood that the Nellie imprisoned in Kent was the unmarried Nellie Neave (b.1867) recorded in the 1901 census as living on her own means. She lived in Stapleton Hall Road, Hornsey, Middlesex with her two single sisters, Maud M. and Annie Neave. From other earlier records it appears that Nellie's father, Thomas, had been a pawnbroker.

When arrested for her part in the window-breaking in March 1912, Nellie was sentenced on Tuesday, 12 March at Bow Street alongside Vera Wentworth.[55] Vera was one of three women involved in the 'attack' on Mr. Asquith and Mr. Gladstone in Lympne, Kent in 1909 (see Chapter 7). Nellie was charged with causing '£25 damage to the premises of Messrs. T.J. Harries and Co. Limited, drapers, Oxford Street.'[56] Home Office records state that while imprisoned in Maidstone Prison, Nellie suffered from indigestion and a 'probable gastric ulcer'.[57]

Reported in the Home Office Records is a 'List of Medical men, with their qualifications, who forcibly fed suffragist prisoners.'[58] At Maidstone Prison in Kent these were listed as the following:

Name	Qualifications
Hoar, Charles Edward	Member of Lic. Midwif., Royal College Surgeons Eng., Licentiate Royal College Physicians, Lond., M.B., M.D. London University
Ground, Edward	Member Royal College Surgeons, Eng., Licentiate Soc. Apoth. Licentiate R. College Physicians Lond. M.B., M.D. Cambridge University
Southey, Herbert Watson	Member Royal College Surgeons, Eng., Licentiate Royal College Physicians, Lond.

By way of background, both Dr. Edward Ground (noted below as present at the forcible feedings in the Kent prison) and Dr. Charles Edward Hoar (absent but clearly the most senior at the time of these forcible feedings) were long-standing surgeons to Maidstone Gaol. In *The Courier* newspaper on 10 April 1891,[59] both are reported as witnesses in two separate inquests into male prisoner deaths.

Dr. Charles Edward Hoar was married to his second wife, Nora Mansfield, according to the 1911 census, and at 35 years old (he was 63), she was younger than his daughters. One of his daughters, Katherine Mildred Hoar, 36, was secretary to the Chelsea Branch of the Charity Organizational Society. This was a society with the aim of organizing charitable effort and improving the condition of the poor. At the time of this census, they were living at 32 Bower Mount Road, Maidstone, Kent which is close to Maidstone Gaol. Interestingly, Bower Mount Medical Practice in Maidstone continues to operate today. In 1919 it is noted that Dr. Charles Hoar resigned the post of medical officer at Maidstone Prison after forty-two years' service.[60] He had 'given evidence in numberless cases at the Kent Assizes'.[61]

Dr. Edward Ground, aged 51, was married to Eleann, aged 50, in 1911 and living at 1 Ashford Road, Maidstone with his two sons and daughter. Again, his home was close to Maidstone Gaol.

The locum standing in for Dr. Charles Edward Hoar during the forcible feedings (see below), namely Dr. Herbert Southey, was 43 in 1911 and married to Violet, 42. They lived at 114 Tonbridge Road, Maidstone which is further from Maidstone Prison than the other surgeons, closer to the village of Mereworth in Kent.

From some brief medical notes for all four prisoners it appears that Dr. Southey led the certification of fitness and unfitness for forcible feeding and the forcible feeding itself, supported and assisted by Dr. Ground. As is seen from these notes (reproduced below), Dr. Southey took Dr. Charles E. Hoar's place as the lead medical man with Dr. Edward Ground supporting and assisting him.

The medical notes written and signed by Dr. Charles Edward Hoar, dated 5 July 1912, read:

> Ref No 760 Hope Jones was suffering from palpitation and was not fit to undergo forcible feeding on June 23 1912. She was released on that date. She served 3 months and 4 days.
>
> Ref No 758 Maud Joachim
>
> Ref No 759 Ethel Lewis
>
> Were both found fit for forcible feeding on June 23 1912 and were force fed twice on June 23rd and twice on June 24th. On June 25th they were nervous and very shaky and were certified unfit for forcible feeding. They were both released on June 25th 1912. They served 3 months and 6 days.
>
> Ref No 761 Nellie Neave was found fit for forcible feeding on June 23 1912 but was overwrought and hypersensitive and took some milk. She was found unfit for forcible feeding on the 25 June 1912 and was released on that day. She served 3 months and 6 days.
>
> These certificates were given by my Locum [Tenens][62] Dr. Southey and were in all cases supported by Dr. Ground who assisted.[63]

These medical men would have been required to comply with the new Prison Rule instigated by Secretary of State Winston Churchill in early 1910, which required that forcible feeding be instigated if prisoners began self-starving and doing so before any weakness of a serious character was produced. Dr. Charles Edward Hoar, Dr. Herbert Watson Southey and Dr. Edward Ground were also required to provide certificates of fitness for forcible feeding and not force-feed if the prisoner was deemed unfit. Reported in *Votes for Women* of 28 June 1912 is Maud Joachim's account of the four prisoners commencing hunger strike and three being forcibly fed. Maud's account of her challenging the doctors about how early they commenced forcible feeding is very much at odds with the 1910 Prison Rule. The account reads as follows:

> Miss Joachim states that last Friday, in order to secure the definite status of political prisoners, the four in Maidstone undertook to hunger-strike. On Sunday Miss Hope Jones was released on account of her health, but that day and on Monday feeding by force was practised on the others. On Tuesday morning the prisoners were medically examined and released on grounds of 'health'. The doctors admitted having standing orders from the Prison Commissioners to begin forcible feeding after twenty-four hours – a curious fact, as Miss Joachim pointed out to them, in view of the common statement that the operation is undertaken by the doctor's own judgement to prevent danger to life.[64]

Some three years earlier, in 1909, Dr. Forbes Ross of Harley Street had made a strong public protest against the forcible feeding of suffragettes in prison. Printed in the *Observer* on Sunday, 3 October 1909, his protest read:

> As a medical man, without any particular feeling for the case of the Suffragettes, I consider that forcible feeding by the methods employed is an act of brutality beyond common endurance, and I am astounded that

it is possible for Members of Parliament, with mothers, wives and sisters of their own, to allow it, however wrong the methods for the women may be. It is a procedure only adopted in regard to lunatics as a last resource; and forcible feeding in asylums, owing to the injurious effect which it has upon the digestion, is frequently followed by an intractable and well-known disease, chronic asylum dysentery. Any Suffragette subjected for long to this method of feeding is likely to contract chronic pigmentary colitis. Even in unconscious typhoid and brain cases artificial feeding cannot with safety be long continued, and asylum cases that have to be fed in this way die as a rule. I have myself seen a man die after being fed artificially for one or two weeks, and the post mortem examination revealed unmistakably chronic pigmentary colitis. I am not advocating the cause of the Suffragettes. I am protesting against the brutality of Englishmen who can treat women in this way. To me it seems typical of the brutality that in the last century could hang a man for stealing a sheep, or transport him for life for shooting the squire's partridges. No other nation in the world does such a thing.[65]

This public protest was contested by the Home Secretary Herbert Gladstone, using information from pathologist Frederick Walter Mott. The debate raged on for many years. A prison medical officer from Gillingham in Kent had also written to the Home Office. Dated 6 July 1912, shortly after the release of the four suffragist prisoners from Maidstone Prison, Dr. Iain Jefferiss[66] of 260 Canterbury Street, Gillingham, wrote:

Dear Sir,

You are welcome to use this letter in any way you wish as I see that a female member of the medical profession is writing in the medical press protesting against the forcible feeding of prisoners on medical grounds. I have been a prison medical officer for some time and again and again forcibly fed lunatics who were unwilling to take food and at no time did I ever see a case any the worse for this necessary treatment. I am not a prison surgeon now but my experience in this matter is I believe greater than that of the woman who writes without experience [and of those who uphold her].[67]

I am yours faithfully,

Iain Jefferiss. MACS. LACP.[68]

The female member of the medical profession he refers to could have been Agnes Savill, a consultant in dermatology and electro-therapeutics, and a suffragette. A distinguished doctor, she joined forces with two male doctors to conduct an inquiry into the treatment of women hunger-strikers in prison. Agnes Savill, MD, C. Mansell Moullin, FRCS and Sir Victor Horsley, FRS, FRCS, wrote a preliminary report[69] on the forcible feeding of suffrage prisoners which was published in the *British Medical Journal* on 31 August 1912. In it was stated that 'Mr. Ellis Griffith admitted in the House of Commons that on one day [26 June 1912], from three prisons [Holloway, Maidstone and Winson Green, Birmingham], no fewer than twenty-two prisoners had to be released and placed under the care of their friends in order to save their lives.' Three of these twenty-two would have been Maud, Ethel and Nellie. The report continued that 'Again, at the commencement of the hunger strike, twelve prisoners were immediately released, upon whom forcible feeding was never attempted, because the doctors of the prison were afraid to risk the operation upon them.' Hope Jones was one of these twelve prisoners released by Dr. Edward Ground, Dr. Herbert Watson Southey and Dr. Edward Hoar. This section of the report concluded with the following:

Further, out of a total of 102 cases of prisoners who joined in the hunger strike we have investigated, forty-six were released long before the termination of their sentences, because their health had been so rapidly reduced as to alarm the medical officers. In many cases the forcible feeding with the nasal or oesophageal tubes had been carried so far that the condition of the prisoners was so enfeebled thereby as to compel the authorities to release them under the care of a special attendant, who accompanied them to their homes, and remained with them until the assistance of their friends could be obtained. It is therefore not correct to say, as the Home Secretary did in the House of Commons, that he ordered his forcible feeding in order to preserve the health of the prisoners.[70]

No evidence has been found of any of the four released from Maidstone Prison having a special attendant. However, the following account of forcible feeding evidences the stark reality of the horrors and danger Maud, Ethel and Nellie would have faced and the pain they would have experienced, both physically and mentally:

During the struggle before the feeding, prisoners were held down by force, flung on the floor, tied to chairs and iron bedsteads. As might be expected, severe bruises were thus inflicted. The prisoners, however, did not complain of these. They regarded them as the inevitable consequences of political war. Forcible feeding by the oesophageal or nasal tube cannot be performed without risk of mechanical injury to the nose and throat. Injuries to the nose were especially common, owing chiefly to the lack of previous examination and skill in operating. Though the medical officers were informed in several cases that the nasal passage was known to be blocked and narrowed from previous injury, no examination was made. The prisoners were usually flung down or tied and held while the tube pushed up the nostrils. The intense pain so produced often forced uncontrollable screams from the prisoners. In most cases local frontal headache, earache, and trigeminal neuralgia supervened, besides severe gastric pain, which lasted throughout the forcible feeding, preventing sleep. One says:

'After each feeding it [the nasal pain] gets worse, so that it becomes the refinement of torture to have the tube forced through.' The nasal mucous membrane was frequently lacerated, as evidenced by bleeding of the nose and swallowing of blood from the back of the nose. Sometimes the tube had to be pushed up the nostrils three to five times before a passage could be forced.[71]

In terms of what Maud, Ethel and Nellie experienced, the only account available is that from Ethel in which she describes the nasal tube curling up in her mouth. There were, however,

> various means of carrying out (what would be rightly called) artificial feeding. They are (1) By a feeding cup; (2) By means of a spoon or bottle, as with a baby; (3) By a rubber tube with a funnel attached, the tube being passed through the nose; (4) By a large rubber tube, with funnel attached, passed through the mouth; (5) By means of enemata. By forcible feeding we mean any of the above procedures, when in addition the patient actively resists their being carried out, thereby necessitating the use of attendants to overcome struggling, and a gag to force open the mouth.[72]

All four Kent suffragette prisoners were released in June 1912 on medical grounds. Hope was released first on 23 June and Maud, Ethel and Nellie two days later on 25 June. This was reported in newspapers with titles like 'More Starvers Released' and 'From Maidstone Gaol – Miss Maud Joachim, Miss Hope Jones, Miss Ethel Lewis, and Miss Nelly [*sic*] Neave. There are no Suffragist prisoners at Maidstone.'[73]

Kent women to be forcibly fed in prisons outside of the county included Helen MacRae of Edenbridge and Miss Georgina Fanny Cheffins (1863–1932) of Hythe in East Kent. Helen lived in Edenbridge, West Kent but operated for 'the cause' in the neighbouring county of East Sussex. She received a medal which was inscribed 'Fed by Force 1/3/12'. She had been imprisoned for her part in the window-smashing in London and forcibly fed in Holloway Prison. Miss Georgina

Cheffins of Hythe in East Kent was sentenced to three months' imprisonment on 19 March 1912 for her part in the WSPU window-smashing, breaking windows in Gorringes' store. While in prison, Georgina was forcibly fed for ten days. Georgina was the daughter of a Portland cement manufacturer and lived with Miss Eva (Evangeline) Lewis (1863–1928), first in Cheshire and by 1912 in Hythe, East Kent. Together they opened and ran a Suffrage Shop at 83 High Street, Hythe.

The following year, in 1913, Kent's Maidstone and Canterbury prisons held two suffragette prisoners found guilty of attempting to blow up the Birmingham and Stratford-upon-Avon Canal. Maidstone and Canterbury prisons released these two suffragette prisoners on licence under the 'Cat and Mouse' Act. This was an Act introduced by the government in an attempt to deal with the problem of hunger-striking suffragettes. The Act provided for the 'Temporary Discharge of Prisoners whose further detention in prison is undesirable on account of the condition of their Health' and its proper name was 'Prisoners (Temporary Discharge for Ill-health) Act, 1913.'[74]

Annie Kenney (b.1879), the London organizer of the WSPU, was released from Maidstone Prison and Miss Rachel Barrett, assistant editor of *The Suffragette*, from Canterbury Prison on 21 June 1913. Both were released because they had begun to hunger-strike immediately on arrival from the Old Bailey in London. A statement by Rachel Barrett was included in *The Suffragette* and is included

Annie Kenney who was imprisoned in Maidstone Prison, Kent, in 1913
© *LSE Women's Library collection*

in full below as it provides an insight into the part Kent's Canterbury Prison played:

> After we left the dock in the Old Bailey, we waited some time in the cells below – each in a separate cell. Some of our number saw a visitor; then we were taken to the yard where the prison van was standing. We got into it with the wardresses who had attended us in the dock. Annie Kenney was not there, and this gave us some uneasiness, but we concluded that she had been sent on alone for some reason.
>
> On arrival at Holloway, I went through the usual formalities of giving up my property and signing a book for it. I noticed, when I signed that Annie Kenney's name was not there, and I felt certain that she had been sent to some other prison.
>
> From the reception cell I was taken to a first division cell in Ward E, where I passed the night. In the morning, about 9 o'clock, one of the wardresses came into my cell, and said I was to get up as I was to be taken away by train. She was not allowed to tell me where. I was surprised, and rather alarmed for a few minutes; however, I dressed and got ready to go. When I was ready and waiting to go, one of the doctors came in and tried to persuade me to take some tea before I started on the railway journey, as I had had nothing since I left the Old Bailey. I refused, of course.
>
> I drove away in a taxi with two wardresses and a man. I asked the wardresses where we were going, but they said they did not know themselves. Finally, we arrived at Victoria. The man took our tickets, and we got into a reserved carriage marked 'Faversham'. We changed at Faversham, and then I learnt that we were going to Canterbury. A cab was awaiting us at Canterbury Station, and we were driven to the prison. The matron met us at the door, and I was taken to a cell. She asked me at once whether I intended to refuse food. I said I did,

whereupon she made the staggering statement that if I did I should lose all my privileges and have to wear prison clothes. I said I absolutely refused to do so. She appealed to me not to give unnecessary trouble to other people. I replied that I was prepared to give a great deal of trouble to other people if it was for something that I thought right.

After a little more parleying, the matron and two wardresses forcibly removed my clothes and dressed me in the hideous prison garb. I was then taken to another cell – of the usual prison pattern, containing a plank bed, rolled-up bedding, tin utensils, and a shelf.

In the afternoon I was taken to see the governor. I told him I did not intend to take any food while I was in prison, and he did not argue with me or try to persuade me – which was a relief. I told him I protested against wearing the prison clothes, and should continue to protest. Later on I saw the doctor, who examined me. He also neither argued nor persuaded.

I went to bed early, and was very sick all through the night. The next day, when the prison doctor came, he ordered me to be taken upstairs to the hospital, where I remained for the rest of the time. In the afternoon the governor came and told me they would have to take my finger-prints. I said I absolutely refused to have them taken, and would resist with all my strength if they attempted to do it. He said it had to be done, and he and two wardresses tried to do it. I struggled hard all the time, with the result that all they got were a few black smudges not at all like finger-prints, so far as I could see.

In the evening the doctor again examined me, and a wardress sat up with me all night. Again I was very sick. On Friday the governor informed me that he had received orders from the Home Secretary that I was to be allowed my own clothes.

Soon after, the matron came in and said they must take my finger-prints again, as those they had were not satisfactory, and I prepared myself for another fight. This time the matron, two wardresses, and a man (I thought possibly a warder from the men's prison) came in to do it. I struggled very hard. The wardresses and the man seemed very unwilling to hurt me, but at last, when they were not succeeding, the man adopted the plan of pushing his nail under my nail to the quick – which hurt very much, and caused me instinctively to keep my finger still for an instant. Then the paper was quickly pressed on, and some sort of an impression produced. They were very dubious about it, but they thought it might do. From what I saw of it, however, I do not think will be set up as a model in Scotland Yard.

That night again a wardress sat up with me. On Saturday, at about one o'clock, the governor and doctor came in and told me I was to be released, and that Miss Sprott was in Canterbury and would come and fetch me. I then took some Brand's Essence and hot water, and soon after got up and dressed, with the help of the matron.

At three o'clock the governor read to me my licence, liberating me under the usual Cat-and-Mouse conditions until Saturday next. At half-past three, Miss Sprott came and took me away in a taxi, and we drove away to the station and came by the first train to London.

All the time Rachel was in prison they brought her prison food at every meal-time, as if she had been an ordinary prisoner. This food they left in the cell until the next meal-time came. She says: 'I was not tempted to eat it, however, and I think it would have been just the same if the food had been much more appetising than the prison food. I felt as if, for the time being, food and I had nothing to do with one another. Of the two wardresses who accompanied me from Holloway to Canterbury, one remained in Canterbury all the time I was there.'[75]

Miss Sprott, a WSPU organizer, met Rachel from Canterbury Prison and an account in a Nottingham newspaper provides an insight:

> Miss Barrett left the prison at 3.30, joining a friend, who, earlier in the day, had visited the prison, evidently in anticipation of the release. They at once entered a motor car and drove to the station, returning direct to London. A Canterbury message states that the released Suffragist showed little outward evidence of serious illness, and laughed and talked with her companion.[76]

While in the Old Bailey after sentencing, Rachel Barrett had noticed that Annie Kenney was missing from the exercise yard. This was because Annie had been taken directly to Maidstone Prison accompanied by two wardresses and a man. 'Contrary to the customary practices, the ladies were not all kept at Holloway, but were divided amongst the various women's prisons throughout the country.'[77] It seems that Mr. Justice Phillimore when sentencing these women on 17 June to long prison sentences (Annie to 18 months and Rachel to 9 months) at the Old Bailey had said:

Annie Kenney, possibly in prison clothing. Annie was imprisoned in Maidstone Prison, Kent, in 1913
© *LSE Women's Library collection*

> The time for leniency is past. I do not think you will meet with the leniency other people have met with. And I am bound to tell you that if the Home Secretary consults me, as he very often consults the judge, I shall take on myself the responsibility of saying that, at any rate, the ringleaders of you should not be released on any consideration.[78]

Upon arriving at Maidstone Prison, it is reported that Annie Kenney immediately adopted the hunger strike. In her statement she said that within twenty-four hours she was so weak she stayed in bed. Like Miss Barrett, she also had her fingerprints taken. When leaving Maidstone Prison on Saturday, 21 June it is known from Annie's own statement that

> While coming down the garden on leaving the prison, I had just turned a corner, when I realised that before me was a man with a camera, to take me unawares. My hair was down, as I was feeling too ill to do it up, and whether or not they got a real photograph of me I do not know.[79]

Annie was reportedly 'brought in a cab, accompanied by a nurse, down to the Central Hotel, a few minutes after her discharge was written out. She was helped upstairs, and though she had kept up wonderfully until then, collapsed as soon as she got into bed.'[80] A friend of Annie had written:

> The prison doctor had warned her that it would be most unwise indeed risky to attempt to come up to London until after 24 hours, and later (about 8 pm), when Dr. Johnston saw her, he absolutely refused to allow her to travel up to town on the Sunday unless we could procure a motor-ambulance for the journey. Both doctors told us that Miss Kenney's heart was bad, and that the greatest care must be taken of her.[81]

It appears that Annie heeded the doctors' advice and agreed not to travel to London until the following day. Her diet was restricted to peptonized milk and brandy-and-soda. Annie's friend reported that 'On the journey to London yesterday (Sunday) she had to be given brandy twice, and was in a very low and completely exhausted condition when we arrived at our destination, the ambulance man having to lift her bodily out of the ambulance and take her up to her room.'[82]

Annie had dictated her statement (referred to in part above) a week after her release when she was reportedly[83] still confined to her room. A medical report for Annie stated that she 'has improved since her release. She is still extremely thin, and her heart has not yet recovered from the strain which she has undergone. She is quite unfit for further imprisonment.'[84] Rachel Barrett had been taken to a nursing home to recuperate and her medical report read: 'Miss Barrett has suffered greatly from indigestion during the week since she left prison; she has had much pain and discomfort. On the whole her condition has improved and she has gained in strength. Her health is still much below the normal level.'[85] Both women were rearrested on Wednesday, 2 July 1913, their licences under the 'Cat and Mouse' Act having expired on Saturday, 28 June. Both were taken to Holloway Prison where it was reported that Annie 'immediately resumed the hunger-strike'.[86] Both were released three days later on 5 July with Annie reportedly very ill. However, newspaper reports from local and national papers as well as those publications associated with the women's suffrage movement tell of Annie joining Mrs. Pankhurst to speak at the WSPU during her periods of release from prison. At these meetings, she auctioned off her licences, donating the £6 to the WSPU fund. This included the licence she was given from Maidstone Prison.

Annie and Rachel were rearrested and released subsequently numerous times under the 'Cat and Mouse' Act but never again held in a Kent prison.

CHAPTER SIX

Irene McLeod: The Young Suffragette

One story of a young suffragette who it might be argued was inspired by her education in Coombe Hill School situated in the West Kent countryside is that of schoolgirl Irene McLeod (b.1892). Irene would have benefited greatly from attending this school as it was set in its own private grounds[1] and seemingly provided an innovative, holistic education to the female pupils. The school appears to have been ahead of its time, as it was singled out in an official report of the 1902 Nature-Study Exhibition as a school in the first flight that showed 'how much can be done by means of Nature Study'.[2] By this they meant conducting education outdoors utilizing the nature around them. Over 100 years since this report, it is noted that 'forest schooling' is beginning to feature in many educational institutes as an intrinsic part of learning.

In 1909 Irene wrote to the editors of *Votes for Women*, the WSPU-dedicated newspaper. In it she declares herself a suffragette and refers to a plan that she and some older pupils have to convert their mistress to support the women's suffrage campaign. The letter reads:

> A School girl's letter to the Editors of *Votes for Women*
>
> Dear Sir,
>
> I just want to tell you that I am quite sure being a Suffragette makes a great difference to one's life. At our

school we are all obliged to learn housework just as we learn any other lesson, and a great deal of this is done by the girls. Now housework here involves the brushing of polished floors, which is a thing I never liked, and didn't trouble much about, before I became a Suffragette. But somehow, if there is a scratch or a dull mark left on any floor now, I don't feel worthy of being a Suffragette, and I just polish until all the stains disappear. I feel as though I couldn't leave a thing unless it is well finished, now that I am trying to work for women. I am so very glad I am a Suffragette. I think it is the grandest thing in all the world, and I do believe that when women have the vote they will obliterate many of the dull spots and ugly stains which are so plainly to be seen in the social affairs of England to-day. The elder girls of the school have promised to come with me one Monday to the Queen's Hall, and with them will come one of our mistresses, who is quite unconverted, but perfectly open-minded. I have no doubt that after hearing our side of the question from our speakers, she cannot fail to sympathise with us.

Yours etc.,

Irene McLeod,

Coombe Hill School, Westerham, Kent.[3]

Irene wasted no time in pursuing her idea of converting others to her way of thinking. In November of that year, she and her sister Janet (b.1893), both living at 9 Thornton Avenue, Streatham, had formed the Drummers' Union. Irene and Janet were the daughters of Frederick H. McLeod, a civil servant, specifically a Labour Investigator for the Board of Trade, and Anna K. McLeod. They had two older brothers, Donald and Keith. It appears that at ages 16 and 17, Irene and Janet were young supporters of the WSPU and had 'decided to form a union of boys and girls between the ages of six and eighteen who wish to give active and independent help to the cause'.[4] They apparently had 'commendable energy' and arranged 'an entertainment at the Rehearsal Theatre in Maiden Lane on January 15, at which Mrs. Lawrence and Miss Pankhurst will speak'.[5] In a report of this evening, it was said that the entertainment provided by the Drummers' Union 'was a delightful success'.[6] At this performance, a play written by Irene called *The Reforming of Augustus* was performed and it 'simply brought down the house'.[7] The play was a translation of 'the process of reformation into the language of light fantastic comedy' transporting the audience 'to the shadowy Forest of Dreams'[8] showing Augustus being reformed by good fairies. As a 17-year-old playwright, Irene was reportedly inspired by 'The spirit of Youth, and Spring, and Morning, of lambkins frisking in meadows, and of Puck laughing in the tree-tops'.[9] How greatly her education at the forward-thinking Kent school influenced, inspired and enabled Irene to hone her writing talent is difficult to say, but it must have had some impact.

'The play grips the eager and delighted attention of the audience from start to finish. It is full of incident, humour, quaint fancy, charm and real wisdom.'[10] An extract from the play was included in the 25 March edition of *Votes for Women* and is reprinted here as it shows the tremendous gift for writing that Irene possessed:

> The sprite Joy, and Jingles (who is Puck under another name), visit Mary Godfrey as she sinks into an armchair wearied out with the rudeness and stupidity of her brother Augustus, and his mulish refusal to understand her revolt against his notions of the subjection of women. Then occurs the following dialogue:
>
> **Jingles**, sitting cross-legged on the floor beside Mary, speaking in a dreamy voice: I came through the clouds, hidden in the streaming hair of the East Wind…the East Wind chanted a wailing song, and I wept, for your world is sad, Child of the Earth, your world is sad.
>
> **Mary**, sniffing audibly: Don't talk like that, or you'll make me cry!

Jingles (springing to his feet): Yes, 'tis folly to be sad. Let's be jolly, let's be mad. (Dancing)... But come, tell me all about it.

Mary: All about what?

Jingles: Your amiable brother.

Mary: I suppose it's my fault as much as his. I've been too patient, and I've only just begun to see –

Jingles: You've only just begun to see that too much patience is inglorious. Ah, Mary, too much patience is no good! When some people are too patient, some people become tyrants, and that's no good. Oh, no good at all.

Mary: You are talking just like a Suffragette.

Jingles: Talking like a Suffragette, am I? Oh, that's good, that's one of the best jokes I've heard during all the billions of years I've existed! And supposing I am a Suffragette!

Mary: How could you be, you queer creature?

Jingles: Why shouldn't I? Why, Portia is a Suffragette. Portia and I live together in the same house – at least, our shadows do.... Now, listen carefully while I describe the house. It has two arms, two legs, and –

Mary: Why, you mean a person!

Jingles: Don't interrupt, it's rude – and a head, covered with brown hair, that is soft as the softest silk, and is always tumbling about in little wavy strands. She has blue eyes – bluer than yours, bluer than mine. Our eyes beside hers are like grey pools, that lie in the shadow, for they cannot flash as hers flash, nor laugh as hers laugh. This glorious house is slender and graceful as a sapling silver-birch.

Mary: Why, that's Cr–

Jingles: Now, didn't I tell you not to interrupt? If you know who it is, so do we all, don't we? (To audience)

Anyway, it's the most delicious house to occupy. Portia and I snuggle up together in the cosiest corner of that house, the corner of the Heart, and when she is tired or sad she calls, 'Spirit of Youth, Spirit of Youth, where are you?' and I answer, 'Here am I, here am I.' Then she has no more fear. (Laughing) When she is cross-examining Cabinet Ministers she calls, 'Portia, Portia, I want you: and Spirit of Youth, you too.' Then stupid, dull Earth people wondered 'how she kept up for so long'. Why, some of them even called her Portia.'[11]

Another extract from this play was the following:

The Queen of Justice is receiving reports from the fairies' Deputation, By-Election, Protest-Maker, Hunger-Striker, Courage and Stone-Thrower:

Hunger-Striker: I left a dark punishment cell, and the last thing I saw was a white face peering out of the darkness, and a flame of golden hair. That was all. The girl was ill but still determined.

Queen: Of course, thank you, sister. Tell us your thoughts, Jingles.

Jingles: Your Majesty, they are about the Forest of Dreams. Then there is soft music; the fairies take up the strain: 'The Shadowy Forest of Dreams', and Jingles tells how a woman went seeking the Land of the Free; how she lost the Forest of Dreams but found her Soul.[12]

This play was performed again in London and books with the printed words of the play were available to purchase in April 1910.

The Drummers' Union continued to exist through to May 1910 when it was recruiting boys and girls less than 18 years of age. By this time, Irene had written a further two suffrage plays. These two plays were performed at the Boudoir Theatre in London's Kensington in May. The first, *How Spring came to*

Nutts Alley which Irene had co-written with a Rachel Ferguson, was about a flower girl and a suffragette. It conveyed 'the hard lot of the working woman that the Suffragettes are out to improve'.[13] The authors of this play were also two of the actresses, while Irene's younger sister Janet 'took Miss Vera Wentworth's part at the last minute, played the part of a woman whose baby had been starved to death, with a restraint and feeling that showed real promise'.[14] Reportedly the cast did not always remember their lines but this did not detract from the overall performance. The second play, a one-act farce written by Irene, was called *The Boot* and 'kept the audience in roars of laughter from start to finish'.[15] The amusing play is told via a report in the WSPU's *Votes for Women* and once read is easily pictured:

> The scene, laid in a pre-historic cave, between primeval man and primeval woman…culminating in a delightful parody of the Salome dance in which the masculine boot was the head on a charger, reached a high level of accomplishment; and the scene in which the modern Suffragettes, at the instigation of outraged Womanhood, do a tug of war in order to pull off the boot from the neck of the woman who had made a doormat of herself was truly funny, with the right amount of serious meaning underneath.[16]

Irene was noted as playing the pianoforte at the Hither Green (Lewisham) branch of the Church League for Women's Suffrage meeting in November 1910. This was reported in the *Kentish Mercury* on 18 November.

By 1914, Irene is listed as an actress taking part in suffrage plays for the Actresses' Franchise League.[17] She also wrote articles for *Votes for Women*.

CHAPTER SEVEN

1909: Mr. Asquith 'Molested' by Suffragettes

Having previously been accosted by two suffragettes at Toynbee Hall in London and forced to listen to them in November 1908, Prime Minister Mr. Asquith was 'molested' by three suffragettes in Kent in September 1909. Home Secretary Mr. Gladstone was also present and targeted at this time in Kent. Such was the level of interest in this story that many newspapers published statements. This chapter uses statements and reports from different peoples' and organizations' perspectives to piece together this Kent-based story.

During the summer Mr. Asquith spent his weekends at Lympne, a village on the sea cliffs above the agricultural plain of Romney Marsh in East Kent. He frequented the nearby Littlestone Golf Course and liked to relax with his family while also attending Lympne Church on a Sunday.

A clearly outraged *Daily Mail* questioned: 'What Privacy remains to a pestered Premier pursued by the shameless kind of Suffragette?'[1]

With police protection for Cabinet members being stepped up in London to prevent suffragettes' 'approaches', it seems that this Kent-based action was a deliberate and strategic move by the WSPU. For Jessie Kenney, one of the suffragettes involved, stated:

'Having ascertained that Mr. Asquith would be going to Lympne this week-end, Vera Wentworth, Elsie Howey and I arranged our plans accordingly, and we decided that we would go down[2] too,' and, in closing her account, 'I am sure Mr. Asquith and Mr. Gladstone had had enough for that week-end, and were only too glad to get back to their public duties, where, at any moment if Suffragettes came on the scene, they could command a force of the big Metropolitan Police to protect them.'[3]

Jessie had also reported that the three women wished to 'remind Mr. Asquith, as we did at Clovelly[4] (only more forcibly), that he would not have much peace until he did his duty to the women of the country'.[5]

According to a statement made at the WSPU's offices,[6] the three suffragettes that carried out this 'attack' were Miss Jessie Kenney, Miss Elsie Howey and Miss Vera Wentworth.

Jessie Kenney (1887–1985) was the younger sister of Annie Kenney, the well-known WSPU member and paid organizer in the west of England. Annie actually spent some time imprisoned in Kent's Maidstone Prison during 1913 where she went on hunger strike (see Chapter 5). Both women were born near Oldham in Lancashire and from a young age worked in a cotton mill. Aged 16, Jessie completed a typing course. In 1905 both sisters went to hear Christabel Pankhurst and Teresa Billington-Greig speak at the Oldham Trades Council. This was to change the course of their lives. By the age of 19, Jessie had become Mrs. Pethick-Lawrence's[7] private secretary and then at 21 she was the youngest paid organizer for the WSPU. Jessie was arrested and imprisoned in 1908 for her part in the disturbances at Parliament Square. By the time she was embarking on her 'attack' of Mr. Asquith and Mr. Gladstone in Kent in 1909, Jessie was clearly very committed and determined.

Miss Elsie Howey (1884–1963) was a member of the WSPU and for her part in campaigning for women's suffrage was arrested, imprisoned and force-fed. She rode as Joan of Arc at the head of the 16 April 1909 procession to welcome Mrs. Pethick-Lawrence on her release from Holloway and in March 1912 participated in the window-smashing campaign.

Jessie Kenney, 3rd from left, sitting at kitchen table working with other WSPU members, c. 1906 - 1907. From left, Flora Drummond, Christabel Pankhurst, Jessie Kenney, Nellie Martel, Emmeline Pankhurst, Charlotte Despard
© LSE Women's Library collection

Jessie Kenney's office at WSPU, circa 1911
© LSE Women's Library collection

In June 1913, Elsie rode as Joan of Arc again but this time beside Emily Wilding Davison's coffin in the procession through London. In 1909 when involved in the Kent 'attack' on the prime minister and Home Secretary, Elsie had been a member of the WSPU for about eighteen months and spent around nineteen weeks of this time imprisoned. She was known as a wonderful speaker and in 1909 became paid organizer for Paignton and Torquay and opened a WSPU shop in Torquay. She frequently campaigned with both Vera and Jessie.

Miss Vera Wentworth (1890–1957) was another extremely determined member of the WSPU. For her part in the campaigning she experienced arrest, imprisonment and forcible feeding. In 1908 and 1909 she worked with Annie Kenney and Elsie Howey for the WSPU in the west of England. She had participated in a tour of Devon and Cornwall earlier in 1909 and had 'served two if not three terms of imprisonment since then'.[8] She was described as 'a lovely girl, and a younger sister of the well-known actress, Miss Patricia Wentworth, who takes a leading part in the work of the Actresses' Franchise League'.[9] She went on to take part in the 1912 window-smashing and was arrested with Nellie Neave, the WSPU member imprisoned and forcibly fed in Kent's Maidstone Prison (see Chapter 5).

Fellow WSPU member Mrs. Mary Blathwayt described Elsie and Vera as 'the two Hooligans we know'[10] in her diary entry for Tuesday, 7 September 1909, referring to their Kent 'attack' on Mr. Asquith and Mr. Gladstone.

Preparations by the three women appear to have included Vera being disguised as a nurse. There may have been other disguises too as reference is made by Jessie in her account to parts of their disguises being left behind when they fled the scene. Jessie's account provides an insight into their planning:

> ...we had thoroughly mastered the whole plans of the Castle grounds and the surrounding country, and so were quite ready to begin our plan of campaign. The Castle is high up on a hill, and commands a view of the English Channel and the surrounding country, and the walls adjoin

the churchyard, to which admission is gained by a private door. So on Sunday morning we disguised ourselves ready for the occasion, Miss Vera Wentworth's disguise as a nurse being especially successful.[11]

The local Kent paper covering the area of Lympne was the *Folkestone, Hythe, Sandgate & Cheriton Herald*. Its headlines included the words 'Disgraceful Proceedings'.[12] Their account tells of the three suffragettes first approaching Mr. Asquith at Lympne Church on Sunday, 5 September:

> The walls adjoin the churchyard, to which admission is gained by a private door. Disguised, the three suffragettes, who had information that the Premier would visit the church for the morning service, stationed themselves in a position which commanded a view of the door. They saw Mr. Asquith, unattended, enter the church, and they waited until he reappeared, and crossed the churchyard. Miss Kenny thus described what followed: 'He was slipping through a side door when we caught him. He was wedged in the door, and a little struggle ensued, in which Mr. Asquith lost his hat. It was a soft felt hat and he recovered it. We got hold of his arm, and tried to pull him back into the churchyard but he escaped through a door, and it was banged in our faces. Not a word was said. Mr. Asquith was so quick, and it all occurred so hurriedly.'[13]

The statement issued by the Press Association as the 'Official Version of the Affair'[14] did not refer to a 'struggle' but stated that 'After service at Lympne Church on Sunday morning the Prime Minister, on leaving the church, was molested by three women, one of whom struck him repeatedly.'[15]

On Sunday afternoon, Mr. Asquith and Mr. Herbert Gladstone met at Littlestone Golf Club

> and as the Cabinet Ministers were leaving the golf clubhouse together, the three women again waylaid them.

One said 'Now, Mr. Asquith we have got you again, and this is what we shall continue to do until you give justice to the women of England.' Mr. Gladstone came up, and in an endeavour to escape the attentions of the women something in the nature of a struggle is alleged to have ensued, and Mr. Asquith's hat was knocked off. Two men arrived in time to enable the two Ministers to regain their car in which they drove away.[16]

The account given in the 'Official Version of the Affair' read:

About 6 pm, Mr. Asquith, who was accompanied by Mr. Gladstone, Mr. Cust, Mr. Dudley Ward, M.P., and Mr. H. Asquith, was preparing to return by motor to Lympne from the Littlestone Golf Club. Mr. Asquith was entering the main door of the club house when the same three women rushed after him and again molested him. Mr. Gladstone, who happened to enter the passage leading the entrance door, saw what was happening, and, coming quickly up, forced the three women outside the double entrance door, only half of which was open. He stood there and prevented the women from re-entering the club house. Beyond that he used no force, and, needless to say, struck no blows. One of the women, dressed as a hospital nurse,[17] knocked his cap off and repeatedly tapped him on the shoulder. After a minute or two he was joined by Mr. H. Asquith, and the women were quietly removed from the doorway to the lawn. Mr. Gladstone and Mr. H. Asquith were joined by the other members of the party, and, entering the motor, left the club house.[18]

The official report stated:

Mr. Gladstone, who happened to enter the passage leading to the entrance door, saw what was happening, and, coming quickly up, forced the three women outside the double entrance door, only half of which was open.

He stood there and prevented the women from re-entering the club house. Beyond that he used no force, and, needless to say, struck no blows.[19]

Jessie Kenney's account, however, was that

> a real fight ensued. Mr. Gladstone and Mr. Asquith tried to push us down the steps, but we pushed back as hard as they pushed forward. There were blows received from both parties, and plenty of jostling. Mr. Gladstone fought like a prize-fighter, and struck out left and right. I must say he is a better fighter than he is a politician! The Suffragettes have often been called hooligans, but certainly the two Cabinet Ministers showed they could also be hooligans when there was no one looking. They got two other men to help them, and we all came down the steps somehow, and by this time were quite out of breath.[20]

Jessie's account pertains to threats being made on both sides. She stated that Mr. Asquith 'said to Miss Howey, "I shall have you locked up", but she promptly returned, "I don't care what you do, Mr. Asquith!"'[21] Jessie also made reference to them giving the men some home truths as they prepared to leave the golf club:

> We told them the leaders of this Movement would not be able to control the women much longer. Our parting words as they drove off in the motor were that worse things would happen to them unless they put an end to this fight, and gave the women their just rights.[22]

Undeterred, the three suffragettes carried out a third 'attack' on Mr. Asquith, when that evening they took a boat on the canal and rowed to Lympne Castle where he was dining with his wife and guests. The suffragettes intended to

> scale the castle wall, and to speak through the window of the dining-hall. 'We helped each other up,' said

Miss Kenney, 'and we had a lot of slips and scrambles, falls and tumbles. At last we reached to within a short distance of two open windows from which light streamed. We judged, by the sounds of the table furniture, that the party were at dinner, but I cannot say whether Mr. Gladstone was there. We hoisted one of the party up to a window, and she peeped through, and saw them at dinner. She reported her observations to us, and, standing on the wall, we decided upon a plan of action. Up again we hoisted her, and thrusting her head through the window, she cried: "Mr. Asquith, we shall go on pestering you." And then the window went smash. How we got down off the wall, and scrambled over the fences and through the ditches I don't know. We heard a commotion behind us in the castle, and a man's voice on the terrace cried out: "There they go down the steps." We got quietly into our boat, and looked behind us. The glare of lanterns flashed about the castle grounds, and voices called. But they never thought of casting the light on the Canal, or looking for us there. And so we got away.'[23]

The Press Association statement does not differ too much from this account. It reads:

About 10 pm Mr. and Mrs. Asquith were sitting in the dining-room with their guests when two large stones were thrown through one of the windows, and a woman[24] shouted some words through another window which was open. This woman and the others with her ran away, and, owing to the darkness of the night, were not seen again. In the hurry of their flight they left a small bag containing a light rope.[25]

However, a reporter from Lympne who may have had access to witnesses soon after this action provided the following account, which identifies the man's voice referred to by Miss Kenney as the butler. However, it disputes the report of lanterns, stating that only one meteor lamp was used, the police not arriving until 11 o'clock:

> Lights were not flashing. Only one meteor lamp was used; no policemen's lights. The police were not there until about 11 o'clock. The dining-room window was open. A woman put her head in and shouted something. Then two stones were thrown and two panes of glass were broken. The butler went after the women. In the darkness he went one way and they another. They left behind two coils of rope and some webbing containing stones. A county policeman is now on duty day and night. There is so much indignation in Lympne among Conservatives no less than among Liberals.[26]

Another newspaper reported that the words shouted through the open window by one of the women were 'This is what the women of England think of you.'[27]

It is believed that Elsie was the woman lifted up to the open window and the one to shout these words and throw the stones that broke a window.

The report of a Kent county policeman being on duty day and night concurs with Jessie's account that the WSPU had heard that Mr. Gladstone went 'to Hythe Police Station and gave information to Superintendent Holland, of the County Police, who came attended with constables to the Castle and left them on guard during the night'.[28]

These events are referred to by Clementine Churchill, wife of Winston Churchill, in a letter to Winston dated 11 September 1909: 'Venetia Stanley [Montagu] is staying with the Asquiths – A letter came from her yesterday describing how both the P.M. & Herbert Gladstone are black & blue from the repeated pummellings of the 3 suffragettes.'[29]

The determination of these three women was noted in a rather brief account by the *Daily Chronicle*:

> Premier's Adventure – Suffragettes 'Storm' Lympne Castle. – Women scale Wall. – Mr. Asquith, who spent

the week-end with his family in the solitude of Lympne
Castle, eight miles from Folkestone, with Mr. Herbert
Gladstone as his guest, had the quietude of yesterday
sadly marred by a Suffragette raid. The assailants,
although only three in number, were very determined.[30]

A term that, unlike 'suffragette' coined in 1906 by the *Daily
Mail*, did not catch on following this event was to call Jessie,
Elsie and Vera 'Lympne-pets'![31]

Clearly affected by and agitated about the incident,
Mr. Gladstone wrote in a memorandum to Sir Edward
Troup, Permanent Secretary at the Home Office:

'Where did the Lympne gang come from? Who housed
and cooperated with them at Hythe? It is not enough to
deal with these people if and when they come. We ought
to know what they are up to locally and all the more
dangerous should be known.'[32]

An intriguing statement, suggesting that Lympne in Kent
and other remote areas outside of London may have been the
subsequent focus of the Home Office.

Clearly Jessie, Elsie and Vera lodged somewhere in the area
as they were all London residents. One idea is that they stayed
on a boat, for in Jessie's report, she refers to them going down
to their boat and in her words: 'as soon as we had had a little
lunch we began to walk to Littlestone.'[33] The discovery of the
lodging address and those 'housing' them would be interesting
to explore and ideal for a future study.

CHAPTER EIGHT

1909–13: Suffrage Plays Performed in Kent

The Actresses' Franchise League was founded in London in December 1908. It did not align itself with any suffrage society and was a league open to anyone involved in the theatrical profession.

In the early days, AFL members were asked to inform the secretaries of the suffrage societies to which they also belonged,

Suffrage theatricals performed by the Actresses' Franchise League, c1909-1914. Photograph by F Kehrhahn & Co, Bexleyheath, Kent
© LSE Women's Library collection

of the AFL and it's services. The services were the performance of suffrage plays, recitals, songs and speeches. As a result the AFL services were more widely used at provincial societies' meetings.

In 1910–11 the AFL opened its own provincial branches with the closest to parts of Kent being Eastbourne in East Sussex. Membership rose steadily from 360 in 1910 to 550 in 1911 and 900 by 1914. Some AFL suffrage plays were performed in Kent.

The play *How the Vote was Won* was first performed in London in April 1909 and by July of that year was being performed in Dover, East Kent. This play was first performed at the Royalty Theatre in London on 13 April 1909 and first published, by the Women's Press, in 1909. It 'quickly became a favourite amongst suffrage audiences and was played all over the country with many different casts'.[1] It re-enacted the community of women on stage, brought together by a common cause in spite of their varied social positions.

This play was performed at Dover Town Hall on Wednesday, 14 July 1909. The play dealt with the idea of a general strike

Suffragette Play, 'How the Vote was Won'. A production of Cicely Hamilton's play 'How the Vote was Won'. This same play was performed in Dover, East Kent in July 1909 and subsequently in Sevenoaks, West Kent in 1910
© *LSE Women's Library collection*

among women, who decide to stop all work until the vote is conceded, and in the meantime to plant themselves for support on their nearest male relative, in this case Mr. Cole. When all his female relatives (see the list below) arrive for support, Mr. Cole rushes with all the other men of London to Parliament to demand the vote for women. Reviews of this popular suffrage play were glowing and in East Kent Mr. Ernest Chitty who played Mr. Cole was said to bear his worries under his female relatives circumstances very amusingly.[2]

Below is the cast list from this Dover performance of the play:

Horace Cole (a clerk, about 30): Mr. E. Chitty
Ethel (his wife, 22): Miss Adams
Winifred (her[3] sister): Mrs. Jellicoe
Agatha Cole (Horace's sister): Miss Crookewit
Molly (his niece): Miss Bishop
Madame Christine (his distant relation): Miss Marchant
Maudie Spark (his first cousin): Miss Fry
Miss Lizzie Wilkins (his aunt): Mrs. Carson
Lily (his maid-of-all-work): Miss Villiers
Gerald Williams (his neighbour): Mr. Wigley

The running time of the play was about forty-five minutes and the introduction to the published play tells of the scene set, at what time and which characters are in the opening scene:

> **Scene**: Sitting-room in Horace Cole's house at Brixton. The room is cheaply furnished in genteel style. The window looks out on a row of little houses, all of the Cole pattern. The door leads into a narrow passage communicating at once with the front door. The fireplace has fancy mantel border, and over it is an overmantel, decorated with many photographs and cheap ornaments. The sideboard, a small bookcase, a table, and a comfortable armchair, are the chief articles of furniture. The whole effect is modest, and quite unpleasing.

> **Time**: Late afternoon on a spring day in any year in the future.

When the curtain rises, **Mrs. Horace Cole [Ethel]** is sitting in the comfortable armchair putting a button onto her husband's coat. She is a pretty, fluffy little woman who could never be bad-tempered, but might be fretful. At this minute she is smiling indulgently, and rather irritatingly, at her sister **Winifred**, who is sitting by the fire when the curtain rises, but gets up almost immediately to leave. **Winifred** is a tall and distinguished-looking young woman with a cheerful, capable manner and an emphatic diction which betrays the public speaker. She wears the colours of the WSPU.[4]

The following year, in 1910, the AFL performed three plays, this time in Sevenoaks, West Kent:

Theatricals – A very successful evening performance was given at the Club Hall on Thursday, January 13th, by the Actresses' Franchise League. There were three plays performed. The first one, *The Pot and the Kettle*, was an amusing play which poked good-humoured fun at the anti-suffragists. The second play, *A Change of Tenant*, was notable for the finished acting of Mr. Roland Pertwee and of Miss Agnes Thomas, who as Mrs. Bassett, the widow, showed the unfair treatment to which women householders may sometimes be subjected. The last play, *How the Vote was Won*, was a farce. The acting throughout attained a high standard. The Sevenoaks Women's Suffrage Society is much indebted to the members of the Actresses' Franchise League who came down from London and so kindly gave their services. During the intervals the audience much enjoyed some delightful songs from Mademoiselle Violette D'Athos.[5]

The first play, *The Pot and Kettle*, was written by Cicely Hamilton and Christopher St John. With a running time of approximately fifteen minutes, it was first performed at the Scala Theatre in London on 12 November 1909[6] by the AFL, so this performance in Sevenoaks was one of the early showings of it. There are five characters: Mr. and Mrs. Brewster; Marjorie Brewster and her fiancé Ernest Hobb; and Nell Roberts (Marjorie's cousin and a suffragette).

Set in a sitting room in a Suburban Villa, Mrs. Brewster is sitting by the fire with a small table by her side on which is placed 'the greatest thing that the English have ever done in fiction' – Debrett's Peerage.[7] Mr. Brewster is steadily playing Patience at another little table and counting out loud. Ernest Hobb is fidgeting about the room.[8]

Ernest is waiting impatiently for Marjorie to get back from the Anti-Suffrage Society meeting. The audience learns from Mrs. Brewster that Lady Shiplake had called at the house and personally asked Marjorie to buy a ticket for the meeting. Mrs. Brewster is excited that being part of the Anti-Suffrage Society will put her 'in the way of meeting some really nice people'.[9] Ernest says: 'I'm very glad that Marjorie's on the right side, anyhow – with ladies, who are really ladies – not with a lot of female roughs who bite policemen, and actually think the word "obey" ought to be left out of the marriage service!'[10] Nell replies: 'What a strikingly faithful description of Suffragettes!'[11]

Ernest leaves, saying that he may call in later in the evening. Marjorie then returns in floods of tears. '*Pot and Kettle* is a comic pleasure – a young woman returns to the bosom of her family in great distress having assaulted a suffragette who was sitting near her at an anti-suffrage meeting.'[12]

On returning from the Anti-Suffrage Society meeting, Marjorie says: 'There was a – a lady sitting next to me at the meeting – She had on a fawn coat and a black hat with daisies in it; but she was really a suffragette – though I didn't know it. She looked just like anyone else.'[13] Nell replied: 'Some of us do. Go on.'[14]

The play reveals that the suffragette Marjorie has assaulted is Nell's good friend, Lady Susan Pengarvon. Mr. and Mrs. Brewster are hysterical, saying things such as

'These women are following in the tracks of the suffragettes! They are spreading the doctrines of the suffragettes, and like the suffragettes, they are wrecking the home they profess to stand for, and they are too stupid to see it.'[15]

Nell resolves the situation over the telephone, much to the relief of a shaken Marjorie. *Pot and Kettle* is a very funny piece in which the audience is as surprised and intrigued as the characters in the play as to why Marjorie returns from the meeting so distressed and enjoys the playing out of the story.[16]

Nell, the suffragette, speaks the last lines: '...I should make her[17] chuck the Anti-Suffrage League, if I were you. It's too strenuous altogether. If she must belong to something let her pick out something quieter – the Women's Freedom League, or the WSPU.'[18]

Intriguingly, a note in the programme for the performance at the Scala Theatre states: 'The idea of this play was suggested to the Authors by an incident which occurred at a Meeting by the Anti-Suffrage League at Queen's Hall, in March 1909.'[19] It is unknown if this level of information was shared with the Sevenoaks audience in January 1910.

The second play, *A Change of Tenant*, was published by the Woman Citizen Publishing Company and is undated, although the Bodleian Library dates it as 1908. The British Library stated that the author was anonymous, but later it was recorded by the Players Library (British Drama League, 1950) as being by Helen Margaret Nightingale. The play was toured by the AFL in 1910, so again it would have been an early performance seen by those attending the Sevenoaks meeting. Miss Agnes Thomas who played the widow, Mrs. Bassett, had been involved with the AFL for some time. She had been praised previously, in 1907, for her 'rasping Cockney tones' and 'termagant attitude that are required'[20] when she played a working woman in the play *Votes for Women!*' Mr. Roland Pertwee, referred to as a cast member in this second play performed in Sevenoaks, seems likely to be the English novelist and playwright. He went on to have two sons,

Michael (screen writer and playwright) and Jon (the actor who played Dr. Who and Worzel Gummidge):

> The play examines the reasons why Squire Brooks has decided to evict his longstanding tenant of 30 years, a widow, Mrs. Basset, despite the fact that she is an industrious, reliable tenant who pays her rent on time and looks after his property well. The Squire reluctantly agrees to her visit to plead her case. He reveals that the insuperable problem is her sex. Not having a vote, she will not be able to support his son in winning a highly marginal election. In the meeting that follows with his prospective new tenant, John Smith, the Squire is forced to question the wisdom of the 'Mrs. Bassets' being disenfranchised when the 'John Smiths' of the world have a say in government. John Smith is a drinker and a fool, in debt and ignorant, and when he has bothered to vote at all, he has spoiled his voting papers.[21]

Mrs. Basset 'is sent away for "a vote is a vote, and nothing else however good and necessary can make up for the lack of a vote". It is only when faced with Smith's record of rent arrears that the Squire relents in this decision.'[22]

The third play performed in Sevenoaks, Kent was *How the Vote was Won*, first published by the Women's Press in 1909. It was first performed at the Royalty Theatre, London on 13 April 1909 and, as referred to above, in Dover, Kent in July 1909.

September 1910 saw the WFL host *The Pageant of Great Women* at the Public Hall in Beckenham. Edith Craig, who later in life lived at Smallhythe in Kent, stage-managed this event.

A dramatic performance was given by the AFL at the Otford Village Hall (near Sevenoaks) on 29 January 1913 and the NUWSS Shoreham and Otford branch secretary, Dorothy Scott, along with a Miss Freeman of Troutbeck in Otford, sold the tickets.[23] Mrs. Henderson and Miss Dorothy Scott were congratulated by the local press for the great success of this performance with over 200 people attending. A play was performed along with two duologues. The play performed was *An Englishwoman's Home* by H. Arncliffe Sennett and the scene was the interior of half a cottage in a London suburb. Reported in the local press, this is how it ran:

> Miss Margaret Busse, as Maria Jenkins, is seen hard at work; she is called here and there by the lodger (Mr. George Carr) and altogether has a very hard time. Her husband enters singing 'Britons never shall be slaves'. He has been looking for work, at the club. He tells his wife never to say die; that was his motto. He then relates the number of things she has to do, and that she ought to think herself lucky. A young lady enters (a suffragette, Miss Victoria Addison). She tells Maria Jenkins about the vote, and eventually succeeds, in spite of John Jenkins' entreaties, in getting her to attend a meeting. Her husband is left to himself, the children begin to cry, he gets desperate and leaves the lodger in charge. Mrs. Jenkins enjoyed herself at the meeting, and on arriving home relates how a person was explaining things to them, when she hears a commotion at the back of the hall, and she sees her 'old man' getting the surprise of his life.[24]

A duologue entitled *The Maid and the Magistrate* by Graham Moffat was performed next. The scene was a sitting room during a dance. The maid played by Miss Victoria Addison and the magistrate by Mr. H.K. Ayliff are talking. He tells her that he is a magistrate and she asks if he has ever tried any suffragettes. He has not but says he has some coming his way the next day and he is going to give them all six months.

> It turns out that his sweetheart is among those to be tried tomorrow, he offers to let her off, but she will not hear of it unless he lets her sisters off. But the magistrate says the law must be maintained. In the end the maid asks the magistrate to give them all a fortnight in the first division, so that they could get their Holloway medal.[25]

During a scenery change, the local Reverend, W.E. Lutyens, told the audience to give their details to Miss Scott should they wish to join the local branch of the NUWSS. He also added that 'this society was not the fighting lot'.[26] He received loud applause.

The final performance was another duologue, entitled *A Chat with Mrs. Chicky* by Eveyln Glover. This was originally performed at the Rehearsal Theatre in London on 20 February 1912. In Otford Village Hall, Miss Victoria Addison plays Mrs. Holbrook, the anti-suffrage canvasser and Miss Margaret Busse plays Mrs. Chicky, the Charwoman. 'The scene is Mrs. Holbrook's brother's house. Mrs. Holbrook is canvassing for names against the women's vote, but each time the tables are neatly turned by Mrs. Chicky who is in favour of the vote.'[27]

It was reported that all three performances went well and without a hitch.

Information about Miss Freeman, Mrs Henderson, Miss Margaret Busse, Miss Victoria Addison, Mr H.K. Ayliff and Reverend W.E. Lutyens has not been discovered at this stage. This would make a great future research project.

CHAPTER NINE

Boycott of the 1911 Census in Kent

On the night of Sunday, 2 April 1911, suffragette organizations urged their members to boycott the census. The idea was to peacefully disobey the Liberal government. The exact number of those who boycotted is not known but it is estimated at several thousand.

In Kent, the total population as at this 1911 census was reported as 1,020,000.[1] A small number of individuals have been identified as boycotting this census and this chapter seeks to provide an insight into their stories.

Two ways were used to boycott the census. One was that the person protesting didn't fill out the form and wrote only a statement of protest on it, such as 'no vote, no census' or 'no vote, no information'. The second way was for the boycotter to stay away from their home for the entire night of the census so as not to be recorded at all. Obviously the latter method makes it impossible to track all stories of those boycotting the census that April night, although in one case, the party in Gillingham organized by Laura Ainsworth, the census enumerator, was still able to count those at the party. A record of the number of individuals could therefore be recorded, although no other details could be.

The following story insights are listed by surname, alphabetically. The surname has therefore been highlighted, as has the name of the place in Kent, for ease of reference:

Abbott and **Ferguson** of Rosemary, Crookham Hill in **Edenbridge**, Kent resisted. They had two servants recorded and for occupation stated 'private means'.

Laura **Ainsworth** of 32 Stuart Road, **Gillingham** was absent from her lodgings. She organized a mass evasion of the census in Jezreel Hall, Canterbury Street, Gillingham. She was a WSPU organizer for the Medway towns area. According to the *Chatham Observer*, there were a total of thirty-nine female and one male census evaders in this hall that night. Miss Boorman was likely one of those evading the census as she was referred to in an article.[2]

Elizabeth T. **Barnes** living in **Sevenoaks**, a ward maid at the Hip Hospital at The Vine (under the control of Emily Jackson) wrote 'no vote, no census' on her census return. Elizabeth was 50 years old in 1911 and lived at Hierpierpoint, Amherst Road with Mr. Henry Ernest Tulley (brewery employer), Mrs. Rose Tulley and their 9-year-old daughter Ethel May.

Miss Gertrude **Harraden**, 'about 30',[3] of Stoney Croft, The Bungalows, **Walmer** in East Kent, resisted and hosted an evasion. She had six female visitors and two servants, names unknown. One of the visitors was described as a hospital nurse. She referred to a letter that had been sent to the Census Office on 4 April 1911. Unfortunately a copy of this letter has not been found. Gertrude was local secretary for the WSPU in Walmer in 1910.[4] It was reported that Gertrude travelled from Walmer to Ramsgate once a week on a Thursday to the office at 2 York Terrace to work on and hold meetings, sell the paper and take charge of the office. She apparently left 'evidence of her presence in flowers and contributions to the Pound Stall'.[5] Thanks were given to Gertrude for the 'handsome stair linoleum etc. as well as for beautiful flowers and other gifts'.[6] Gertrude made regular contributions to the suffrage movement and examples of this are recorded in *The Suffragette* publications from 1908 through to 1913.

Mrs. Kate **Harvey** (1870–1946) of Brackenhill, 47 Highland Road, **Bromley** was detailed as 'resister/evader'. The enumerator wrote: 'House filled with suffragettes who refuse information.' The summary gave no figures but Suffrage WFL and the WTRL were cited.

Mrs. Harvey was also known as Catherine Harvey, Felicia Kate Harvey and Katherine Felicia Harvey. She was profoundly deaf and had married Frank Harvey and had three daughters, but was widowed at a young age. Kate lived in Bromley, then Kent and ran a home for disabled children. She was a physiotherapist and an early practitioner of physical therapy with the disabled children she cared for. In the then Victorian era this was extremely unusual. Society was such that women were not encouraged to work in the medical profession and certainly not in roles that required physical contact.

There is a long history recorded of Kate's involvement in the women's suffrage movement. On 4 April 1882 a meeting of the Bromley, Beckenham and Shortlands Women's Suffrage Society was held at Kate Harvey's house when she was the secretary. In 1893, the Bromley, Beckenham and Shortlands branch held its first annual general meeting at Kate's house. The society continued for at least nine more years. It seems that it then lapsed and was reformed as an NUWSS society.

Kate is known to have been a leading member of the WFL by August 1910. She organized the WFL Women's Coronation Procession for King George V that Charlotte Despard led in June 1911. Charlotte and Kate became close friends. Recorded in Charlotte's diary on 12 January 1912 is 'the anniversary of our love' which has caused some speculation as to the exact nature of Kate and Charlotte's relationship. It is also noted that Kate's name appears in the WFL publication *The Vote* as 'Press Department'.

Kate also became a member of the WTRL and engaged in a two-year battle with Kent County Council for refusing to pay a stamp to obtain a licence for her gardener, who was named Asquith (unrelated to but with the same name as the then prime minister). For eight months, Kate barricaded herself into her home to avoid being arrested. In *The Vote*, 1912, p.231, Kate is described as taking the stance of refusing to pay taxes without the right to vote for her representation. When the barricade was broken by bailiffs, Kate still refused to pay the taxes and was arrested and taken to Bromley Police Court. At her hearing in August 1913 she again refused to pay and was sentenced to two months in prison at Holloway. As reported in the *Guardian* in 1913, p.7, Kate was the first person sentenced under the Insurance Act. Protests about Kate's sentence were made, arguing inequality of treatment between men and Kate as her fines were far higher than those imposed on men committing the same offence. Kate only served one month of her sentence and was released due to concerns for her health. She received a suffragist's prison medal for her courage.

During the war, Kate and Charlotte continued to campaign for reform. In 1916 they bought a large house in Hartfield, Sussex and created a hospital for women and children that they named 'Kurundai'. Despard initially paid expenses, but in 1917 the Theosophical Society became involved. The hospital was renamed 'Brackenhill Theosophical Home School'. By 1921 Kate and Charlotte no longer lived together as Charlotte had moved to Ireland.

Alice R. **Rollinson** of Kismet, Pier Road, Northfleet, **Gravesend** was 35 at the time of the 1911 census and although she complied with the census, she must have referred to the WFL as it was mentioned by the enumerator. She was a teacher in a county council school and boarded with another county school teacher and his wife and their three children. In the 13 February 1914 *The Vote* journal, Alice is listed as taking the chair at a London meeting of the WFL.

Mrs. Margaretta **Wightwick** (1850–1921) of 3 The Drive, Barton Fields in **Canterbury** resisted the census. She was a 60-year-old widow living with her son, a solicitor, and two daughters. She lived in a large house with sixteen rooms and three servants. It appears that Margaretta's husband William Norman Wightwick died in 1902 aged 52 and had been a solicitor. In a 29 March 1902 local newspaper,[7] Mrs. Wightwick is named as Margaretta Charlotte, the second daughter of Mr. James Haig of Lincoln's Inn, barrister-at-law. Margaretta died in August 1921. The author has not found any links to any particular suffrage organization.

Rose Lamartine **Yates** (née Janua, b.1875) and her husband Tom resisted the census while on holiday in Kent. They lived in Wimbledon. Their holiday home address was The Cottage, Preston Parade, **Whitstable-cum-Seasalter**, near Blean. Tom was a barrister-at-law. Suffrage organizations mentioned were the WSPU and MPU.

In 1907 Rose became the first woman elected to the Cyclists' Touring Club (CTC). There were sixty-eight councillors at the CTC, and Rose was the only woman. She also served as the only woman on the Roads Improvement Council.

Joining the Wimbledon branch of the WSPU in 1909, Rose marched in February that year to the House of Commons. She was one of the twenty-eight protesters arrested and charged with obstruction. During her trial she said:

> I have a little son who is only eight months old…when the boy grows up he might ask me, 'What did you do, mother, in the days of the women's agitation, to lay the views of the women before the Prime Minister?' and I could not blush if I said to him, 'I made no attempt to go to the Prime Minister.'[8]

Rose was a regular speaker in Kent. In Canterbury in September 1909, Rose Lamartine Yates and Gertrude Wilkinson had attempted to address a meeting, but owing to the conduct of some attending had needed to stop. In a letter they shared an apology and their willingness to try again:

> *Votes for Women*
>
> To the Editor.
>
> Sir – Will you allow us through your columns to express our regrets to those persons interested in this movement who asked us to hold an evening meeting and those who attended last night to hear us speak that, owing to the outrageous conduct of the Whitstable hooligans

we were unable to carry the meeting through. We persisted as long as it was humanly possible, but when dastardly attempts at personal injury to the speaker were indulged in, it became perilous to life to continue. We should like to thank those few who had the courage to come to the rescue of two unprotected women, who, but for their stubborn help, might have been seriously injured. Needless to say, we shall not be intimidated from continuing to address those who wish to hear us. We should be glad if the man who so courageously protected the speaker would communicate with her at Belrapar.

Yours etc.,

Gertrude Wilkinson, Rose Lamartine Yates.

Belrapar, Whitstable, August 31st, 1909.[9]

Mrs. **Smart**, suffragette, 'about 60 years', of 30 Bouverie Road West, **Folkestone** resisted. Her occupation was described as 'Boarding House Keeper' and listed were **two visitors**, both unnamed and about 40. Also one servant was mentioned. The registrar recorded that 'Mrs. Smart refused to fill up a Schedule and the others refused information for the reason that they state women have no Vote. This schedule is filled up on the authority of the Registrar General.'[10] These three females were likely to have been **Mrs. Smart** (boarding house keeper), **Miss Florence E.M. Macaulay** (she was known to be living here by June 1911 as she was the WSPU organizer for Canterbury and South Kent) and one of the **Misses Key** sisters. One resided with Mrs. Smart at 30 Bouverie Road West and the other at 32 Bouverie Road West with Miss Annie West recorded as a visitor on the 1911 census.[11]

Lydia Judith **Le Lacheur**, a 68-year-old widow living at The Wilderness in **Tunbridge Wells** stated that her occupation was 'Treasurer, Tunbridge Wells Women's Suffrage Society' and two of her staff said that they are 'suffragist' next to their names. These were **Sarah Turner Reynolds** (cook, aged 60, single) and **Caroline Marchant** (nurse, aged 64, also single). This is interesting as they are the only servants found resisting the census in Kent during this research. It is known that the cook, Sarah, had been with the Le Lacheur family for at least twenty years and the nurse, Caroline, for at least ten. No other information about their interest and any involvement has been found at this stage.

CHAPTER TEN

1912: Militant Action in Kent

The struggle for votes for women continued. During the year of 1912 there were a number of events connected to Kent. This chapter takes a brief look at some of these events. These include Mr. Winston Churchill being accosted by suffragettes, a Pankhurst visit, and incendiary devices being used to explode Kent letter boxes.

In June of 1912 reports were made of six compartments of a train arriving in London Victoria from Kent's Tunbridge Wells being damaged. It was alleged that 'Cushions had been cut and turned upside down, straps had been severed, and no fewer than eleven windows broken.'[1] This was associated with suffragettes because there had apparently been papers pasted in the carriages with messages condemning the government's treatment of suffragist prisoners. One message read: 'We wish the release of Mr. Pethick Lawrence and women's rights.'[2]

The train went from Tunbridge Wells to Croydon, then to Clapham Junction, before terminating at London Victoria. Apparently the carriages were empty when the train reached London Victoria, suggesting that the perpetrators had boarded at either Tunbridge Wells or Croydon and alighted at either Croydon or Clapham Junction. This makes it possible that those involved were from Tunbridge Wells.

During the summer of 1912, Mr. Winston Churchill was the target of suffragettes. It is noted that Mr. Churchill's wife, Clementine, was, pre-marriage, often seen in the tie-and-shirt-collar combination favoured by suffragists. Churchill never publicly opposed the principle of giving women the right to vote (unlike Asquith, who was unwavering in his antipathy to the idea). Clementine strongly supported the Suffragists, an organisation which sought by legal and constitutional methods to press for the right to vote, but which was opposed to the militant, law-breaking activities of the Suffragettes...Clementine publicly declared that she was 'ardently in favour of votes for women'[3] and privately lobbied Winston, but she had ruefully to acknowledge that she was never able to make him support the cause, except in carefully qualified terms.[4] However, upon the announcement in 1908 of Clementine's engagement to Winston Churchill, one newspaper commented that

> With Miss Clementine Hozier, Mr. Churchill will find life much easier, and should the Suffragists rage too fiercely round him, he also will have a wife to suggest counter plans and rescue him from the hands of infuriated women anxious to shed the blood of the latest addition to the Cabinet.[5]

In one letter to Clementine from Dundee in October 1909, Winston Churchill wrote:

> I hope you will not be angry with me for having answered the suffragettes sternly. I shall never try to crush your convictions. I must claim an equal liberty for myself. I have told them that I cannot help them while the present tactics are continued. I am sorry for them. The feeling here is very hot against them.[6]

'Clementine's disapproval of the violent aspects of the Suffragettes' campaign was, not surprisingly, strengthened by the quite frequent attacks on Winston himself.'[7] He had been struck with a horse whip and pushed towards the edge of a railway platform while in Bristol, and protection had needed to be put in place for his young family as reports of threatened kidnap were received.

In Kent, the Churchill family spent the summer of 1912 at Rest Harrow near Sandwich. The home was lent to them by Waldorf and Nancy Astor.[8] Winston Churchill visited his family there when he could. While there in August, Churchill encountered the attentions of two suffragettes on bicycles. The reports of this ran with headlines like 'Mr. Winston Churchill held up by Suffragists'[9] and 'Waylaying Mr. Churchill – Suffragettes' Ruse At Sandwich Bay.'[10] The accounts of the incident included the following:

> Mr. Winston Churchill had an unpleasant adventure with Suffragettes at Sandwich on Monday evening.[11]

> As Mr. Winston Churchill was driving back to his house in Sandwich Bay his car was stopped by two Suffragists, who formed a barricade across the road with their bicycles. When he had thus been compelled to receive their message, they allowed his car to proceed. Mr. Churchill seemed much perturbed by the risks taken by these women.[12]

> Fortunately for the women who adopted this foolhardy method of interviewing the First Lord the speed of the car had just been reduced, and the skilful way in which the car was handled and pulled up by the chauffeur averted a very serious accident. The road through the bay is a private one, and it is a long sweep downhill. Cars usually travel along it at a great pace. If Mr. Churchill's car had been going even at the regulation speed of 20 miles an hour the result of the women's mad freak would have been certain death. As it was, the car by a quick pull-up got clear of the shrieking women.[13]

In reply to these accounts the WSPU newspaper *Votes for Women* published the following personal account:

A PERSONAL ACCOUNT. The following account has been sent us by the two ladies who are spending their summer holidays at Ramsgate:

On Friday [9 August 1912] we cycled to Sandwich Bay for a day's picnic. On the bleak, windswept foreshore we could find no shelter, so we pitched our camp at the roadside, and as we waited for our kettle to boil, a car drove past. In that car we saw Mr. Winston Churchill! We waited patiently for his return, so that we might speak to him; but he did not come back, and we went home that time disappointed.

The next day [Saturday, 10 August 1912], as we were propping our cycles against the wall of the Coastguard Station we saw two men who, shadowed by a car, were walking along the road some distance away. We strolled gently towards them, but even the distant vision of two women was enough to make Mr. Churchill realise that 'discretion is the better part of valour'. And once again we saw the First Lord of the Admiralty whirl past us in his car.

Three hundred yards down the road he got out and went into the Golf Club. A few hours later we saw the same car bringing Mr. Churchill back. It deposited him on his doorstep, and we were forced to realise that any attempt to interview Mr. Churchill was, under such conditions as these, an absolute impossibility. He was always accompanied by men, evidently detectives, one of whom never left his side. His house is only a short distance from the Golf Club House, yet the car always fetched him from home, and one of the detectives would walk down to the gate to see that no Suffragette was on the horizon before Mr. Churchill ventured on to the doorstep. Then he would be pushed hurriedly into the car, which would start at once at lightning speed, and deposit him at the Club House. The process was repeated on the return journey. There was evidently nothing for it but the desperate method of holding up his car.

On Monday [12 August 1912] we established ourselves by the roadside in time to see Mr. Churchill motor away, presumably to lunch, and we waited in patient content for his return. Presently, as we were making tea, we saw the car coming towards us, and seizing our bicycles, we rushed into the road and barred the way. The car pulled up with desperate suddenness, and one Cabinet Minister at least was compelled to listen to what we had to say with regard to the enfranchisement of women.

Then the car drove on again, and we went back to our deserted tea, only to be interrupted once more, this time by a messenger, who came to tell us how great were the risks we had run, and how deeply perturbed was Mr. Churchill lest we should have suffered an injury.[14]

In the *Western Daily Press* is the WSPU's reply to Mr. Churchill's released account of this event. It reads:

In a statement issued yesterday, the Women's Social and Political Union state that they have noticed with astonishment Mr. Winston Churchill's statement that the present Government seek 'to liberate, not to enthral: to conciliate, not to coerce'. Their policy concerning votes for women and its advocates is regarded by the union as a policy not of liberation, but of enthralment and of coercion, not conciliation. The statement proceeds: 'The militant suffragists desire it to be clearly understood by Mr. Churchill that they are certainly the women to dare and suffer all things in resistance to the tyranny of disfranchisement imposed upon them by the Government. The Ulster revolution may not be a serious matter, but the women's resolution is. The Women's Social and Political Union, while expressing no dissent from Mr. Churchill's proposition that in a constitutionally governed country there is no need and no excuse for violence, would point out that so far as women are concerned, this country is not governed constitutionally because women have no share in electing the House of Commons. Consequently the use of militant methods has been found imperative, and will be continued until votes are granted to women on equal terms with men.'[15]

The names of these two suffragettes are not known. The road leading to Mr. Astor's house on which the suffragettes had positioned themselves was a private one. This and their own account of how they checked out all the details of Mr. Churchill's movements and protection speak of a planned encounter.

This planned campaign to target Mr. Churchill continued when several groups of suffragists gathered again to try to intercept his car. However, as reported under the heading 'Suffragettes after Winston' in the *Framlington Weekly News* on Friday, 16 August 1912, 'Mr. and Mrs. Churchill left Sandwich to-day for Scotland. The Suffragettes' attempt to waylay the First Lord was frustrated.'[16] The suffragettes were described as being 'outwitted' by Mr. Churchill in the *Leeds Mercury*[17] and Mr. Churchill as 'dodging the Suffragists'[18] in another newspaper. In the *Scotsman* newspaper it was reported that 'Several parties of suffragettes had assembled on the road from Sandwich Bay yesterday [Friday, 16 August 1912] to waylay Mr. Churchill, but the motor had passed an hour previously, the women apparently having had wrong information as to the time.'[19]

Reportedly, on the night of Thursday, 15 August 1912, 'the police found four women loitering around Mr. Astor's house in Sandwich Bay, where Mr. Churchill has been staying. When questioned, they stated they had come to see about votes for women. The police saw them out of the vicinity.'[20] In the *Nottingham Journal* of 17 August 1912 it was reported that 'They were ordered off the premises and left without creating any disturbance.'[21]

In the nearby Whitstable and Herne Bay areas, the following was included in the 17 August edition of their local newspaper:

'It is to be hoped that the Suffragists will learn thoroughly the lesson taught them by the sentences of five years' penal servitude passed on two of the women responsible for the dastardly outrages in Dublin at the time of the Premier's visit.' It continues: 'and we repeat that it is sincerely to be hoped that they will now mend their ways. We can put up with a good deal of speech-making and minor disorderliness, but it is too much when hatchets are thrown at prominent politicians, and attempts made to burn down public and private buildings when people are in them. Nor will the cause of Female Suffrage be advanced a single stage by such heinous crimes, and we refuse to believe that any sane person favourable to the enfranchisement of women for a moment defends the perpetration of outrages of this description, however much he or she may be inclined to favour the use of force for the furtherance of political ends.'[22]

On 18 November 1912, the second anniversary of Black Friday, Miss Sylvia Pankhurst, sister of Christabel Pankhurst and daughter of Mrs. Emmeline Pankhurst, visited Kent's Tunbridge Wells to address a meeting of the local WSPU. Miss Sylvia Pankhurst was greeted with cheers and said that she had just come from the East End of London where she had been carrying out a campaign. The following year, Sylvia's work participation with the East London Federation of Suffragettes saw her dismissed from the WSPU by her sister and mother. At the Tunbridge Wells meeting she spoke about 'lukewarm Suffragists who said they believed in women having the vote, but spent most of their time in criticising other people who were working harder than they were' and of there being too many others who 'had no very great faith in the use of women's suffrage'.[23] Ironically, given her subsequent rift with her family, she concluded her address in Tunbridge Wells with an appeal for unity among the various bodies working for women's suffrage.

Sylvia Pankhurst went to Hythe in Kent later in November to address their WSPU members. The hall was almost full, despite a charge on the door being made. Miss Sylvia Pankhurst referred to the March window-smashing campaign, saying: 'Stone-throwing only began after "Black Friday". It was felt then that something ought to be done to draw the attention of the country to their claims, and it was thought, too, that stone-throwing at windows endangered no lives.'[24]

By December of 1912, militancy had definitely arrived in Kent when reports circulated about tar being poured into some post boxes. In the seaside town of Margate, tar was poured through some post boxes and it was assumed that this was the work of suffragettes, while in Tunbridge Wells 'considerable indignation was expressed'[26] when a postman emptying a box in the Pantiles discovered 'black fluid and sticky substance, and some acid'[27] which had been contained in a package but this package had broken when forced into the postbox. There were reports that other post boxes in the town had also been targeted in this way. Some at the time believed this to be worse than the window-smashing as people were unable to trust important communications to the post. In Kent a newspaper[25] article appeared about this latest suffragette campaign and spoke of the Post Office authorities refusing to offer an alternative free way to safely post letters. However, it was reported that although suffering some delays, the Post Office was able to deliver all correspondence posted.

CHAPTER ELEVEN

1913: Arson Attacks and Militant Action in Kent

By 1913, suffragette prisoners were receiving longer sentences with more commencing hunger strikes and being forcibly fed. Arson attacks by militant suffragettes had increased throughout the country. Kent was no exception, having an eventful year. This chapter sets out some of the key developments in Kent, together with some unusual ones.

In Ashford, a report was made of fourteen plate-glass windows being damaged in February. It was noted in the report that 'Suffragettes have been busy in the district lately.'[1] Not far away in Canterbury, members of the Canterbury Corporation and other citizens like magistrates, solicitors, clergymen, schoolmasters and councillors were targeted, rather oddly, by Manchester suffragettes. They sent them unstamped letters containing a halfpenny coin and a *Votes for Women* circular entitled 'WSPU. Suffragette Tactics'. To accept the letter, the individual needed to pay a fee of 6d.

Further east in Kent, railwaymen mocked suffragettes when they competed against each other in a mock suffragette riot. On the podium were Ramsgate in third, Faversham second and in first place, Deal.[2]

The militant action was not only resulting in this kind of mockery, but concern from those women campaigning for women's suffrage. In Folkestone, for example, the NUWSS reiterated via the local press that militant suffragettes were 'a small, though zealous and noisy section' and that the 'thousands of law-abiding men and women who comprise the other Suffrage Societies'[3] needed also to be remembered. Miss Hilda Stainer of the Folkestone NUWSS replied to an article about militant action in the Folkestone Baptist magazine, and it read:

> We regret that the action of the ladies leading the campaign on behalf of the enfranchisement of women makes it necessary for many who support the movement to stand in opposition because of the methods pursued. We hear that Folkestone is to have its 'outrage'. We do not know whether it is to be letter-burning, window-smashing or breaking up public meetings, but either will only cause damage to the cause and provide another reason for keeping women out of politics.[4]

She concluded in her response that she was not aware of any 'outrages' and reiterated that the NUWSS did not agree with violence. Her stance was supported weeks later in an article in another local newspaper. It read:

> Besides the NUWSS there are the New Constitutional Society and about thirty other non-militant societies, possibly more. It is well for this to be clearly understood, for in various directions, either from ignorance or malice, it is being industriously circulated that all suffragists are militant, of course, quite inaccurately.[5]

It was decided in Canterbury in 1913 to have monthly meetings for members and 'Friends'.[6] As in Ramsgate, a scheme had been introduced called 'Friends of Woman Suffrage' to enable the enrolment of sympathizers who did not want to become members of the society. Given the challenges experienced at this time by those for women's suffrage, this seems like a clever and sensible method of more discreetly engaging with supporters and making their input flexible and any associated challenges less onerous.

While the Kent constitutional societies worked hard to remind Kent inhabitants of their non-militant methods, activities by the WSPU members continued. For in 1913 the first Cabinet minister to ever be disturbed in Kent at a political meeting by suffragettes proved to be Earl Beauchamp. Speaking at the Opera House in Tunbridge Wells, Earl Beauchamp was far into his speech when two suffragettes revealed themselves from under the stage. They were Miss Olive Walton, Hon. Secretary of the Tunbridge Wells WSPU, and Miss Emily Wilding Davison, who died just two months later in an attempt to stop the king's horse at the Epsom Derby. They had attended a performance at the Opera House the evening before and hid until everyone had gone. When interviewed, Olive had said:

> We then explored the building in every part, and I know every cranny of it. On Friday we of course had to hide, and we found a place under the stage, where we remained

Portrait of Emily Wilding Davison. She hid with Miss Olive Walton in the Tunbridge Wells Opera House in 1913 just two months' before her death at the Epsom Derby.
© *LSE Women's Library collection*

all day. We were in a very cramped position and got very tired indeed. We had only a few biscuits to eat. During the day a search was made for suffragettes, but the searchers failed to find us.[7]

Olive, described as 'that remarkable young lady who is one of the acknowledged leaders of local workers for "The Cause"',[8] ran into the orchestra and intended to say more but was quoted as saying that 'when you are dead tired, and men are rushing towards you it is not so easy to say all you would like.' Meanwhile, Emily had rushed on stage and was calling out 'No peace until you give the vote' and 'Stop forcible feeding when we are in prison.' Olive recalled a handkerchief being applied to Emily's mouth to stop her from speaking. Meanwhile, Olive was removed from the Opera House, first 'Without any violence, gently carried' by a Mr. Lang, son of a Liberal candidate, where others came to his aid and she was summarily removed.[9] Another local report said that 'after a short struggle' she was 'forcibly ejected'.[10] Despite some reports alleging that Olive had something alight in her hands at the time, she denied this. The following morning, undeterred, Olive was selling copies of *The Suffragette* journal outside the Opera House. She was clearly a very determined individual, having been imprisoned and forcibly fed in spring 1912.

In March 1913, a fire broke out in a block of flats in Tunbridge Wells. The affected premises included the Fine Art Gallery which was completely burned out, and the Constitutional Club which was wrecked. After the fire an examination revealed that attached to a picture on the staircase leading to the Art Gallery, an area untouched by fire or water,

was a quarto-size sheet of paper on which was written in blue pencil in printed characters the words 'Votes for Women', while pinned to the adjoining shelf was a cutting from a recent issue of the *Daily Telegraph* of the protest against the forcible feeding of Suffragettes in prison.[11]

However, after further consideration it was reported that

> 'A general examination of the staircase had, of course, been made several times previously, but these papers had not been noticed by anyone. The question arises whether they were placed there before or after the fire' and finally, 'the opinion of the authorities is that the discovery represents a stupid and, under the circumstances, very reprehensible joke.'[12]

While all of this raged on, Sarah M.K. Kingsley, the Hon. Secretary for Hythe's NUWSS, wrote to an East Kent newspaper calling for readers to remember that those from 'constitutional' societies continued to work tirelessly for votes for women. She informed the readers that the NUWSS now had 43,000 members countrywide, that there were other similar societies operating in Kent like the New Constitutional Society (NCS), and proclaimed that 'The militants are, in reality, a small body. Their courage all would do well to imitate, but not their methods.'[13]

The following month, a further destructive fire in Tunbridge Wells was to intensify backlash on those campaigning for women's suffrage. On the morning of 11 April 1913, the Nevill Cricket Ground in Tunbridge Wells, which cost several hundred pounds (although *The Suffragette* claimed £1,500),[14] was burned down. The building was apparently insured, but a greater loss was the collection of sporting trophies and archive records. Near the ruins was found a photograph of Mrs. Pankhurst, leader of the WSPU. 'The fire was discovered by a lamplighter at 3.50 am and about the same time the groundsman was aroused by the barking of his dog.'[15] Although it didn't take the fire brigade long to arrive, such was the intensity of the fire that the building could not be saved and was burned down completely. In another newspaper there were reports of an explosion being heard, the cause of which was unknown.[16]

This incident was recorded in a growing list of arson attacks in the 18 April edition[17] of the *Votes for Women* journal. By this time this journal was not controlled by the WSPU but published by the Pethick Lawrences who had split, after disagreeing over the militant action, from Christabel Pankhurst.

A local Whitstable newspaper printed the story of four women acting suspiciously on the afternoon prior to this arson attack. It gave an account of a locally-employed carter witnessing four women in a motor car while on Mount Ephraim on the afternoon of 10 April. 'Three of them, carrying parcels, alighted, and he heard one of them ask: "You are sure the bombs will go off all right?" another replying: "Oh, yes, they will do so right enough."'[18] The carter was said to have recorded the car registration details and mentioned it to his father. However, he could not be contacted as immediately following that he had apparently left for a neighbouring town.

Christabel Pankhurst made the following bold statement about the destruction of the cricket pavilion:

> Tunbridge Wells is up in arms, it appears, because of the burnt pavilion. That is good: it shows that the inhabitants of that town do not like the present state of affairs. There is to be a meeting to demand immediate Government action. The only action that will do any good is to give votes to women and so the meeting had better pass a Woman Suffrage resolution, otherwise it will be wasting its indignation and its breath. The Mayor of Tunbridge Wells is greatly incensed. 'Bats, net, bows and arrows have been sacrificed, shamelessly sacrificed,' says he. Let him remember that the Suffragettes are protesting against the sacrifice of women's happiness and honour and life. Surely these are of more value than bats, nets, bows and arrows![19]

In *The Suffragette*, the newspaper that Christabel controlled and the new official organ from 1912 for the WSPU, the following almost 'poetic' report of the fire burning was included:

> The fire presented a magnificent sight, and could be seen for a very good distance around. The fierce glare of the

blazing woodwork mingled with weird effect with the soft light of the approaching dawn. The flames roared like a furnace, and the 'sissing' of the water from the firemen's hose as it fell upon the blaze and mingled with the incessant cracking and spluttering which told of the fast advance of fire.[20]

A meeting was held on Monday, 28 April to protest against the burning down of the Nevill Ground pavilion. Local anti-suffrage campaigner Sir Arthur Conan Doyle spoke to a 'densely packed audience'[21] in the Great Hall, Tunbridge Wells. 'He referred to the malicious monkey-tricks of the militants, and added: "It would seem that the only thing left for them to do in the way of meanness is to blow up a blind man and his dog."'[22]

Olive Walton, Kate Le Lacheur and Miss Haynes attended this meeting and interrupted and interjected questions to those speaking against women's suffrage. The following is an extract from a report that appeared in a local newspaper:

> They kept on interjecting questions and remarks, and holding up their posters. They were appealed to by several level-headed bystanders, but all in vain, and the crowd began to wax excited. They began to surge, and the ladies were pushed hither and thither. Once the ball was set rolling things became worse. The Suffragettes were booed and severely hustled. Their placards were torn from them, and their literature scattered all over the place. Eggs in a somewhat advanced state of decadence were thrown at the ladies, and some of them found their mark. Several people in the crowd tried to protect the interrupters, but mob passion soon spread, and in a very short time the crowd became thoroughly aroused. They pulled off the hats of the Suffragettes, and tore their clothing. Matters had gone quite far enough when the police pushed through the crowd, and with considerable difficulty rescued the ladies and escorted them to the police station for safety.[23]

Olive, Kate and Miss Haynes were followed to the police station by a shouting jeering crowd and they hung outside, hissing and booing. The following day Olive was interviewed by the local newspaper reporter and 'was apparently none the worse for her adventures the night before'.[24] Olive was keen to emphasize that there were only three of them there from the Tunbridge Wells branch of the WSPU and they were challenging the speaker 'because he misinterpreted'[25] their motives. Olive recalls being attacked more than her companions, although they were all pelted with eggs with one striking her in the face and running down her clothes. She had felt her head being pulled back and her hat dragged off. Olive said that 'the crowd was composed of irresponsible boys and a general assortment of loafers. There were practically no decent men there at all with just a few exceptions.'[26]

When the replacement pavilion was opened in July, it was reported that a number of Suffragists visited and distributed literature. It is not known if one of these was Olive Walton. Not surprisingly, these visitors were not warmly welcomed there.[27]

This progression by suffragettes from pavement-chalking to window-breaking, bombing and arson sparked much anger and disgust. In April 1913 a new word was used by the press to describe this new kind of suffragette: 'Outragette':

> A new kind of woman has been created by the present Government, and the sooner she disappears the better for law and order and national dignity. This new woman is the Outragette. She began simply as one asking that women should have votes. Later she became a Suffragette and then a Militant, and finally, exasperated by the pettifogging evasions which are possible under our so-called system of representative government, she became an Outragette, window-smasher, a rioter, wrecker, and incendiary.[28]

A Kent newspaper later termed the women carrying out these attacks as 'female incendiaries'.[29]

Not surprisingly, the Kent inhabitants also became wary of those involved in the suffrage movement. One illustration of this was the following advertisement in a newspaper: 'Passengers as well as letters are to be carried in a motor mail-van which serves a number of villages in the neighbourhood of Ashford, Kent. Suffragettes are requested to declare themselves on applying for seats.'[30]

During June in Bromley attempts were made to destroy letters in letter boxes. The perpetrators left behind the following message: 'Asquith, do your duty and give votes to women.'[31]

Meanwhile, in North-West Kent, a meeting by the Gravesend branch of the WFL was reported to have been successful after a previous meeting was forced to be abandoned. A 'packed audience listened attentively and most courteously to Miss Boyle for upwards of an hour, breaking up without the slightest disorder and with no evidence of hostility.'[32] Miss Nina Boyle would go on to join the WFL caravan tour in Kent's Herne Bay later in the year. The success of this Gravesend meeting was attributed to the presence of a Mr. Smith, reportedly a well-known local Socialist. He had taken the chair, apparently,

> not so much in the interests of Women's Suffrage as in a chivalrous determination to secure fair play and a fair hearing for the women, who on a recent occasion were mobbed and prevented from holding a meeting. His frank and manly appeal was eminently successful in securing an orderly and quiet attendance.[33]

The need for this approach gives an insight into how the women's suffrage movement was being perceived and reacted to in Kent. This reaction of 'outrage' would be further fuelled when in September another arson attack took place, this time on a house with occupants inside.

In September 1913, Penshurst Place, the home of the de L'Isle family at Tonbridge was set on fire. The house dates back to the fourteenth century and is the seat of the Sidney family. In the early hours of this September morning, the housekeeper

Miss Stowasser was disturbed by the sound of the fire. 'She saw the reflections of a bright flare outside, and rushed to the window, which occupies a commanding position on the West side of the building.' She opened the window to find the source of the noise and saw two women walking away from the house to the road. However, her attention was turned towards the bright flare which was fire. She woke up maids Stenner and Johnson, and together they rushed to the scene:

> They worked like Trojans, and succeeded in a short time in subduing the fire before the arrival of the male servants, who sleep in another wing of the building. Every credit is due to these three women. It was only their promptness which saved the mansion. They were only just in time.[34]

The damage was only slight. No furniture or pictures were damaged. They had all been under wrap as the family was absent at the time. On examination it appeared that a considerable amount of wadding saturated with paraffin had been put in the framework. It was reported that there was sufficient evidence to prove conclusively that the fire was started by two suffragettes. It is believed that they were disturbed when the housekeeper opened her window to find the source of the noise and therefore did not ignite all of the incendiaries and left behind the following items:

One new gallon can of paraffin oil
A 1 1/2 pint empty bottle, which had evidently contained paraffin
A tin of powdered resin
A packet of cotton wool
One sock
A piece of brown paper, with 'Moss' Stores, Chapel Street' written thereon
A tin of soft soap
Two copies of *The Suffragette*
One copy of *The Awakener*
One copy of *Votes for Women*

On one of the papers left behind was scrawled in blue pencil: 'Votes for women; militancy will not cease until women have the vote.'[35]

Later enquiries revealed that two women unknown to those in the village of Penshurst had been making enquiries about Penshurst Place in the days leading up to the attack. Reportedly, the questioning included some about the family that lived there and whether they were home or away. They were away at the time and so the women are likely to have assumed the house was empty. As local women may well have known about the presence of the family's servant employees and how they took care of the house while the family was away, this is most likely to have been the work of suffragettes from another area. Following this attack, the house was closed to the public.

On Christmas night 1913, in Eastchurch on the Isle of Sheppey, two haystacks, about three-quarters of a mile apart, were destroyed by fire. This was reported in *The Suffragette* and detailed that

> the first outbreak occurred in Water Lane, between the village and Sheppey Cliffs, and near the burning stack was discovered some Suffragist literature. The second fire broke out at 11.45 pm, where a large stack on Parsonage Farm, between Eastchurch Village and the Naval Flying Grounds, was found to be ablaze. Assistance was rendered from the Naval Flying School, Eastchurch. The stack was valued at £140.[36]

The arson attacks continued in Kent into 1914 as in June the parish church in Beckenham was set on fire and slightly damaged. Suffragettes were blamed for this attack.

CHAPTER TWELVE

1913: NUWSS Pilgrimage from Kent to London

In 1913 three women's suffrage societies involved the county of Kent in their campaign work. In July the NUWSS called on their Kent members to join 'the Women's Pilgrimage' to London. In the same month, the WFL completed a 'Holiday Campaign' in Kent, while one month later, in August, the WSPU arrived with their 'Campaign Kent' consisting of eight active members travelling between Tunbridge Wells and London. These next three chapters will explore these in turn, beginning with the NUWSS July 1913 pilgrimage from Kent to London.

Following the defeat of the third Conciliation Bill in March 1912 and the withdrawal of the Reform Bill in January 1913, the NUWSS sought to change its strategy. Having previously lobbied for any measures promoting women's suffrage, they turned their attention to the public. As part of this switch in focus, 'the Women's Pilgrimage' was proposed by the then president Mrs. Harley.[1] Plans were made for NUWSS supporters to march to London for a Hyde Park rally on 26 July 1913 via one of six routes. The routes were the Great North route from Newcastle and East Anglia; the Watling Street route from Carlisle, Manchester and North Wales; the West Country route from Land's End and South Wales; the Bournemouth route; the Portsmouth route; and the Kentish Pilgrims' Way route.

NUWSS poster from 1913 advertising the Kentish Pilgrimage to London
© LSE Women's Library collection

Kent's Madame Sarah Grand[2] made a speech with the rather accurate proclamation that 'No history of this Empire could be faithfully written in the future without containing mention of this unique event.'[3]

The look and feel of this huge procession of women travelling through Kent can be captured through the examination of the communications provided to the pilgrims. For example, the June edition of *The Common Cause* had the following text:

> Questions have also been asked about dress, especially as to the correctness of wearing grey. Grey is one of the shades specially recommended by the Pilgrimage Committee, and since there seems to be a certain amount of misunderstanding still as to these recommendations, we beg to point out that their object was not to make each individual look as nice as possible, but to ensure some degree of uniformity. There is no one colour of which every member of the NU has a costume, and it was not desired that Pilgrims should be put to unnecessary expense in buying a uniform. The only alternative was to banish colour altogether, except the NU scarlet, white, and green,[4] in badges, haversacks, and banners. Therefore, black, white, grey, and navy blue were chosen, and surely almost everyone has some garment in one of these shades.[5]

The NUWSS further emphasized that wearing a set outfit was not a mandatory requirement of a woman wishing to join the pilgrimage when inside the same 6 June edition they stated:

> Dress for the Pilgrims. – We have received a large number of letters on this subject, but all may be answered together: (1) Grey is one of the shades recommended by the Committee; (2) the object of the recommendations was to obtain some degree of uniformity – not to put Suffragists to unnecessary expense; (3) therefore, all Pilgrims will be welcome whatever they wear. – Ed., C.C.[6]

'All Pilgrims will be welcome whatever they wear' portrays the quality of a fully inclusive affair and of course the NUWSS were aiming for large numbers of pilgrims so this would have been essential. However, in order to satisfy another aim, that of fund-raising, the NUWSS clearly used the pilgrimage to generate revenue from advertising. A variety of businesses advertised their goods; their marketing of them linked directly to the NUWSS and in some cases the pilgrimage itself. Examples include women's clothing, shoes and even soap! Advertisements included a soap manufacturer announcing that they could supply vegetable oil toilet soap in boxes bearing the NUWSS colours and letters. Society secretaries could purchase the soaps at 'a price which enables the Societies to obtain a good profit and increase their funds by its sale.'[7] This also provides an insight into one of the responsibilities of the societies, namely, to fund-raise, further evidenced by the following communication:

> Orders for haversacks, badges, posters, &c., still pour in. We should be very glad if Secretaries of Societies would let us have their orders at once, giving the latest date on which they should receive the goods. The haversacks are meant to wear across the shoulders (after a messenger-boy's satchel). The length of ribbon supplied and the price of the haversack are both calculated on this method of wearing.[8]

One of these haversacks or leaflet bags owned and carried by Amelia Scott of Tunbridge Wells in Kent is now preserved in the LSE Women's Library in London. The carrying of these by about 100 women walking from Tunbridge Wells is described in a report by a local newspaper, the *Kent & Sussex Courier*.[9]

Perhaps more obvious items to be marketed for purchase were women's clothing. There were numerous such advertisements included in *The Common Cause* in the run-up to the pilgrimage. In one edition, next to a large half-page advertisement for the Ladies' Wear specialists Swan & Edgar of Regent Street and Piccadilly in London, the NUWSS commented: 'For useful articles of attire for the Pilgrimage, Messrs. Swan & Edgar are specially catering, and in the ribbon department they are stocking the National Union colours, 3 3/4 ins. wide, at 1s.2d. per yard, suitable for millinery trimming, sashes, &c.[10]

In one edition of *The Common Cause* was an advertisement for Burberry with an illustration of a woman wearing a coat and in their words, 'The Ideal Coat for The Pilgrimage.'[11]

The NUWSS also appealed directly to its members for funds, including a coupon that could be cut out and posted together with a donation to their head office in London. The small print on this coupon read: 'The whole or part of the Special Offering may be earmarked for any local Society or Federation within the National Union, or for the Election Fighting Fund.'[12]

Clearly stated and reiterated throughout the pilgrimage was that the NUWSS was a non-militant women's suffrage organization. For the promotion and advertising of the Kentish Pilgrimage and while the Kentish Pilgrims were making their way through the county, reiterations of this position were necessary. NUWSS leaflets were given out that read as follows:

Protest Against Violence

The National Union of Women's Suffrage Societies has always worked for Votes for Women by peaceful and constitutional methods.

It has always condemned violence. It did so in 1908, in 1909, in 1911, in 1912, and in 1913. It does so now.

We who belong to it call on all men and women who love justice and fair play to come forward and help us in our law-abiding propaganda. Help us to show that peaceful methods are the only ones which can advance our great cause.

Do not stand aside because a few suffragists belonging to another organisation have done things of which you disapprove and we disapprove.

Our Union is quite distinct from theirs, and is far the oldest and the largest. We have now got 424 societies all over the kingdom.[13]

The organization of the pilgrimage also extended to a uniform song to sing while marching. NUWSS members were asked to send in songs for consideration and the following was chosen:

> A good heart and a steady mind,
>   Our purpose clear in view,
> And we will show our country now
>   What women folk can do.
> From Land's End by the blue sea coast,
>   From far beyond the Tweed,
> We march that all the countryside
>   May know the women's need.

> CHORUS
> And shall they scorn the women's voice
>   When we for justice cry?
> We're marching in our thousands now
>   To know the reason why.

> Outspoken our leaders every one,
>   A goodly band were they:
> 'We claim the right to serve our land,
>   And who shall say us nay?'
> And we have heard our country's call,
>   Can we stand idle by?
> If still we may not serve, we come
>   To know the reason why.

> CHORUS
> What do they fear who hold us back,
>   Who number half the race?
> Do we the needful courage lack
>   To fill a worthy place?
> The sex that toils in home and mill
>   That shares their smiles and tears,
> The sex that graced our country's throne
>   For half a hundred years.

CHORUS
From West and East we gather now,
But one in purpose set.
Oh! ye who need the women's vote,
We'll be victorious yet.
Then join the women of our land
And march with us to-day,
Come one and all, a dauntless band,
And who shall say us nay?

LAST CHORUS
They shall not scorn our just demand,
Our freedom still deny;
We're marching in our thousands now
And this our reason why.[14]

The first pilgrims began their journey on 18 June, and from that date groups began to set out all over the country, discreetly in some places, with bands and banners and a civic send-off in others. Most travelled on foot, though some rode horses or bicycles, and wealthy sympathisers lent cars, carriages, or pony traps for their luggage. The intention was not that each individual should cover the whole route but that the federations would do so collectively. This led to some taunts that they were not a 'proper' pilgrimage, but the sharper suffragists turned these round in claiming that even feminists had homes, and that contrary to popular belief, virtuous suffragists did not neglect them. They held innumerable meetings, gathered petitions, sold *The Common Cause*, literature and accessories, and enlisted sympathisers as members or 'friends'. They found accommodation from fellow suffragists and in small hostels and boarding houses along the route, paying their own expenses. And on Sundays they went to services at which sympathetic Anglican vicars preached from ingeniously selected texts.[15]

The Common Cause in late June 1913 promoted the Kent Pilgrimage: 'The Kentish Pilgrim's Way will also see its regiment of blue and grey and white women, tramping Londonwards under their red, white, and green banner, later on in July, coming from Canterbury, Margate, Dover, Folkestone, and marching through Rochester, Maidstone, Tonbridge, and Sevenoaks.'[16]

There were two starting-points for the Kentish Pilgrims' Way route, described in *The Common Cause* on 4 July 1913 as Westgate to Blackheath (known as 'the Northern Route') and Sandwich to Blackheath (known as 'the Southern Route'). This same edition of the NUWSS journal confirmed that Miss Griffith Jones was the Federation's secretary or organizer in charge. She was later confirmed as the lead on the Northern Route. In a separate article in a Kent newspaper[17] it was confirmed that Miss Ward was in charge of the Southern Route. In terms of organizational responsibilities, it was also communicated that 'The last halting-place given for each route is the point at which the London Society will probably take over the arrangements.'[18] For Kent this was Blackheath.

The Kentish Pilgrims' Way route was not ready for publication by the NUWSS on 20 June as 'the complete time-table has not been received',[19] but a map showing all routes was published in a later edition.[20] However, in addition, the *Dover Express* of 4 July included a detailed article which had the following call for help:

All non-militant associations and friends and sympathisers, both men and women, are invited to join in the pilgrimage, and help in any of the following ways:- (1) Walking (specify how far); (2) Driving in brake (specify how far); (3) Giving money; (4) Hospitality to workers (a meal, meals or bed for pilgrims, and date); (5) Lending cars or carriages (on which date); (6) Selling *Common Cause* and other literature; (7) Exhibit large or small poster; (8) Distribute handbills; (9) Attend final meeting, Hyde Park, July 26th. The local Secretaries, the Head Organiser for Kent, Miss Griffith Jones, 88 Vauxhall Bridge Road, London, S.W., or Miss Ward, 25, Bennett Park, Blackheath, London, who is in charge of the

Southern Route, will be very glad to hear from anyone who can possibly help in any way, however small.[21]

Prior to the pilgrimage, Miss Griffith Jones wrote to local newspapers calling for 'all Non-Militant Suffragists, friends and sympathizers, both men and women' to 'co-operate'.[22] She referred to all areas of Kent that were to be visited on the pilgrimage and gave hers and Miss Katherine Ward's contact details. During the pilgrimage itself, both women used the Post Offices in each of the places they stopped at to receive communications.

There was, in fact, a third Kentish Pilgrim route that local active suffragists engineered and organized. It commenced at Tunbridge Wells, and went via Southborough to Tonbridge. From Tonbridge the pilgrims from all three routes marched through Hildenborough, Sevenoaks (also visiting villages Brasted and Knockholt), Bromley and Dartford before converging at Blackheath. From there they marched to the Elephant and Castle in London and finished in Hyde Park on Saturday, 26 July. To provide further clarity, detailed below are the routes, stopping-places and dates:[23]

Northern Route

Garlinge, Westgate (NB: In her planned route, Miss Griffith Jones cites Margate as the starting place on Tuesday, 1 July 1913.)	Monday, 30 June 1913
Margate	Tuesday, 1 July 1913
Broadstairs	Wednesday, 2 July 1913
Ramsgate	Thursday, 3 July 1913
Minster and Monkton	Friday, 4 July 1913
Sarre and St Nicholas	Saturday, 5 July 1913
Birchington	Monday, 7 July 1913
Herne Bay	Tuesday, 8 July 1913
Tankerton	Wednesday, 9 July 1913
Whitstable	Wednesday, 9 July 1913

Canterbury	Thursday, 10 July 1913
Faversham and Boughton	Friday, 11 July 1913
[Green Street and] Sittingbourne	Saturday, 12 July 1913
Newington and Rainham	Monday, 14 July 1913
Gillingham	Tuesday, 15 July 1913
Chatham	Wednesday, 16 July 1913
Rochester	Thursday, 17 July 1913
Strood	Friday, 18 July 1913
Maidstone	Saturday, 19 July 1913
Tonbridge	Monday, 21 July 1913

Southern Route

Sandwich	Thursday, 3 July 1913
Eastry	Friday, 4 July 1913
Deal	Saturday, 5 July 1913
Great Mongeham	Monday, 7 July 1913
Walmer	Tuesday, 8 July 1913
Kingsdown	Wednesday, 9 July 1913
St Margaret's Bay	Thursday, 10 July 1913
Dover	Friday, 11 July 1913
Whitfield and Ewell	Saturday, 12 July 1913
Folkestone	Planned for evening of Monday, 14 July 1913. Postponed, owing to rain, to afternoon of Tuesday, 15 July.*
Cheriton	Tuesday, 15 July 1913 (evening)
Sandgate	Wednesday, 16 July 1913
Saltwood	Thursday, 17 July 1913
Hythe	Friday, 18 July 1913
Ashford	Saturday, 19 July 1913
Tonbridge	Monday, 21 July 1913

* According to report in the *Folkestone, Hythe, Sandgate & Cheriton Herald*, 19 July 1913, p.9.

Tunbridge Wells and Southborough Suffragists join in	
Tunbridge Wells	Tuesday, 15 July 1913
Southborough	Monday, 21 July 1913
Tonbridge	Monday, 21 July 1913

Pilgrims from the above three routes travel from Tonbridge to Blackheath	
Tonbridge	Monday, 21 July 1913
Hildenborough	Tuesday, 22 July 1913
Sevenoaks	Tuesday, 22 July 1913
Brasted	Tuesday, 22 July 1913
Knockholt	Wednesday, 23 July 1913
Bromley	Thursday, 24 July 1913
Dartford	Thursday, 24 July 1913
Blackheath	Thursday, 24 July 1913
New Cross Gate	Friday, 25 July 1913
Elephant and Castle	Friday, 25 July 1913
Hyde Park	Saturday, 26 July 1913
St Paul's Cathedral	Sunday, 27 July 1913

Also useful for examining established NUWSS branches and active members' names at the time of the pilgrimage is the information below (from *The Common Cause*, 4 July 1913, pp.220 to 222).

Federation or Society	Honorary Secretary and Key to Letters
Kentish Federation	Miss Bence, Tintoch, Canterbury covering the area of the county of Kent
Ashford Society	Miss Clemetson, 2 Castle Street, Ashford, Kent
Canterbury Society	Mrs. Harold Wacher, 72 St Dunstans, Canterbury, Kent
Deal and Walmer Society	Mrs. Clare Royse, 2 Herschell Road, Walmer, and Miss Marsh, The Manor House, Upper Deal, Kent

Folkestone and Hythe Society	Pro tem. Miss Bence, % Mrs. Sturt, The Priory, Folkestone, and Mrs. Henry Kingsley, Yewlands, Napier Gardens, Hythe, Kent
Maidstone Society	No details included
Margate Society	Mrs. B.E. Chapman, 2 Lyndhurst Avenue, Cliftonville, Margate, Kent
Pembury, Matfield and Brenchley Society	Miss Mabel Symonds, The Grange, Matfield, Kent
Ramsgate Society	Miss Margaret E. Sale, 19 Royal Crescent, Ramsgate, Kent
Rochester Society	Miss V. Conway-Gordon, Longley House, Rochester, Kent
Sevenoaks Society	Miss Crosbie Hill and Miss Hemmant, Bulimba, Sevenoaks, Kent
Shoreham and Otford Society	Miss Dorothy Scott, Shoreham, Sevenoaks, Kent
Tonbridge Society	Mrs. Ridgway, Greatham, 8 London Road, Tonbridge, Kent
Tunbridge Wells Society	Mrs. Tattershall Dodd and Miss Moseley. Office: 18 Crescent Road, Tunbridge Wells, Kent

In July 1913 the NUWSS described itself as

> the largest and oldest of all the Suffrage societies [that] demands the franchise for women on the same terms as it is or may be granted to men. Founded in 1867, it now numbers over 42,000 members, and its 443 branches, organised into 16 Federations, are distributed over England, Scotland, and Wales. Those Parliamentary divisions in which no Society exists, are worked by the Federation in whose area they lie. In 1912 the Union raised £40,000, which was devoted to educational propaganda and political work, on purely constitutional lines. The Union has never sanctioned violence of any kind, and has repeatedly passed resolutions expressing

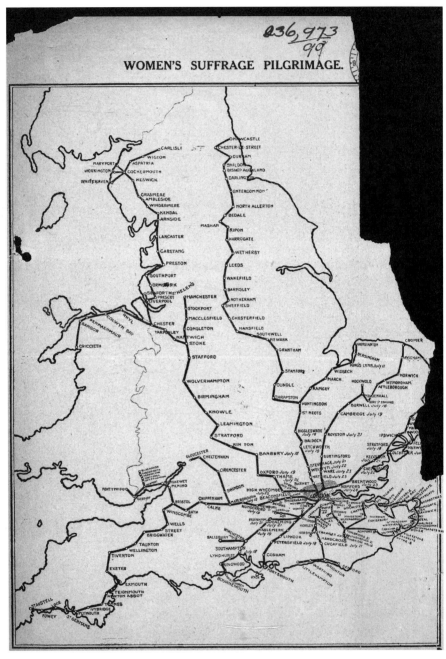

NUWSS published map of the 1913 Pilgrimage to London
The National Archives

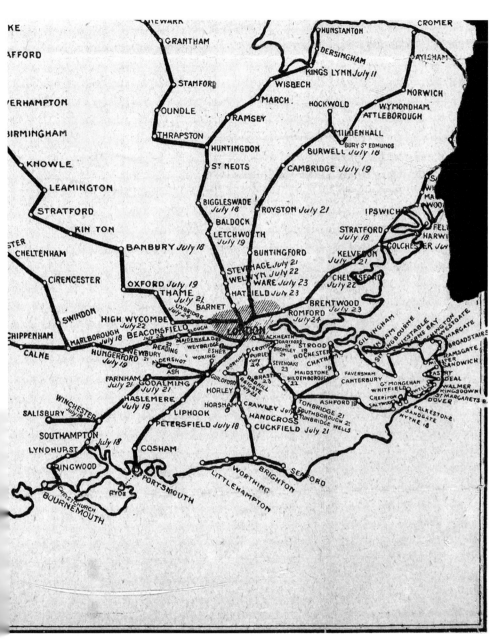

NUWSS published map with South-East England enlarged to show the planned routes of the Kentish Pilgrimage, 1913
The National Archives

the conviction that its use in political agitation was both wrong in itself and harmful to the cause in which it was employed.[24]

Many of those speaking at meetings along the Kentish Pilgrimage routes expressed these values, aims and mission of the NUWSS to their audiences.

The pilgrimage for those furthest away from London started earlier than the Kentish Pilgrimage commencing on Wednesday, 18 June 1913. In the *Votes for Women* newspaper, reference was made to the pilgrims averaging 10 to 16 miles a day. They reported the approach of the NUWSS as a 'go-as-you-please affair through the countryside…some strolling in pairs, some in groups, some whisking ahead in friendly motors, on horseback, or on bicycles'.[25]

Despite reports of 'the "Antics"'[26] in other parts of the country, Kent appears to have had a comparatively peaceful pilgrimage. In fact, in reports of progress in Kent, the word 'peaceful' was often used. In St Neots (Cambridgeshire), for example, there were reports of the police having to get suffragists away to their hotel and guard them for two hours until the mob had stopped shouting and storming in the street outside. As will be told next, the worst that Kentish Pilgrims experienced was a jug and dirt being thrown at them and a great deal of heckling.

The Northern Route was Westgate in East Kent to Blackheath with Miss Griffith Jones as organizer and Miss Muriel Matters as main speaker. This route commenced at Westgate on Monday, 30 June 1913.

The Kentish Federation's secretary or organizer, Miss Griffith Jones, wrote a report that appeared in the 11 July edition of *The Common Cause*, marking the start of the Northern Route Pilgrimage. This report is included in full below:

The Kentish Pilgrims started their operations on Monday, June 30th, with a well-attended and successful meeting addressed by Miss Griffith Jones, at Garlinge in the Square (Garlinge being an outlying portion of

Westgate). The following afternoon [Tuesday, 1 July] an open-air meeting was held in Cecil Square, Margate, the speaker being Miss Muriel Matters, who held the interest of a distinctly sympathetic audience for an hour. Miss Moseley, of Tunbridge Wells, also spoke. In the evening a vast crowd collected to hear Miss Matters again. A disturbing element was present, but disorder was kept well in check by Miss Matters' skilful replies to the hecklers. A good collection was taken, many people signed as 'Friends', and some 160 *Common Causes* were sold, whilst the interest aroused in the town in Woman's Suffrage was beyond the greatest expectations of the workers.

The following morning [Wednesday, 2 July] another open-air meeting was held near the Queen's Bandstand [in Margate], the speaker being Miss Griffith Jones. A letter was read from the Member for Thanet, Mr. Norman Craig, in response to a request that he should attend some of the meetings, stating his inability to do so, and reiterating the extent of his belief in the efficacy of Women's Suffrage. The afternoon was devoted to the distribution of leaflets and selling *Common Causes*, a large sum of money also being collected, after which a procession of Pilgrims on foot, followed by two decorated brakes,[27] left the square and proceeded by the cliff front to the Broadstairs road. The Broadstairs meeting was held in the Assembly Room, opening directly on the front, and in a short time the room was crowded, although the meeting was taken by Mrs. Oat Rhinel, a well-known supporter of the cause, and after her speech Miss Matters addressed an extremely interested audience for over an hour.

At Ramsgate two meetings were held on the sands [Thursday, 3 July], both attended by large audiences, all the helpers being entertained by a Committee member in the interval. Miss Matters addressed both meetings, and Miss Moseley again took the chair, many of the audience returning to hear Miss Matters a second time. Again a large number of friends' cards were signed.

The following day [Friday, 4 July] a party of workers motored out to Minster, five miles from Ramsgate, and proceeded to advertise an evening meeting to take place in an open space outside the far-famed old Minster Church. The news of the meeting spread throughout the village like wild-fire, Women's Suffrage being hitherto an undiscussed topic in the immediate neighbourhood. The villagers were evidently extremely shy, in the characteristic Kentish manner, but they gradually collected in good numbers, and drew in slowly as Miss Griffith Jones began to address them, listening with great attention whilst a most imposing police sergeant held the school children in order. Thus ended the first week of the Kent Pilgrimage, leaving the workers most encouraged by the results and proving to them that the Kentish people, though perhaps slow to come forward, and much shocked by militantism, are capable of taking a great interest when once they got hold of their subject.

Many good results are anticipated throughout Kent from the Pilgrimage. Letters with offers of help in various ways are daily coming in from sympathisers, many of whom were hitherto unknown, and Kentish Societies are working hard to make the Pilgrimage a success in their districts. What is perhaps more satisfactory than anything is the attentive earnestness of the audiences, which consist of men and women of every class.[28]

Miss Moseley, mentioned above, was by this time joint secretary, with Mrs. Tattershall Dodd of the Tunbridge Wells branch of the NUWSS (office at 18 Crescent Road).

Well-known leaders of the NUWSS joined the marchers, making speeches at meetings along the way and of course in London where all the pilgrims converged. One was Miss Muriel Matters. She spoke at the pilgrimage meeting in Margate on 1 July and continued to make appearances. Miss Matters was the Australian actress who had already toured Kent with the WFL in 1908.

Information relating to the programmed stops at Minster & Monckton and Sarre & St Nicholas has not been found.

Meetings are known to have taken place at Birchington, followed by Herne Bay and then Tankerton en route to Whitstable. Miss Muriel Matters and Miss Griffith Jones spoke at all three meetings. Miss Griffith Jones reported that the 'reception of the Pilgrims has everywhere been satisfactory; hundreds of members and "Friends" have been enrolled, and many *Common Causes* sold.'[29] This comment applied to Birchington, Herne Bay, Tankerton, Whitstable, Canterbury, Faversham, Green Street and Sittingbourne.

The Whitstable evening meeting was reported in the local newspaper:

> The Kentish Pilgrims, in connection with the National Union of Women's Suffrage Societies, visited Whitstable on Wednesday last. In the evening an open air meeting took place on 'The Cross'. Long before the advertised time a large crowd of people assembled and the speakers had the opportunity of addressing several hundred of the inhabitants of Whitstable. A local celebrity[30] made repeated attempts to disturb the course of the meeting, but, on the whole, the speakers were given a fair hearing. Unfortunately the ladies' opinions of Whitstable must have been sadly marred by several missiles which found their way into the carriage as it was being driven away. No doubt this was the work of youngsters, but none the less it is a matter for regret that it occurred. The police are to be congratulated on the way in which they managed the crowd. The Chairman, Mrs. Packman, the President of the Herne Bay Branch (Ocean View, Beacon Hill Parade, Herne Bay) appealed for a fair hearing for the speakers.[31]

Mrs. Packman, in 1912, was a known leading member of the WSPU as well as a member of the Rochester branch of the NUWSS.

Mr. Lang MP spoke at the Whitstable meeting, reiterating 'his belief in women's enfranchisement from the Suffrage platform'.[32]

On Thursday, 10 July a party of fifty assembled in the market place in Canterbury and marched through the streets to the cathedral in time for the 3 o'clock service. From an account given in *The Common Cause*[33] it is known that fifteen local Canterbury sympathizers joined the rally in the Market Square. This suggests that the Northern Route Pilgrimage consisted of thirty-five pilgrims as it arrived in Canterbury and gives an indication of the scale of the march at this point.

In a report entitled 'Peaceful Kent', *The Common Cause* spoke of

> successful meetings held all along the route; at some of these there was an audience numbering thousands of people. The speakers included Miss Courtney, Mrs. Stanbury, Mrs. Ruth Young, Mrs. Rackham, Mrs. Venning, Miss Mercer, Miss Talmer, Mr. Bart Kennedy, Miss Griffith Jones, and the Rev. T.M. Tamplin. Among the Chairmen have been Canon Horsley, the Rev. Baird Turner, Councillor Tapp, Mr. H.W. Clouting, and Mr. Bray.[34]

Reference was made to the vicar of Sittingbourne preaching on Sunday, 13 July a 'sympathetic sermon, urging that men and women should found their opinions on "knowledge, not prejudice".'[35] This followed the arrival of the pilgrims in the town on Friday, 11 July of which the following was reported: 'After an enormous and very successful meeting at Faversham, the pilgrims were entertained to supper by the Liberal Club.'[36]

There is a gap of approximately three days when the plan for this route was for the pilgrims to go via Newington and Rainham, Gillingham and then Chatham before reaching Rochester. No details of this period have been found.

The pilgrims arrived in Rochester on Thursday, 17 July and *The Common Cause* reported that 'At Rochester thirty to forty Pilgrims marched to and from the Cathedral, and afterwards, received a kind message of encouragement of people accompanying them to the afternoon service.'[37]

The scale of the marching pilgrims appears to be similar to that reported in Canterbury. The weather in Rochester was wet, but an attentive audience listened under umbrellas. Rochester did, after all, have an NUWSS branch and member Mrs. Packman was a leading member of the WSPU. Furthermore, one month prior to the pilgrimage, Miss Griffith Jones spoke at a meeting with Miss Christabel[38] at which 'six new members enrolled'.[39] Alarmingly, however, an adult is reported to have thrown a jug at the speakers and 'hooligan children' to have thrown dirt. The report concluded with 'the North Kent Pilgrims have fared well, and feel that their work is already bearing fruit.'[40]

Advance warning was given of the demonstration that was to take place outside the Sessions House in Maidstone on Saturday, 19 July.[41] Miss Palmer of Hadlow near Tonbridge was announced as one of the speakers and Canon Horsley as chairman (Canon of Rochester Cathedral from 1905 and a previous Chaplain at Clerkenwell Prison, he was well known in Kent). However, no record of this meeting has been traced.

Meanwhile, the Southern Route was Sandwich in East Kent to Blackheath. Miss Katherine Ward was organizer, Mrs G.F. Abbott main speaker and Miss Geraldine Cooke spoke until reaching Tonbridge in West Kent. This route commenced at Sandwich on Thursday, 3 July 1913.

In *The Common Cause* on 18 July it was reported that 'By this time, those who are on pilgrimage have reached an audience which must be piling up to hundreds of thousands. No effort made by the Union in the past has ever justified itself more triumphantly.'[42]

It was stated:

> Day by day news comes to us from all parts of the country of the Women's Pilgrimage, which, by the force of its gathering strength and extending influence is awakening the intellectual sluggards of the British Isles. 'What then is this Women's Pilgrimage?' some enquire, and 'what its relationship to modern life? Pilgrimages belong to the

ritual of the past, and their artificial revival is a mockery of the progress of civilisation. But such are the ways of women.' 'The ways of women' are, however, not to be so easily dismissed. Those of us who work at the heart of the women's moment, and have had, perchance, some vision of this vaunted modern civilisation, may well reply: 'This pilgrimage of ours is no vain show; no gaudy spectacle devised behind the scenes for the capture of the goodwill of unthinking mob and a hide-bound Ministry, but a spontaneous efflorescence, the expression of the spirit of our times'.[43]

This same edition of *The Common Cause* included a short article on 'Waking up South Kent'. Route organizer Miss Katherine Ward was the author and wrote: 'It is my part to tell of perhaps one of the most difficult routes which the pilgrims have attempted. In the first place, there are few societies in South Kent, and secondly, the societies that there are, are very small.'[44] Miss Ward continued to tell of an evening meeting at the starting-place of the Southern Route, Sandwich on Thursday 3 July. Mrs. Abbott spoke and Miss Katherine Ward and Miss Gimingham, the treasurer, were also in attendance. Mrs. Abbott is recorded in one Kent local newspaper as being 'a speaker from headquarters' and from 'Chelsea', London.[45] Katherine wrote: 'As a matter of fact, that was the noisiest gathering that we have had (do the children ever go to bed in South Kent?).'[46]

Katherine travelled to Eastry for an evening meeting on Friday, 4 July. Local reporters told of Mrs. G.F. Abbott addressing the audience, saying that

a great deal is heard of the Militant Suffragettes, while comparatively little is known of the enormous educational work that is being done by the many thousands of peaceful, law-abiding men and women suffragists, whose work and aims she expounded in a practical and lucid manner, and advanced logical reasons for her advocating of the enfranchisement of women.[47]

At Eastry, Katherine reported via the NUWSS journal[48] that they were sent off with a hearty cheer and received good wishes from gypsies.

In Deal on Saturday, 5 July Katherine reported that they 'had a most orderly meeting, and sold a large quantity of *Common Causes*'.[49]

Great Mongeham had a planned meeting for Monday, 7 July and Waller for Tuesday, 8 July, but no accounts of these have been found. A meeting, however, was reported[50] as having taken place at the Girls' School in Elham on the evening of Wednesday, 9 July. It was largely attended, with speakers Miss H.M. Stainer (of the NCS, Folkestone and Hon. Press Secretary of NUWSS) and Mrs. Venning of Faversham (likely to have been Mrs Katherine Venning who became one of the Hon. Secretaries of the Tonbridge branch of the NUWSS by 1914). Mr. L. Hubble of Elham chaired the meeting.

Reaching the coastal town of Kingsdown on Wednesday, 9 July, Katherine remembered a 'small straggling crowd and the cold wind blowing from a grey sea'.[51] In contrast at St Margaret's Bay the following day (10 July 1913) she recalled 'brilliant sunshine and white cliffs'. She also reported receiving 'assurance from the villagers that we looked "too sensible to be militants"'[52] at this open-air meeting which took place 'at the Post Office Corner'.[53]

The following day, on Friday, 11 July, the pilgrims reached Dover and a 'band of a dozen or so, marching in their colours through the town' was noted together with a description of the 8.00 pm meeting 'on the Sea Front, near the Stone Apron',[54] having a 'dense black crowd and the play of a lighthouse on the sea and on the speaker'.[55] This description conveys such a clear picture of the setting and the view seen by the speakers at this Dover meeting. From the account given by Katherine in *The Common Cause* of 18 July, it seems that the Dover Constitutional Society provided support both by attending the meeting and collecting subscriptions. The *Dover Express* included a lengthy article about this meeting with some interesting accounts of the general mood there and issues raised. The speakers were given 'a decidedly sympathetic hearing, although one or two would be wags who occasionally tried to be funny.'[56] The speakers were Mrs G.F. Abbott and Miss Geraldine Cooke. At this meeting the issue of the pilgrimage being by non-militant suffragists was highlighted when someone in the audience wanted to know whether the speakers had paid for the damage done by fires in Regent's Park and Kew Gardens. Interestingly, the questioner did not refer to the recent April Kent arson at Tunbridge Wells Nevill's Cricket Club. Miss Geraldine Cooke replied that they were members of the non-militant society, the NUWSS, and had no connection with these fires. The questioner replied, saying 'that they were all the same – six of one and half a dozen of the other'. Miss Geraldine Cooke said that they had no connection with the society responsible for the outrages, and disapproved of its methods.[57] In her speech, Mrs. Abbott

> pointed out that the Anti-Suffragist League, which claimed to represent the women of the country, largely comprised business men, and never published a balance sheet or list of subscribers. On the other hand, every organised body of women in the country had passed resolutions in favour of the vote being granted to women.[58]

From Dover, the pilgrims travelled to Whitfield and Ewell for a meeting on Saturday, 12 July. A short report was included in Dover's local newspaper, but it only detailed that it was 'an open-air meeting held at Ewell near the Flour Mill on Saturday evening'.[59] The report provided no insight into the audience size, speakers or how the views expressed were received.

Marching on to Folkestone, the pilgrims planned to hold an open-air meeting at the Fountain in Harbour Street on the evening of Monday, 14 July. Owing to the rain, this was postponed to the afternoon of Tuesday, 15 July. Katherine fed back to readers of *The Common Cause* that 'At Folkestone we received a good deal of heckling from a large but not inspiring audience; nevertheless an auditor, who proclaimed himself a Quaker, came forward spontaneously and said how in all their undertakings women were equal with men, and how helpful they found it.[60]

A report in the local newspaper described how 'One man mounted the wagon from which the ladies addressed the meeting. He arrogated to himself the position of Chairman, but as the meeting progressed, became so loquacious in the performance of his duties that he was ultimately forcibly removed by the police.'[61] The use of these words – 'arrogated' (to take claim of something) and 'loquacious' (keen to talk, talkative) – vividly conveys the actions of this man and the impact they had on the lady speakers and the meeting in general.

Miss H.M. Stainer (Hon. Press Secretary of NUWSS, Leonard Lodge, Folkestone[62]) chaired the Folkestone meeting and in her speech, set out the aims of the pilgrimage and called for a fair hearing of the women's suffrage question. She emphasized the non-militant and wholly constitutional nature of the NUWSS and pilgrimage.

Mrs G.F. Abbott was also present and gave a lengthy speech, emphasizing that only some women's suffrage groups used militant methods and that the NUWSS did not. She continued that 'Women formed the only class which was excluded absolutely from participation in the electoral system of the country, and she protested against the insult which placed women in the same category as criminals, paupers, and lunatics.'[63] She referred to improving the position of working women by giving them the vote. She 'also dealt with the assertion that suffragists merely courted notoriety, and appealed to the reasonableness of her hearers to consider whether it was enjoyable or pleasant for a woman, for the sake of notoriety, to shout at the street corners in almost every town in the United Kingdom'.[64] There were a number of questions mainly relating to militancy to which Mrs G.F. Abbott responded. In her report to the NUWSS, printed in *The Common Cause*, Katherine wrote: 'The help given us at Folkestone by the Society, and by members who are spending their holidays in the town, must be gratefully acknowledged.'[65]

In a letter to her local newspaper, Miss H.M. Stainer wrote:

To the Editor. The work of the local branch of the National Union of Women's Suffrage Societies in connection with the great suffrage pilgrimage is now over, and I beg a little space in your friendly columns in order to offer our sincere thanks to all who helped to make the week's activities successful in this constituency. Our speakers were given a fair hearing, our paper, *The Common Cause*, was largely bought, and the crowds appeared to be convinced that the vast majority of women suffragists are entirely innocent of unconstitutional and outrageous methods of promoting their cause. On behalf of the local branch of the Union, I offer our gratitude to the Press for their valuable assistance in advertising and reporting our meetings, to the Superintendent of Police and the constables for their kind and courteous supervision, and to the members of the general public who gave us their support at our meetings. Any person wishing to help us in our struggle to obtain votes for women can greatly assist us by joining our Union, or by sending a donation towards the heavy expenses of the pilgrimage. Yours faithfully.[66]

Rather interestingly, the letter appearing immediately below Miss Stainer's was from an anonymous author clearly upset by the non-militant pilgrimage on account of its effect on the militant societies and of confused information given to members of the public about the fight of women's suffrage. It read:

To the Editor. Sir, The ladies belonging to the non-militant Society who are now promenading the country show clearly by this very action that they owe to the militants, whom, at the same time, they are abusing, for they would never have undertaken even this mild form of advertisement if the militants, by numerous processions and outdoor meetings, had not shown them the way. The defence of all militancy is contained in the undisputed fact that it has familiarised the whole population of this country with the claim of 'Votes for Women'. In the space of a few years, whilst the tactics of the National Union, who had the whole suffrage campaign in their own hands for over forty years, had for its result the fact that the great mass of the people never knew that such a claim was made or any suffrage society existed. One of the militant speakers said the other day that she was addressing an outdoor meeting, and happened to mention that she had belonged to a suffrage society for forty years, when a voice from the audience shouted out 'That's a lie; they only started six years ago.' The militants are quite content to hear all the misunderstanding and abuse of such ignorant persons as that interruptor; but it does seem rather unfair that the National Union, which is now profiting from the interest which has been aroused all over the Kingdom by the actions of the militants, should fail to acknowledge their indebtedness to the self-sacrificing women of the Social and Political Union, who are now, and have been all along, bearing all the hard blows, and doing all the hard work of the campaign. Truly yours, Sussex.[67]

That evening, the pilgrims marched on to Cheriton and held a meeting near the White Lion. The feedback given by Miss Katherine Ward was that 'The crowd of about 700 was entirely sympathetic, and the owner of the lorry from which we spoke refused to take more than half the original price, saying that the speeches were well worth half his charge!'[68] The reporter for the local press supported this feedback in their report which read: 'A very large crowd assembled, and the speakers were given a good hearing. Indeed, the attitude of the crowd was distinctly favourable, and a few half-hearted interrupters were sharply called to order by the remainder of the crowd.'[69]

There were three speakers at this large Cheriton meeting:

Miss Ward, in the course of her speech, briefly outlined the object of the suffrage pilgrimage. She said that their Society, although the oldest, had never had the same advertisement as the militant societies had. They did not break windows or fire letter boxes, and many people had, in fact, never heard of them. The pilgrimage had been organized as a great living advertisement and a protest against the militant tactics.[70]

Miss Stainer called for support for the movement in her address, while Mrs. G.F. Abbott 'spoke of the value of the vote to women as an instrument whereby they could make their desires known and a weapon to obtain their desires'.[71]

On the evening of Wednesday, 16 July, 'a dozen or so marched to Sandgate',[72] and a meeting was held near the Sir John Moore Memorial. Presiding was the Folkestone & Hythe branch of the NUWSS Hon. Secretary, Mrs. Henry Kingsley. It appears that Mrs. Kingsley had been speaking at women's suffrage meetings for forty-one years while undertaking social work. 'Her experience, she said, had taught her to realise that the vote was needed if anything was to be done.'[73] Mrs. G.F. Abbott, continuing her journey with the Southern Route Pilgrims, also spoke, along with Miss Cooke. Miss Cooke referred to militancy and 'admitted that the women's movement had been disfigured by militancy, but she appealed to her hearers to judge fairly, and not condemn the whole movement because of the doings of a comparatively small section'.[74] At Sandgate, 'The speakers were all listened to without interruption, and apparently with appreciation.'[75]

On Thursday, 17 July 'Mrs. Henry Kingsley presided again at Saltwood'.[76] It was reported that 'four suffragists with a van took up a stand at Saltwood Village Green. Mrs. Henry Kingsley, Mrs Cooke,[77] and Miss Ward addressed a fairly large assembly. There were no interruptions, but when questions were asked there was some good-humoured banter.'[78]

The meeting in the Market Square of Hythe on the evening of Friday, 18 July was reported in a local newspaper. The report said that 'there was a large crowd, which was addressed by Mrs. Henry Kingsley and Mrs Cooke.[79] A number of questions were put and answered. The listeners were very orderly and generally sympathetic.'[80]

Reporting in the NUWSS journal of 'perhaps the best meeting of all',[81] Katherine cites Ashford. This meeting took place on Saturday, 19 July.

The pilgrims following this Northern Route reached Tonbridge to converge with the other Kentish Pilgrims on Monday, 21 July 1913. The scenes there are described below.

The unofficial route was Tunbridge Wells through Southborough to Tonbridge. This took place on 21 July 1913. Appearing in the *Hastings and St Leonard's Observer* for residents from this East Sussex area was the following notification:

> Late last night we received a circular letter from Mrs. Strickland and Miss Kate Rance, stating that, as suggested by Countess Brassey, it has been suggested that those marching from the local Society shall join the Kentish Federation Pilgrimage at Tunbridge Wells or Tonbridge on July 21st. Hospitality will be provided when possible, but at any place where it is not available, Pilgrims will pay their own expenses, which, it is anticipated, will not amount to more than 5s. a day, and may be considerably less. Pilgrims who would like to march, but are prevented from doing so by the outlay required, should make applications at once to the local Hon. Secretary for a grant towards expenses out of money that may be given for that purpose.
>
> Pilgrims joining the procession at Tunbridge Wells on July 21st start by the 10.50 train from Hastings and arrive at Tunbridge Wells Station 11.48, from whence they will march to the Suffrage Office, 18, Crescent-road. Those joining at Tonbridge on July 21st should arrive at the station no later than 6.52, where Miss Rance will meet them.[82]

A number of meetings were held in the Tunbridge Wells area prior to the pilgrimage to Tonbridge. One was organized for Penshurst on the afternoon of Saturday, 5 July.[83] A garden party was held at Clare Lodge with speakers Miss Ward and Miss Moseley, and chaired by Madame Sarah Grand.[84] One open-air meeting was held on 7 July at Pembury Green, organized and chaired by Mrs. Perkin (of Matfield Grange), with speaker

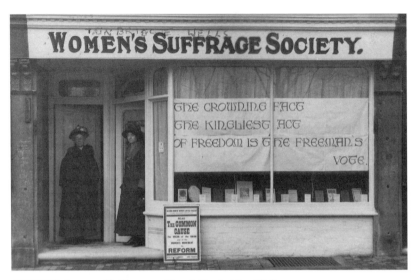

NUWSS shop on 18 Crescent Road, Tunbridge Wells
© LSE Women's Library collection

Mrs. Stanbury (of the National Union Executive[85]). There were 'about a hundred people. The colours red, white and green, flew gaily, and the whole scene looked very picturesque. Much interest was shown, and a large quantity of literature was distributed.'[86] This was described as 'A successful meeting in breaking new ground.'[87] Two days later on Wednesday, 9 July, Miss Anna Martin, B.A. chaired a meeting in the Town Hall at which Miss Geraldine Cooke spoke.[88] It was explained that 'the meeting was held for the purpose to arouse interest and enthusiasm in the Suffragist pilgrimage.'[89] However, there was reportedly only a moderate attendance at this meeting.

In the *Kent & Sussex Courier* on 18 July 1913 (p.7), it was reported that

> On Tuesday [15 July] Mrs. Le Lacheur entertained between thirty and forty people, and many more guests would have been present had the rain been not so heavy during the afternoon. Miss Geraldine Cooke, in a very eloquent speech, explained the pilgrimage in detail, and asked the Society to make its colours widely known – red,

white and green – and also urged each member to support and read the official organ of the National Union of Women's Suffrage Societies, *The Common Cause*.

The *Kent & Sussex Courier* gives a fantastic description of the procession of women making their way from Tunbridge Wells, via Southborough, to Tonbridge. This account includes reference to women all having a satchel slung over their shoulders, likely the haversacks that could be purchased through the NUWSS:

> Although comparatively small, this effort was most impressive and provocative of thought. One saw over 100 ladies, including some of the best-known and most influential residents of this town [Tunbridge Wells], marching, enthusiastically over the long road to Southborough and Tonbridge. Progress was necessarily slow, as some of the participants were advanced in years, but nevertheless they bore up bravely. The procession started from the offices of the Tunbridge Wells Branch in Crescent road. The ladies formed up in twos. Each of the pilgrims had slung over her shoulder a satchel [haversack], supported by a red, white and green band, and bearing on it the legend in red letters, 'Kent Pilgrims' Way'. Rosettes in the same hues – the colours of the cause – adorned the hats of the ladies, whilst they also carried small red, white and green pennants and wore on their breasts similarly coloured badges. To a short-sighted onlooker the battalion of suffrage aspirants must have looked something like a red, white and green kaleidoscope.[90]

The same article detailed that at the front of the procession was a banner that read in huge lettering 'Non-militant'. Other banners advertised the meeting that was to take place in Southborough later that day and one read 'Do well, doubt not!' Two police constables and two young women on 'gaily decorated cycles' led the way with the young cyclists collecting donations from and selling copies of *The Common Cause* to 'the crowds that lined the route'.[91]

Behind the first banner were Madame Sarah Grand, the president of the Tunbridge Wells branch of the NUWSS, and Miss Moseley, their Honorary Secretary. The report suggested a hierarchy for the procession as it said: 'The ladies of the Committee followed, and then came the rank and file.'[92]

On the way to Southborough there were reports of five carriages and a motor car joining the procession. 'The actual march was uneventful. One could not help remarking upon the absolute respect and deference with which the crowds who lined the kerbs at various busy spots on the route treated the pilgrims. Salutations and encouraging utterances were frequent; coarse criticism entirely absent.'[93]

The Tonbridge and Langton Green pilgrims joined this Tunbridge Wells procession at Speldhurst Road. 'A round of applause greeted the newcomers, who brought with them some imposing banners. One of these stated the object of the NUWSS, another bore a picture of Tonbridge Castle, and another said boldly, "Long live the Scottish bailies!" a cry which quickly caught on'.[94] This was a tribute to the many members of the Northern Men's Federation who were bailees and councillors from Glasgow and Scotland who used their status to press for women's suffrage.

'All Southborough turned out to witness the march to the Victoria Hall which was somewhat in the nature of a triumphal procession'.[95] The same newspaper article that described this also listed the names of most of those that were in the procession who arrived at Southborough. The meeting at Southborough was large and the hall crowded. Madame Sarah Grand presided and in her speech

> said that some people thought only exceptionally gifted people could make history. Doubtless it would come as a surprise to some of them that they had been helping to make history. They had had records of many a pilgrimage, but that undertaken by the devoted women then marching from all parts of the United Kingdom at

a great expenditure of mental and physical strength was an event unique in their annals.[96]

During the course of her speech she went on to say that

> women were not claiming the vote because they were the same as men, but because they were different. They are the other half of the race – the unrepresented half. They had their own duties to perform, and very important ones. The Suffrage agitation had proved that when it came to public work there was nothing to choose between the abilities of men and women. They were the equals of men in courage, work, argument, organisation and administration (hear, hear).[97]

Miss Amelia Scott called for a resolution at the meeting: 'That this meeting, believing that the exclusion of women from the Parliamentary franchise is unjust and contrary to the principle of representative government, calls on His Majesty's Ministers to introduce a measure removing this injustice without further delay.'[98] This resolution was carried unanimously. She described the object of the pilgrimage as being 'to demonstrate that quiet, home-loving women are not against this movement' and highlighted 'such women on the road, coming out of every town and village'.[99] Amelia Scott also spoke of all the meetings taking place along the route and that at their meeting today were representatives from areas such as Matfield, Pembury, Brenchley and Tunbridge Wells.

Portrait of Ameila Scott. She led the organisation for Tunbridge Wells (West Kent) of the 1913 NUWSS Pilgrimage to Kent
© *LSE Women's Library collection*

Her speech also touched on the suggestion that women are hard on other women. She agreed that in a time gone by women would be competing for the best marriage to gain material advantage over other women. She argued that this was no longer the case, because 'education, scientific research, the invention of machinery and many other forces have changed the whole outlook of humanity, and of women as part of humanity' and so women now compete with each other and men 'in the labour makers for her daily bread... Women are learning that if one member of the body politic suffers all the members suffer with it.'[100]

Mr. Malcolm Mitchell, a past founder member and secretary of the Men's League for Women's Suffrage, also spoke at this meeting. He referred to the current politics and of how he believed that those in Parliament were beginning to see how important it was for women to have the vote. He said that 'From the moment women had the vote the Government would suddenly discover that women's grievances must be looked into the same as men's.'[101]

Miss Griffith Jones was also known to have been at this Southborough meeting as she was recorded as proposing gratitude to all speakers. This could therefore mean she arrived with other pilgrims from the Northern Route.

After the Southborough meeting and some tea, the procession continued its march to Tonbridge. The local press published a list[102] of those people ending their pilgrimage in Southborough, and those continuing to Tonbridge. It was recorded that there were fifteen women from Tonbridge who joined the pilgrimage. There were notably women coming 'from outlying districts'. They included three women from Matfield; two from Goudhurst; two from Wadhurst; several from Crowborough and Rotherfield; one from Groombridge and several from Hastings.

Prior to all Kentish Pilgrims converging at Tonbridge, the Tonbridge Branch of the NUWSS held meetings in outlying villages. Reported in the *Kent & Sussex Courier* newspaper, the details of two were 'In connection with the Women's Suffrage Pilgrimage two very successful open-air meetings were held locally during the past week.' A meeting was held at the village of Hadlow (on the outskirts of Tonbridge) in the Broadway on Saturday, 12 July from 7.00 to 8.00 pm:

> The chief speaker was Miss Mercer, Organising Secretary of the Conservative and Unionist Women's Franchise Association, and also a member of the NUWSS, who was listened to with great attention. At the close of her address questions were asked, leaflets were distributed, and copies of *The Common Cause* were sold.

On Tuesday, 15 July

> members of the Tonbridge Branch held a meeting at Golden Green, near Hadlow where the speakers were Mrs. Venning, Miss Palmer, and Mr. Bart Kennedy. In spite of the rain there was a good attendance, and much interest was shown. The proceedings lasted nearly two hours, many of the audience remaining to discuss the question with the speakers long after the meeting closed.[103]

NUWSS Kentish Pilgrimage of 1913 marching through Tonbridge High Street.
© *Dennis Goodland and Tonbridge Historical Society*

*NUWSS Kentish Pilgrimage of 1913 marching through Tonbridge High Street.
Note the banners on display: 'Tonbridge' specific, 'Non Militant' as a reminder
to those they passed and 'Long live the Scottish bailies!' which was reported as
a cry that quickly caught on*
© *Dennis Goodland and Tonbridge Historical Society*

*NUWSS Kentish Pilgrimage of 1913 marching through Tonbridge High Street.
Close up of one of the banners seen to refer to the 'Kentish Pilgrimage'*
© *Dennis Goodland and Tonbridge Historical Society*

The planned Tonbridge to Blackheath route allowed for halting in the village of Hildenborough, between Tonbridge and Sevenoaks on the Tonbridge Road. No record of this has been found.

The pilgrims arrived at Tub's Hill Station (in Sevenoaks) on Tuesday, 22 July at 7.11 pm[104] 'where they were joined by a number of sympathisers'.[105]

> A procession was formed, and with banners flying, they marched slowly towards the town. Large crowds patiently awaited their arrival. No blaze of trumpets or brass bands heralded their coming, but silently and with slow and measured tread, the little procession mounted the hill, turned by the fountain at the top of London-road, and took up their stand in the market place, where their first meeting was to be held. Very soon an exceedingly large crowd had gathered round.[106]

Describing the banners and flags being carried was a report in the *Sevenoaks Chronicle*, which read: 'They carried banners and flags, amongst them being notably the Sevenoaks W.S.S. banner and another one bearing the inscription "Long live the Scottish Bailies", a tribute to the Scotchmen that had succeeded, where the Suffragists had failed, in interviewing the Prime Minister.'[107]

A description of this first meeting at Sevenoaks was also in a report:

> A large number of adherents[108] gathered en route, while in the Market Place, the few small knots of people swelled to a large crowd upon the arrival of the processionists. Miss Hemmant took the chair, the rostrum being a van. The first note of the pilgrims' message was struck by Miss Muriel Matters. Her first sentences were followed by some derisive laughter, the experience of hearing a lady orator probably being strange to a section of the audience. But Miss Matters was soon well under sail in a most interesting exposition of the women's cause. A few interrupters were present, but the speaker gave them an uncomfortable time and they thought better to hold their peace. The meeting proceeded orderly, and even at

question time – a time that hecklers' love – there was comparative quiet, only two questions being put.[109]

Also on this Tuesday, 22 July at 7.30 pm pilgrims held a meeting on the village green in the nearby village of Brasted. To target as many areas of Kent as possible, including the more rural ones, pilgrims formed groups and split off. With Miss Muriel Matters speaking in Sevenoaks, Miss Griffith Jones travelled to Brasted to address their meeting.

On Wednesday, 23 July at 3.00 pm an open-air meeting was held at a village near Sevenoaks, called Knockholt. The speaker was Canon Beanlands.[110] At 5.30 pm on the same day a meeting was scheduled at The Vine (cricket ground) in Sevenoaks with Muriel Matters speaking. Then, later that evening, a further meeting was organized for the Market Place in Sevenoaks, again with Muriel speaking. It was reported that 'At the evening meeting a large number were again attracted.'[111]

The pilgrims left the Market Place on 24 July, and proceeded to Bromley:

> On Thursday morning the march to London was resumed. The pilgrims assembled in the Market Place at 9.30 and with banners and flags flying set out to carry their messages into Bromley. The local arrangements were made by Miss M. Crosbie-Hill, Miss Mary Hemmant, and Mrs. Percy Thompson, who are to be congratulated upon the complete success of the pilgrims' visit.[112]

Press in Bromley reported that the pilgrims had been long expected and that therefore 'a very large number of people'[113] arrived to meet them. 'Contrary to the expectations of the crowd, the pilgrims arrived in two waggonettes. It transpired that they had driven from Sevenoaks, and held meetings at Bromley and elsewhere on the way.'[114]

One newspaper described the pilgrims looking 'bronzed by daily exposure to the weather and country marches'[115] and another 'as fresh as the proverbial daisy'.[116] There were reports of the show of red, white and green, the colours of the law-abiding suffrage societies. Leading the procession was a lady in white, carrying a banner that clearly stated 'law abiding'. The Blackheath members carried their banner next and then came the pilgrims and banners from Kent. They read: 'It is not to be thought that the flood of British Freedom should perish' and 'Home-makers Demand the Vote'.[117]

Other banners from Kent were said to have inscriptions referring to Joan of Arc, Jane Austen, Caroline Herschel and other famous women. The procession was joined by a brass band of sixteen performers from Stepney.

Miss Griffith Jones, the Northern Kent route organizer, spoke to the crowd and was treated less graciously than other speakers by some youths in the crowd heckling her. She was interrupted, but dealt with it well. However, 'a dog fight in the crowd caused another diversion.'[118] Miss Ward, organizer for the Southern Kent route, also spoke.

An advertisement appeared in the Sevenoaks local press urging NUWSS members and sympathizers wishing to attend the Hyde Park demonstration on Saturday, 26 July to either 'join the Sevenoaks contingent at the Sevenoaks Railway station, in time to catch the 1.33 train, or else to join them in Trafalgar Square at 2.30'.[119] This is telling of the many different groups of supporters of this pilgrimage and Hyde Park demonstration. Some members and supporters would have left Sevenoaks on Thursday, 24 July but others, perhaps unable to spare the time, the cost of travel and/or stay away from home etc., travelled into London by train on the Saturday to participate in the demonstration.

The entry into London for the Kentish Pilgrims was detailed in *The Common Cause* of Friday, 25 July 1913[120] and included marching along Deptford Broadway to a meeting at New Cross Gate, followed by rest and refreshments, then assembling at Pepys Road and marching via the Old Kent Road to the Elephant and Castle's King's Hall for a meeting.

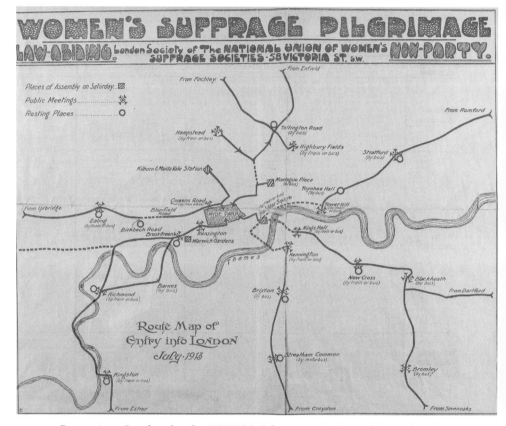

Routes into London for the NUWSS Pilgrimage 1913, including that from Dartford and Sevenoaks in Kent
© *LSE Women's Library collection*

The arrival of the Kentish Pilgrims in Lee Green on Thursday, 24 July was recorded in an August 1913 account by the NUWSS:

> The Blackheath Branch met the Pilgrims at Lee Green on Thursday, July 24th, at 5.30, and marched to Whitfield's Mount, where a meeting was held. At platform 1 the chair was taken by Richard H. Green, Esq., and the speakers were Miss Maud Royden and Miss Ruth Young. At platform 2, G.H. Monk Esq., took the chair, the speakers being Miss Fielden, and Miss Griffith Jones. Collection realised £1 3s. 2½d, and over 150 'Friends'

of Women's Suffrage cards were signed. The Pilgrims re-assembled on Friday morning at the same spot, and marched to Pepys Road, New Cross Gate, when a meeting was held, with Mrs. Stanbury in the chair, the speakers being Miss Muriel Matters, Miss Griffith Jones and Miss M. Goddard. Collection realised 9s. 2½d, and over 100 'Friends' cards were signed. In the evening the Pilgrims marched to the King's Hall, Elephant and Castle, joining in the meeting there. Special thanks are due to those local men who came forward and helped at the meetings.[121]

The King's Hall speakers were recorded as Mrs. Philip Snowden, Miss Ward, Mr. Mirrlees and Mr. S. Pascall.[122]

On Saturday, 26 July 1913 all pilgrims met at Hyde Park for a demonstration. The details for this were included in the *Votes for Women* newspaper. This included a map of Hyde Park with meeting-up points for each stream of pilgrims shown. The eight routes would converge at Hyde Park, meeting at four points. The Kentish Pilgrims assembled with those from the East Coast at Trafalgar Square at 2.30 pm and marched via Cockspur Street, Pall Mall, Waterloo Place, Piccadilly and Hyde Park Corner. It was reported that 'Nearly thirty meetings were held in various parts of London last night. This morning the Pilgrims and their friends were parading the main London streets selling copies of *The Common Cause*, and wearing their haversacks, badges and colours.'[123]

There were 50,000 spectators and 19 platforms with between 80 and 90 speakers.

On Sunday, 27 July 1913 the pilgrims were invited to attend the afternoon service at St Paul's Cathedral. This occasion was reported in *The Common Cause* in the following way:

Pilgrims assembled in Trafalgar Square and marched to St. Paul's, where they attended the afternoon service. Long lines of women, wearing red, white and green sashes, filed into the Cathedral for about half an hour, and the quiet assembly gathered in thanksgiving at the end of its long

Millicent Fawcett's Hyde Park address on 26 July 1913
© LSE Women's Library collection

Pilgrimage made a very impressive spectacle. Outside the procession, organised by the WSPU, was making its way from the East End to Trafalgar Square, and later in the day I found Whitehall still thronged by people who had been watching the arrest of Miss Sylvia Pankhurst, and were perhaps waiting in hope of her reappearance. Some militants asked me why the Pilgrims had not tried to go to Downing Street, why we were not going in procession to the House of Commons, why a few of us who had been invited to tea on the Terrace were not seizing the opportunity to make a Suffrage speech to the members. But our appeal has been, and is, not simply to Ministers or Members of Parliament, but to the people of Great Britain.[124]

On 29 July 1913 Mrs. Fawcett wrote to Asquith on behalf of the pilgrims and requested a deputation of law-abiding suffragists. Asquith replied on the 31st, acknowledging that the demonstration had a 'special claim' on his consideration and stood 'upon another footing from similar demands proceeding from other quarters where a different method and spirit is predominant. But he felt bound to warn her that he had nothing to add to recent statements in the House on government policy.'[125]

The deputation took place on 8 August and those NUWSS members who attended were disappointed. Mrs. Fawcett wrote to Asquith following this to set out their exasperation.[126]

Different to other marches lasting a few hours and culminating in a meeting, the Women's Pilgrimage involved a fluctuating number of participants over a period of more than a month, giving opportunity for meetings, fund-raising and distribution of literature. The members were also able to meet people in towns and villages otherwise missed by the NUWSS campaign.

> We have been urged to 'advertise' ourselves, our objects, and our methods. Here is a giant advertisement, which all the country will hear of and will see…. It would cost hundreds of pounds adequately to post the hoardings and newspapers of this country with the appeal we want to make and the grounds on which we make it. Here is a chance to make it heard by those who have never listened before.[127]

Despite the efforts of the NUWSS with this pilgrimage, the outbreak of war in August 1914 halted any momentum they had initiated.

CHAPTER THIRTEEN

1913: The WFL 'Holiday Campaign'

Towards the end of July 1913, the WFL completed a 'Holiday Campaign' in Kent. The aim of these 'Holiday Campaigns' was to spread the cause of women's suffrage.[1]

The programme for the Kent Holiday Campaign was initially advertised[2] as follows:

Tankerton, Kent, beyond The Lawn daily at 11.00 am	19 to 29 July
Foxall, Kent	21 July
Whitstable at 7.30 pm	22, 25 and 28 July
Faversham	19 and 24 July
Canterbury	23 and 29 July
Blean	26 July

The following week,[3] the programme was amended to:

Tankerton, Kent, beyond The Lawn daily at 11.00 am	25 to 29 July
Whitstable at 7.30 pm	25 and 28 July
Blean	26 July
Canterbury	29 July

However, it seems that they did not follow either programme, starting proceedings in Tankerton on 14 July and setting up their headquarters in Herne Bay, a place not even mentioned in either programme. This demonstrates the organic nature of such a campaign. Miss Katherine Trott was the WFL organizer for the Kent work from the second half of July, and reported back that 'Herne Bay appears to be always swarming with people, so we have determined to make our headquarters there for August.'[4]

There were two lead organizers for Kent. Miss Constance E. Andrews was reportedly in charge of the Kent work in the first part of July, recorded as working in Gravesend, North-West Kent, with Miss Katherine Trott succeeding her later in July. Constance then went to the Devonshire coast to 'open up a new centre of activity'.[5] In an early July[6] edition of *The Vote*, it was said that Mrs. Merivale Mayer was to be the chief speaker in that district.

Constance had worked with Katherine Trott before. She was Hon. Secretary of the Ipswich and County Women's Suffrage Society in 1907–12. She seems to have participated in several WFL tours, including one in June 1912 to Hertfordshire. She was a well-known WFL speaker, and had spoken alongside Mrs. Charlotte Despard at a Trafalgar Square demonstration in September 1912 and in Hyde Park in May 1913 when the Home Office had prohibited such meetings.

In June 1913, just prior to Constance's involvement in the WFL Kent Holiday Campaign, she was arrested outside St James's Palace along with two other WFL members. They were released from Holloway Prison after their fines were paid by an unknown person. The following day, Constance had gone with a Mr. Simpson of the MLWS to Gravesend in North-West Kent. There they

> attempted to address a gathering numbering some thousands at the Clock Tower. The gathering, however, showed such a resentful disposition that the speakers were quickly compelled to find refuge in the home of a local resident. The house was surrounded for two hours, the crowd hooting and discharging rousers and squibs.[7]

A 'squib' and a 'rouser' are fireworks. A squib is a small firework that burns with a hissing sound before exploding. Despite this 'gigantic meeting'[8] having to be abandoned, the Gravesend WFL branch reported that a meeting had taken place in the Labour Hall with Constance giving 'a most delightful speech to a very enthusiastic audience'.[9] This was apparently a surprise visit by Constance, the purpose of which was to spend a few days' organizing work with the branch. The Gravesend branch reported that two new members had joined, that they had sold much suffrage literature, and that progress had been made with the Town Council on the proposed suffrage literature market stall. Feeding back on Constance's visit to Gravesend in Kent, the branch reported that 'Miss Andrew's visit has been a source of great pleasure to all members, and we thank her very much for coming. A good contingent of Gravesend members will take part in our Suffrage Flower Day in London on Saturday.'[10]

There was a Miss F. Taylor detailed as the Honorary Press Secretary of the Kent Federation of Suffrage Societies in March 1913. It is likely that this was the Miss F. Taylor responsible with Miss Katherine Trott for organizing the WFL Kent Holiday Campaign. In the NUWSS newspaper *The Common Cause*, the following interesting report on the county of Kent and the challenges facing the women's suffrage campaigners was included:

> The Kent Federation has been reorganised under the presidency of Countess Brassey, and is now, we hope, on a firm basis. A Federation committee meeting was held at 24, Park Lane on March 12th. All the Societies within the Federation were represented, and the following officers were appointed:- Hon. Sec, Miss Bruce; Hon. Treas., Miss Drace; Hon. Press Sec., Miss F. Taylor. Kent is an extremely difficult county to work owing to the lack of industrial centres, the shifting nature of the population in the garrison and seaside towns, and the apathy of country folk. The organiser, Miss Griffith Jones, and her assistant, Miss Missick, have been energetically touring the county, and give a hopeful account of their district.

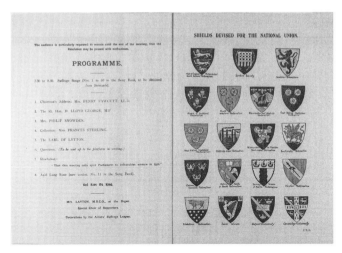

Shown in this Programme for the Royal Albert Hall leaflet NUWSS 23 Feb 1912 is the Kentish Federation shield design. This design represented the Pilgrims' Way bearing as a charge, a Palmer's Hat and Staff. In colour this is shown to have green representing a green field. From the design album of Mary Lowndes © LSE Women's Library collection

A second image of the Kentish Federation shield design representing the Pilgrims' Way bearing as a charge, a Palmer's Hat and Staff. In colour this is shown to have green representing a green field. From the design album of Mary Lowndes © LSE Women's Library collection

All the Societies had committees of special meetings
to meet the organisers, who are now personally known
throughout the Federation. Future propaganda work
was discussed and much useful work suggested and put
in hand. The organisers are proceeding to the formation
of several new societies in important districts.[11]

This report then included specific details on suffrage societies
in Kent towns, villages and districts. These were Ashford,
Canterbury, Folkestone, Hythe, Matfield, Brenchley & Pembury,
Margate, Ramsgate, Rochester, Sevenoaks, Sidcup & Chislehurst
and Tonbridge. All reported meetings; Sevenoaks advised that
their suffrage shop would be moving to other premises; Margate
had been reorganized; Matfield, Brenchley & Pembury –
described as a 'difficult district' – told of a successful drawing-
room meeting; and Folkestone proclaimed very full public
meetings and enthusiasm for the cause in the town. None of
these places were visited by this WFL tour.

Katherine Trott was a very active campaigner for women's
suffrage and member of the WFL. Subsequent to this tour
Katherine was arrested in London along with six other women
for obstruction. Evidence given by the police was that 'the
defendants were addressing three separate crowds. In each case
one was ringing a bell to attract passers-by.'[12] Another report
published about this incident involving Katherine was that the
seven women made 'a raid upon the residence of the Prime
Minister and the Chancellor of the Exchequer [and] went to all
the doors of the principal buildings and commenced ringing the
bells'.[13] Miss Marguerite Sidley, the WFL member that took part
in the WFL 1908 Kent Tour, was also arrested. When replying to
the magistrate, the women said that they had acted in this way
as a protest against the absence from the King's Speech of any
reference to the franchise for women. Marguerite and another
suffragette were ordered to find two sureties of £10 each for six
months, while Katherine and the other four women were ordered
to enter into their own recognizances to keep the peace for six
months. 'They declined to be bound over, and Miss Sidley and

Miss Ball were sentenced to four days' imprisonment, and the others [including Katherine] to one day's imprisonment.'[14]

Starting the Kent Holiday Campaign on 14 July 1913, Katherine and Mrs. Merivale Mayer spoke at a meeting in Tankerton.[15] The headquarters in Tankerton were at 37 Clare Road. Australian Mrs. Merivale Mayer was another well-known and well-travelled women's suffrage speaker. She was described as having considerable gifts as a speaker and being eloquent and charmingly witty. Records show that Merivale and Katherine continued working together long into 1914 as they are named as speakers at an open-air meeting in Brighton and Hove.[16]

The report of the Tankerton meeting on 14 July 1913 was submitted by Katherine and reads as follows:

> Residents and visitors were not at all surprised to see us down here, for the NUWSS were a few days before us to prepare a welcome for the 'Kentish Marchers', who held two meetings on Wednesday. People were quite ready to understand and approve our policy. We have made a number of friends among the fishermen, who have willingly bought *The Vote*; one has issued a pressing invitation to us to go for a trip and hold a meeting in his yacht, which we hope to do soon.[17]

Two weeks later and Katherine continued to report that the

> Tankertonians continue to be most kind and sympathetic to the Cause and make many inquiries about our meetings. Miss Underwood addressed a gathering of excursionists on the shore on July 17, at which Miss F. Taylor presided. It was followed by a capital meeting in the centre of Whitstable town, which evoked nothing but favourable remarks; and nearly all the boyhood and youth of the town turned out to escort us home![18]

A few days later, previous WFL Kent tourer from 1908, Mrs. Margaret Wynne Nevinson, led a meeting. From the report it is not clear exactly where this meeting was held. However, some interest appears to have been generated as reportedly two people remained behind at this meeting to discuss increasing women's suffrage activity.

Aiming to target the Bank Holiday tourists or 'Bank Holidayists'[19] as Katherine Trott referred to them in her reports, the Kent Holiday Campaign moved its headquarters from Tankerton to Herne Bay on 30 July. On 31 July they began a series of meetings at the East Cliff. Miss L.B. Shakespeare had joined them as the lead speaker. This was Lucy Shakespeare, known to have worked in Glasgow in 1913 and 1914.

In August 1913, the Holiday Campaign welcomed Miss Nina Boyle (1865–1943), 'whose splendid speeches, two, three, and four times a day, became quite a feature of the town, and we announced each meeting by a march with the colours through High-street and along the front'.[20] Nina, along with Constance Andrews, had been one of the speakers at the reconvened Gravesend meeting in July. Reportedly, a 'packed audience listened attentively and most courteously to Miss Boyle for upwards of an hour, breaking up without the slightest disorder and with no evidence of hostility'.[21] Nina was one of the WFL's main speakers and had endured imprisonment for her women's suffrage beliefs and actions. A year after her speeches in Kent, Nina founded and became chief of the Women Police Volunteers. She was one of the first women to appear in police uniform. Such was Nina's passion and obvious speaker talents that the following letter was received from an audience member:

> Madam, Recently staying at Herne Bay for a few days, and having had the advantage of hearing Miss Boyle of the Freedom League speak on behalf of Women's Suffrage, I felt bound in common gratitude to testify to the splendid work done by the League through such speeches as hers. They are at once an education and inspiration. The brave way she stood her ground, her fund of information readily placed at the disposal of questioners, impressed many of us who have hitherto been indifferent. Good luck to the Freedom League and

its mission! We workers want such leaders to point out the way. One of the 'Daily Crowd'.[22]

In her reports that appeared in *The Vote*, Katherine referred to a belief that 'a lasting impression has been made on many who attended meeting after meeting, asking intelligent questions and seeking private conversation afterwards.' She referred to a party of schoolboys with their master stopping after a meeting to ask for more information, 'too shy to ask for in front of the crowd!' She also reported that

> Bystanders rebuked us for 'wasting our time on youngsters', but we do not doubt that the seed will bear lasting fruit when, as voters, they may be called to stand up for the rights of their sisters. The rowdy element was present also on some occasions, demonstrating against women's militancy by means of their own militant words and actions; and then we hear of man's logic and women's lack of it![23]

The Holiday Campaign also visited Whitstable and returned to Tankerton to hold meetings at which Nina Boyle spoke. Meetings were held in the town, on the beach and 'in the elite corner as well; at the latter especially we had a splendid reception'.[24]

Katherine Trott reported that

> *The Vote* has sold well all the time, and on the whole collections have been good. On one occasion a slip of paper containing half a crown was found in the box, bearing the words: 'A mark of a working woman's appreciation of Miss Nina Boyle's splendid work on our behalf at Herne Bay.'[25]

She concluded by extending her thanks to all those people who had given up their holiday time to help the WFL in selling *The Vote*, taking collections and canvassing.

The women's suffrage campaigning continued in Kent as in August the WSPU arrived with their 'Campaign Kent'.

Nina Boyle who joined the WFL Kent Holiday Campaign in August 1913. She had also been a speaker, alongside Constance Andrews, at the reconvened Gravesend meeting in July of 1913
© *LSE Women's Library collection*

CHAPTER FOURTEEN

1913: The WSPU 'Campaign Kent'

In August 1913, the WSPU brought their campaigning to Kent with 'Campaign Kent' consisting of eight active members travelling between Tunbridge Wells and London.

Shortly after the NUWSS deputation to Asquith on 8 August 1913, the militant suffrage organization WSPU completed a smaller-scale pilgrimage to Kent. *The Suffragette*, the official newspaper or publication of the WSPU, urged members taking a holiday to spend some of their holiday time keeping 'the needs of the movement in mind' with 'one all-important way for serving the movement during August and September [being] to get new readers for *The Suffragette*.'[1] This same edition of *The Suffragette* referred to the peaceful pilgrimage of the NUWSS:

> The Hyde Park Demonstration which has the culminating point of the great peaceful pilgrimage organised by the anti-militants, has had considerable attention in the Press. But, in accordance with men's favourite policy of playing off one section of women against another, the newspapers in their accounts have laid great stress upon the anti-militants' attacks upon the WSPU. They have, in fact, represented it to be a demonstration against militancy rather than in favour of the vote. *The Times* report actually says: 'The proceedings indeed were as

much a demonstration against militancy as one in favour of the Suffrage.'

The Times adds that 'many bitter things were said of the militant women'. The *Daily Mail* goes so far as to use the demonstration as an argument against votes for women, and makes the truly ridiculous claim that it proves that women could get the reforms they want by means of such demonstrations instead of by means of the vote itself.[2]

This reaction by the Press to the NUWSS pilgrimage would have fuelled the energy behind the WSPU's 1913 Holiday Campaign. A key message to WSPU members was included in their official newspaper:

Members are determined that the 1913 Holiday Campaign shall be bigger and better than that of any previous year. Every post brings letters, every day fresh volunteers.... The latest scheme which is in hand should prove very attractive, especially to the younger members of the Union: this is, that they should band themselves together and become as wandering gypsies, making their way from one village to another, selling and advertising *The Suffragette* and holding village meetings as they go.... This should prove not only of great service to the cause, but also a most agreeable and healthy way of spending a holiday. This scheme also opens up to those unable to take active part in the Holiday Campaign themselves, a new way of joining in and helping to make it a success. Hospitality will be wanted all along the route for the gypsy wanderers, and the organiser would be very glad to have the names of those who will offer to help in this way. This, of course, is only one of the many ideas which we have on hand, and if there are any to whom it does not appeal they may rest assured that there are plans afoot to suit every sort and kind of helper. We have work that everyone can join in, and now is the chance for those who cannot give much time during the year. This is an opportunity for members who are unable to make the great sacrifices that many are now making. Send in your names to Miss Bartels, at Lincoln's Inn House: decide at once that you will be among those to ensure the success of this great campaign, which will help to show the Government that their weapons of tyranny, coercion, and injustice are of no avail.[3]

Later in the same article is written: 'As regards the Suffragette gypsies, it has been suggested that they should take dogs as protection at night, and a mail-cart might also be found useful for carrying papers and any personal luggage that may be necessary.'[4]

One similarity to the NUWSS campaign is that the WSPU sold their branded items to members to fund-raise and publicize their cause. There were suffragette sunshades described as 'invaluable for seaside and country campaigns'.[5] Flags and bunting were also available.

A coupon was included in the Suffragette journal for completion by those wishing to participate in the Holiday Campaign. They advised of their holiday destination and dates together with the time they were prepared to give to the cause.

The initially proposed Kent route was set out in a local newspaper, the *Kent & Sussex Courier*. Described as a 'holiday pedestrian campaign',[6] it went from Waterloo Station and via Kent to Croydon:

Waterloo Station to Woolwich	Wednesday (first day)
Woolwich to Sevenoaks	Second day
Sevenoaks to Tonbridge	Third day
Tonbridge to Tunbridge Wells	Fourth day
Tunbridge Wells to Lingfield, via Groomsbridge	Fifth day
Lingfield to Oxted and Croydon	Sixth day

A few days later in *The Suffragette* was included the object of the campaign, namely 'to boom the sale of *The Suffragette* in holiday places, among all the holiday-goers in the British Isles'.[7] This would explain the choice of the Lake District for Route No. 1 and Kent for Route No. 2. The article continued that the campaign's 'plan is to make use of every member of the WSPU on vacation, or whose home is one of the holiday spots of this country, to carry on this work of the Union through the summer months.'[8]

The description given for the Kent holiday campaign was

> The Gypsy Wanderers. Younger members of the Union in charge of a Gypsy Queen, travelling through the country in bands with their dogs, camping by the roadsides, carrying their supplies in a cart, holding meetings and hawking papers in the villages along their route. They were said to be wanting volunteers to give hospitality to gypsies, speakers and workers; volunteers to take part in the gypsy campaign; paper-sellers, advertisers, stewards for meetings; tents; dogs for gypsies; hostesses for garden meetings; and promoters for single meetings where no campaign has been arranged.[9]

This list of wants covered the majority of people and items needed to successfully run such a holiday campaign and, published on 1 August for an August campaign this seems a bit late in the day. However, Miss Olive Walton, an active WSPU member, was making extensive plans for the campaign in her town of Tunbridge Wells: 'Tunbridge Wells is making special plans for the second half of August, when Miss Olive Walton will be arranging a holiday campaign in this town and in the surrounding villages. Who will come forward?'[10]

The 'Gypsy Queen' for Kent was named as Miss Lily McDonnell.[11] She was a concert singer living at 13 Regent's Park Villas, Oval Road, London. She performed in concerts to support the WSPU.

The revised route was also published in the 8 August 1913 edition of *The Suffragette*.

Leave Lincoln's Inn House	Thursday, 7 August 1913 at 10 o'clock
Stop at Farnborough, Kent	Overnight, Thursday, 7 August 1913
Farnborough to Southborough	Friday, 8 August 1913
Stop at Southborough	Overnight, Friday, 8 August 1913
Southborough to Tunbridge Wells	Saturday, 9 August 1913
Stop at Tunbridge Wells	Overnight, Saturday, 9 August 1913
Tunbridge Wells to Edenbridge	Sunday, 10 August 1913
Stop at Edenbridge, Kent	Overnight, Sunday, 10 August 1913
Edenbridge to Caterham, Surrey	Monday, 11 August 1913
Stop at Caterham, Surrey	Overnight, Monday, 11 August 1913
Caterham to Croydon	Tuesday, 12 August 1913
Stop at Croydon, Surrey	Overnight, Tuesday, 12 August 1913
Croydon to Lincoln's Inn House	Wednesday, 13 August 1913

In one London newspaper the eight members of this 'gypsy band' were described as 'ardent young Suffragettes'[12] intending on pleading 'the cause for women in Kent' by 'spreading the knowledge of their paper, *The Suffragette*, throughout the highways and byways of Kent'. They planned on giving concerts as some of them were concert singers and follow this with talks about votes for women. One young suffragette reportedly said: 'Oh, we shall have a ripping time.'[13] The reporter from the newspaper was apparently decorated with suffragette colours and given ample suffragette literature before the small group left in front of a small crowd of spectators. The *Kent and Sussex Courier*[14] included a photograph of these suffragettes heading

WSPU members making banners
© LSE Women's Library collection

WSPU members heading off to Kent for their 1913 campaign tour
© The March of the Women Collection / Mary Evans Picture Library

off to Kent. This photograph appears both on the front cover and in the images section.

An account from the gypsies' perspectives was included in the WSPU publication *The Suffragette*:

> On Thursday [7 August] eight of us dressed as gypsies climbed into an old decorated cart and made seats for ourselves on our bundles of luggage and provisions. The crowd collected outside Lincoln's Inn House and made a way for us as the gypsy queen took her seat up front, and we flicked the old horse up. We had commenced our journey from the Kingsway to carry our message of hope to the women of Kent. The mare certainly required a good amount of 'wigging' and no one knew her name. It was suggested we should call her 'Christabel' or 'Pankhurst' but we found that neither name was appropriate, as she stopped all the progress and activity of the Strand. What do you think we called her? Why, Asquith, of course! I feel that all my party would like to write pages about the smiling good-natured welcome we received. 'You're the real ones, ain't yer missis?' called one poor woman. 'You're goin' ter win, ain't yer?' cried another. 'Ra-ther!' we shouted back in chorus.[15]

The horse that Charlotte Despard and other WFL members used for their 1908 tour of Kent was named 'Asquith' too.

The first stop for the 1913 WSPU suffragettes was Lewisham to collect another of their party. It is not clear who this was. It is known from an account written by one of the wandering gypsies that the 'Gypsy Queen', Miss Lily McDonnell had Miss May Billinghurst as her driver.[16] May Billinghurst was from Lewisham and could well have been the member collected, for she was disabled and used a wheelchair. She was an active suffragette who throughout her campaigning had been imprisoned many times and forcibly fed. Reports of Miss Lily McDonnell, with driver Miss May Billinghurst, driving to East Sussex 'in a decorated dogcart'[17] after the Kent Tour also suggest that May was the member of their party stopped for in Lewisham. Interestingly, despite May's known record of activity and imprisonment, Lily describes her as 'a "mouse"'.[18] Either this is ironic or May was not the 'mouse' they stopped in Lewisham to collect.

The gypsy band arrived in Halstead, Kent later on Thursday, 7 August and it was there that they spent their first night. They had no plans of where to stay over. Seeing a farm, they approached the farmer to see if they could use one of his fields:

> After dispelling the farmer's idea that we had come to burn his haystacks and the boys' idea that we had come to smash all the windows, the whole family set to work to make us comfortable. They turned out a summer house, where four of us slept, and gave accommodation to the others in the farmhouse, where they served a most delightful breakfast next morning.[19]

1913 WSPU 'Campaign Kent' may have had Miss Rosa May Billinghurst as its driver. She was disabled and used a wheelchair. She was an active suffragette, imprisoned many times and forcibly fed. If she was the member collected on this tour in Lewisham, the description used of her as a 'mouse' was ironic
© *LSE Women's Library collection*

The farm was owned by a Mr. and Mrs. Bowen and *The Suffragette* report included reference to their hospitality, as did a local Kent newspaper. The WSPU gypsies were treated to breakfast the following morning served on the Bowen family's best china. Quoted in the local newspaper was: 'We shall never forget their kindness to utter strangers, whose only recommendation was that they were militant Suffragettes.'[20]

Research suggests that Mr. and Mrs. Bowen operated M.H. Bowen and Son and were fruit-growers. The 1911 census lists 57-year-old Mr. Matthew Henry Bowen as head of the family and farmer of Widmore Farm. His wife was 62-year-old Helen Louisa and their four children: Gertrude, Henry, Charles and Gordon.

About the same time as the suffragettes were staying during August 1913, it is known that the family attended, assisted as committee members, and competed in the local Halstead Sports and Horse Show. Such was the family that the suffragettes travelling from the London WSPU headquarters first stumbled upon when arriving in Kent.

The next stop was Tonbridge where, on the evening of Friday, 8 August, the suffragettes held a meeting. 'We had a most successful meeting in the street, and then a member put up the ten of us for the night'.[21] It was also reported that the suffragettes sang suffrage songs after the meeting 'which the crowd evidently vastly enjoyed'.[22] It has not been possible to find out which member put these suffragettes up in Tonbridge.

On Saturday, 9 August they arrived in Tunbridge Wells, sold papers in the streets and at 3.00 pm held a meeting at Five Ways 'which was most enthusiastically received, and they were most eager for us to come again in the evening'.[23] They held another meeting in the evening at which Miss McDonnell and Miss Gregory spoke. They reported receiving 'vociferous applause at the end of the speeches'.[24] Miss Lily McDonnell, the Gypsy Queen, then sang and told the audience some humorous stories which they reportedly enjoyed so much they didn't want to go home.

On the afternoon of Sunday, 10 August, they held another meeting on the Common and then proceeded to Edenbridge.

The suffragettes provided a positive report back to headquarters, saying 'if the people of Kent are a criterion of the people in the other parts of the realm, our militancy has made the people realise that this question is a living question: a question that cannot be, and will not be ignored.'[25]

The suffragettes returned to London on Monday, 11 August via Caterham and Croydon and they reported that 'Our experiences have been very enjoyable and we have all come to the conclusion it is a splendid way of having a holiday, apart from the work that is done for the Women's Suffrage movement.'[26]

In *The Suffragette* publication towards the end of August, the following overview of and feedback on the tour of Kent was included: 'A caravan tour through Kent has just come to an end, and has been fraught with excellent results, the members taking part in it stating that they were surprised at the enormous amount of sympathy displayed in the small villages through which they passed.'[27]

The larger report on the tour in Kent read:

> Much to the regret of all our party the gypsy tour through Kent has come to an end. We returned to London with rosy cheeks and £7 14s. for the war-chest after all expenses had been paid. Many of the party walked the whole way, and to that fact we attribute the success of having sold 500 copies of *The Suffragette*. The first thing the 'gypsies' feel it incumbent on them to do is to thank through the medium of these columns, all those kind people who made it possible for the party to set out, and all those very hospitable people en route who extended such a hearty welcome to these wanderers. The varied experiences of the kindness and goodwill we met with will always remain in our memories from the village blacksmith who refused to charge for mending the wheels of our cart, and sent us on our way expressing his hope that God would bless us and speed our cause, to the lady of the stately home who placed her house and grounds at our disposal as we passed on our way. Then there was the farmer who let us have the use of his barn, to sleep easily among his

chickens and ducks on the fresh straw which he spread for us and the appetising supper the farmer's wife prepared for us in her warm kitchen. To the policeman, too, our thanks are due who patrolled the field outside the barn to protect us in case of need.[28]

Following the tour, calls were made via *The Suffragette* newspaper[29] for members to volunteer to sell papers and/or speak at meetings:

The result of the magnificent work that is being done all over the country during the holiday months must be kept up, and one excellent way of doing this is to see to it that the newsagents in various districts stock *The Suffragette* and show a weekly poster from now onwards. Another valuable way of helping to introduce *The Suffragette* to new readers is to make a point of leaving a copy of the paper at hotels and boarding houses. Waiting rooms at railway stations present another excellent opportunity, and a strong appeal is made to holiday-makers to remember to spread the light in this way.[30]

While this approach continued in Kent, just a year later Britain was at war and much changed for women and women's suffrage campaigning.

1914–28: The First World War, 1918 Representation of the People Act, 1928 Equal Franchise Act

On 4 August 1914 Britain declared war on Germany. Both the WSPU and NUWSS agreed to cease their campaigning once the war began. Mrs. Fawcett's views on the war were passed to members of the NUWSS, including those in Kent, in 1915 and read: 'I am heart and soul for the cause of Great Britain in the present war. It is the gravest national crisis she has ever had to face, and every British woman is bound to do what she can and give what she can.'[1]

During the war years that followed, an estimated 2 million women replaced men in traditional male jobs. In Kent this included working in the munitions factories. There was an explosives factory in Faversham; gun manufacturers in Erith, Crayford and Dartford; and an ordnance works at Woolwich Arsenal. At the Faversham explosives factory a song called *The Girls with Yellow Hands* had a chorus line that went: 'Who helped them all to do their job? The girls with yellow hands.'[2] The reference to 'them' is the boys or men fighting on the front line and the 'yellow hands' to the discolouration of skin and poisoning of the body that arose from working with TNT. This

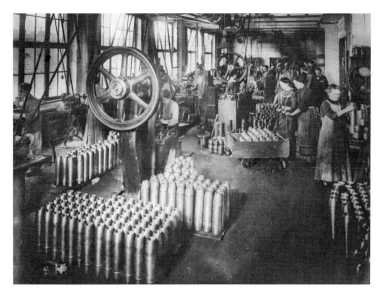

Women working in Munition Factory during World War One
© LSE Women's Library collection

Dame Millicent Fawcett, Miss Fawcett, Miss Garrett and Mrs. Strachey after
Royal Assent to Equal Franchise Act July 2nd 1928. Mrs. Strachey was a guest
speaker at a meeting in Tunbridge Wells, Kent, at the end of 1915. She was Hon
Parliamentary Sec of the NUWSS and appealed to the Kent members to hold
together and maintain their organisation continuing their special work
© LSE Women's Library collection

song portrays an image of women munitions workers seeing themselves as critically important in the war effort.

In Tunbridge Wells in 1917 a scheme operated whereby women were trained as munitions workers. Dr. Lister, head of Tunbridge Wells' Technical Institute, ran the course and once trained, the women would have gone all over the country. It is known that the NUWSS raised funds to improve the hostels in which these women munitions workers were required to lodge.

To assist in the war effort, Kent suffrage societies assisted voluntary and paid workers to find work while also aligning themselves with other local societies and charities, such as the Red Cross. One example discovered is that reported by Mrs. Katherine Venning, one of the Hon. Secretaries of the Tonbridge branch of the NUWSS. It read:

> The NUWSS wishes it to be known that it has suspended its ordinary work for the time being, and is anxious to use its organisation in order to help those thrown into distress by the present crisis. I and my Committee would be glad to place ourselves at the disposal of any Committee you may find it necessary to call together for the relief of distress, and believe that we can count on our members rendering all the assistance in their power.
>
> We are prepared to assist in providing helpers for clerical work, visiting, distribution of provisions and clothing, and in helping to provide shelter, if such be necessary. We will take steps to organise helpers as soon as we hear from you what particular kind of work will be required. I may say we are already in touch with, and helping, the ladies of the Red Cross Society in Tonbridge.[3]

Mr. Peach of the Tonbridge Advisory Committee, appointed for the alleviation of distress and other matters in connection with the war, read this letter out at a meeting at Tonbridge Castle and was applauded.

By the end of 1915 it was clear that all the Kent suffrage societies were involved in some sort of special war work. Miss

Moseley, Hon. Secretary of the Kent Federation, reported at a meeting held in Tunbridge Wells that

> Much energy was being put into hospital, club and patrol work. Maidstone had elected a Woman Guardian, and Walmer possessed a woman Special Constable. The Kent Federation has endowed a bed at the NUWSS Scottish Women's Hospital at Royaumont in France, and is also hoping to assist the Scottish Women's Hospitals in Serbia, if sufficient money can be raised by the Societies for the purpose.[4]

Guest speaker at this Kent meeting was Mrs. Oliver Strachey, Hon. Parliamentary Secretary of the NUWSS. She spoke of the work of the London branch in the past year. The society had been finding work for voluntary women workers as well as paid work. In addition they had focused on training in the semi-skilled areas of the engineering trade. She reported that the War Office had approached them directly requesting experts in testing hay and the society had been able to reach out to their numerous branches and find such experts from 'women who had themselves held farms or reared horses, etc.' The society had also responded to a request from the Woolwich Arsenal and found 500 women to work there.

> 'By doing any work required of us,' said Mrs. Strachey, 'any work that lies before us, we can best help our country and best help the cause of Women's Suffrage, which we all have so much at heart.' She felt sure that when peace came they would find themselves to be nearer to obtaining the vote than they had been before the war. 'Mrs. Strachey appealed to the members of the Tunbridge Wells Branch to hold together, to maintain their organisation, and to continue the special work they had undertaken.'[5]

In 1916 a committee chaired by the House of Commons Speaker was established to begin discussing electoral reform. When it reported in 1917, it recommended limited women's suffrage. Mr. Asquith's response, announcing his conversion to women's suffrage, was as follows:

> Asquith told the House of Commons: 'They fill our munitions factories; they have aided in the most effective way in the prosecution of the war. What is more…they say, when the war comes to an end, and when those abnormal…conditions have to be revised, and when the process of industrial reconstruction has to be set on foot, have not the women a special claim to be heard on the many questions which will arise directly affecting their interests?'[6]

In 1918 an article appeared in a local Kent newspaper about the war and other work undertaken by the Kent Federation of Women's Suffrage Societies. It listed some of the societies, together with the work in which they had been involved. East Kent's Deal and Walmer and West Kent's Tunbridge Wells had worked on the Women's Franchise Clause in the Reform Bill proposed by the committee set up in 1916. Herne Bay, Rochester and Maidstone were listed as continuing societies, but the work they had undertaken was not detailed. For Ramsgate, the report was that 'owing to frequent air-raids, almost all members have left but interest is still there, and all are ready to re-start work as soon as conditions allow this.'[7] Sevenoaks members had reportedly continued with meetings and fund-raised for hospitals. The report concluded that

> The foregoing reports, though necessarily brief, and containing but little account of active suffrage work, show that interest is still alive and keen, and while we rejoice that our cause is won in so wide an extent, determination is steadfast that we shall not cease work until the Franchise is granted on equal terms to men and women.[8]

Miss Lorna Bomford, previous Hon. Treasurer of the Dover branch of the NUWSS, described the war as an 'opportunity to show that love of one's country and fellow men was not the prerogative of the male sex, and that women were perfectly capable and only too keen to shoulder the responsibilities of citizenship'.[9]

Despite an attempt to have the Women's Suffrage clauses omitted from the Representation of the People Act, the House of Lords voted in favour of their inclusion by 134 to 71. As reported in Kent: 'The Bill received the King's Assent and has become an Act upon the Statute Book.'[10] On 6 February 1918, the Representation of the People Act allowed some women over the age of 30 to vote in national elections. This represented 40 per cent of the total population of women. On 14 December of the same year, women were able to vote in a General Election for the first time. There was reportedly a steady stream of ladies attending polling stations throughout the day. In Kent in spite of the miserable weather there were also displays of celebration as processions of women took to the streets. In Tunbridge Wells, 'a procession of women electors, with artistic banners, marched from Calverley Park Gates, through Monson Road, and by the Five Ways to the Town Hall.'[11] Madame Sarah Grand marched with Miss Amelia Scott in the centre of the procession carrying a bouquet of red, white and green flowers:

> At the Town Hall Madame Sarah Grand entered to record her vote, and on returning was received with cheers by the ladies, whose faces showed how profound was the satisfaction felt by them that the long struggle for political freedom was over, and that women had at last entered full citizenship.[12]

In April, Madame Sarah Grand queried with the Tunbridge Wells Women's Suffrage Society if the society was needed any longer. Mrs. Tattershall Dodd – long-standing, ten-year Hon. Secretary – reportedly 'pleaded that though a few women had been enfranchised, the way to equal citizenship between man and woman was still long, and much work was yet to be done before it could be covered, and the full strength of the Suffrage Organisation was needed as urgently as ever'.[13] This was not resolved at this meeting as members Lady Matthews and Miss Scott called for a special meeting to decide it. Also clearly pre-planned was the presentation of a silver tea service to Mrs. Dodd from the Executive Committee. Madame Grand presented it, saying that Mrs. Dodd had 'been the inspiration of the Society, which without her might well have disintegrated. She had carried them through to the triumph of last December, when women first exercised the Parliamentary vote'.[14] It is not clear if this was intended as a presentation to mark the end of this society, but given the nature of the speech and the significant gift it might have been meant that way. This was certainly happening elsewhere in Kent with the closure of suffrage societies and the establishment of local Women Citizens Associations.

Meanwhile in East Kent a woman voter from Hythe using only the initials E.M.M. wrote a letter to the local Press. It is possible that this was Miss Florence E.M. Macaulay, the previous WSPU organizer for Canterbury and Thanet district. If so, she shared a stage with Miss Christabel Pankhurst in July 1910 when Christabel visited the North Kent coastline and in 1913 was arrested for obstruction outside Holloway Prison. It is not known, but in the letter, E.M.M. referred to women entering a Parliamentary ballot box and recording their votes for the first time. She continued: 'they are now citizens of that Great Empire upon which the sun never sets; and on woman's shoulders now rests the weal or woe of the greater portion of the World itself.'[15] Later in her letter she proclaimed that

> woman's sphere is still in the home; the young women are mothers of England's future citizens; it behoves every woman, then, to so equip herself that she can house, feed and teach those embryo citizens in the best possible manner. She must concentrate her energies to improve the conditions of the municipality in which she dwells.[16]

Her final words were interesting, and read:

> Although now woman stands on an equal footing with man, let her still remain a true woman; for in the age of Reconstruction which is dawning it is Co-operation we want, not sex antagonism, so let women work together with the men to make a better England and a saner world.[17]

The Sevenoaks Women's Suffrage Society celebrated the establishment of the principle of women's suffrage but announced via their local newspaper that 'our goal – the obtaining of the vote for women as it is, or may be, granted men – is not yet attained.'[18]

This would take a further ten years to achieve. In the meantime, change to suffrage societies was afoot and steps were being taken to pursue equal enfranchisement. The NUWSS and WSPU disbanded and a new organization called the National Union of Societies for Equal Citizenship (NUSEC) was formed. Eleanor Rathbone succeeded Millicent Fawcett as president of the society. In Kent this resulted in many changes, beginning with the closure of the Kentish Federation in early 1919. Founded in 1909 by Madame Sarah Grand, the president at the time of closure was Mrs. Percy Thompson of Kippington Vicarage in Sevenoaks, the Hon. Treasurer was Miss Druce of Thornhill, Sevenoaks and the Hon. Secretary Mrs. J. Hewlett Hobbs of 13 Hastings Road in Maidstone. It had been unanimously agreed to close the organization, 'as the new terms of the constitution of the National Union of Societies for Equal Citizenship are not such as make necessary the existence of Federations within the Union'.[19]

A July 1919 report in *The Common Cause*, now the organ of the NUSEC, provides an insight into the status of the Kent NUSEC branches at this time. No report was included for Canterbury, just the names of the Hon. Treasurer Mr. E.R.J. Glanville and Hon. Secretaries Mrs. H. Wacher and Miss Carter of 16 The Friars were listed. Mrs. Wacher had been secretary at this branch since its formation as the NUWSS in 1913. Miss Carter could have been the Miss Carter known to be involved in the Rochester NUWSS branch in 1913, but it is not clear if this is the case.

Deal and Walmer reported that a number of members were more interested in the newly-formed Women Citizens Association than the NUSEC. The president was Lady Frances Balfour and the Hon. Secretary remained Mrs. Clare Royse of 2 Herschell Road in Walmer.

The Herne Bay branch had agreed to fold because a replacement Women Citizens Association had been formed the previous year. The chairman at the time was still Mrs. A. Cowper Field of Wivenhoe, Beltinge in Kent. The Hon. Secretary was Miss A. Cross.

However, Kent's county town, Maidstone, reported that it was hoped a small branch of the NUSEC would continue, although the Women Citizens Association had absorbed a number of their members.

NUWSS Procession, 13 June 1908 showing Lady Frances Balfour with Mrs. Henry Fawcett, Mrs. Philip Snowden, Miss Emily Davies and Mrs. Sophie Byrant. Lady Frances Balfour was President of the East Kent, Deal and Walmer Women Citizen Association in 1919.
© *LSE Women's Library collection*

Margate provided no update but listed the president and treasurer as Mrs. Southey with Hon. Secretary as Mrs. Houghton of 54 Warwick Road, Cliftonville.

In West Kent, Matfield, Pembury and Brenchley had Mrs. Perkins listed as president and Miss Symonds of the Grange in Matfield as Hon. Secretary. They reported that 'The political work of this Society has been in abeyance as the members have been occupied in various branches of war work at home and abroad; and candidates for Parliament have been approached concerning their views on the matter affecting women's interests.'[20]

Ramsgate included details of their president Mrs. Oakley Coles and Hon. Secretary Mrs. Howe of 70 Elkington Road, but no other details. Rochester similarly listed its president and Hon. Secretary. They were one and the same person, Miss Vera Conway Gordon of Longley House, Rochester. She had been involved since 1912.

Also continuing to operate was the Sevenoaks branch. The president was Mrs. Deane Streatfield and Hon. Secretary Miss Coleman of 'Babbacombe' in Granville Road. Approximately 7 miles away in Tonbridge, their society was also continuing with Miss Hall as president, Miss Stowes as Hon. Treasurer and Mrs. Gregory of 7 The Terrace, Tonbridge as Hon. Secretary.

The report from the Tunbridge Wells branch was more detailed. It advised that during the General Election the branch had taken a shop on a short lease and the society had provided an enquiry office. The report continued with a list of reasons why the NUSEC branches should continue to work towards equal franchise as opposed to agreeing to merge with Women Citizens Associations which were allegedly addressing more generic issues. This edition of *The Common Cause* finished this section of 'News' with the following: 'We earnestly urge all members not to allow their branches to lapse or to be merged in the larger, but less progressive, Women Citizens Association.'[21]

The WFL continued its campaign, although activity in Kent has been difficult to find with only a branch in Ashford seemingly operating. Meetings took place in Ashford between

1920 and 1928 and in April 1924 the organizer was listed as Miss M.L. White of 8 Holmsdale Gardens.[22] A WFL garden party is known to have taken place in Ashford at 62 Albert Road on Friday, 29 June 1928.[23] This was likely a celebration of the new Equal Franchise Act.

The extension of women's suffrage to give equal representation was debated for ten years. However, the approach to this was as part of wider issues around the role and rights of women in society generally.

In Folkestone in February 1928 Mrs. Emmeline Pankhurst had been due to visit to attend a mass meeting of the Women Conservatives. However, her agent had sent a letter explaining that she was unwell, suffering from gastric influenza. Emmeline died on 14 June 1928 just a few weeks before the Representation of the People Act came into force.

In February 1928, Home Secretary Sir William Joynson-Hicks addressed a meeting of more than 1,500 women at a Conservative rally at Leas Cliff Hall in Folkestone, East Kent. He said that he had never before addressed an audience entirely composed of women of Kent. At this meeting Sir William referred to the pledge given by the prime minister to extend equal franchise to women, saying:

> Let them just consider for a moment the position of the younger women of the country. The woman under thirty was compelled, for instance, to serve on a jury; she might hold the issues between life and death of a fellow man when she was only 21. She might go to the bar and she might plead for the life of a man before she was thirty; she might become a doctor and she might have in her hands the life of one of their children. They could trust her with these matters but not trust her to vote. She had got to stand on one side until she was thirty whilst the young man of 21, the young man of 21 who was only a lodger, with no family, business or profession could vote when he was 21. Why? Was it because he was more intelligent than the girl of 21? Did he know more about

politics than the girl of 21? Was he more loyal to his country than the girl of 21? He would like to find the man who would say so (laughter and applause).[24]

Five months later, in July 1928, Sir William wrote to the WFL about the Equal Franchise Act. In it he spoke of 'irresponsible newspapers' reviling the Bill and of his belief that these would be 'confounded' when enfranchised women 'bring to the discharge of their function, common sense, sounds of judgement and a proper appreciation of their civic responsibility.' He went on to say:

My confident expectations are, I am sure, shared by a vast majority in the country, and it is matter for amazement that in less than twenty years the public attitude should have veered round from one of active opposition to the grant of the franchise to women in any form to one of general support of the grant of the franchise to women at twenty-one. The war – and the part played in it by women – is, of course, in part responsible, but much of the success in educating public opinion can only be ascribed to the tenacious efforts of those who have given most of their lives to further the objects now attained in the new Act, and I would like to add my word of congratulation to them for the work they have done.[25]

This letter was read out in a victory birthday party for Mrs. Despard at 'a record rally at Caxton Hall'.[26] Charlotte Despard 'recalled the day when the Women's Freedom League was founded and took for its motto "Dare to be Free"' and continued: 'I think we all have. I don't think we're of any use unless we take risks.'[27] Charlotte had led the caravan tour of the country in 1908 (see Chapter 4) and this included travelling through Kent. She shared a memory of this tour, although did not confirm where this particular incident had happened: 'Once the caravan was almost knocked to pieces, but a meeting of apology followed.'[28]

She might have been referring to their experience in Herne Bay, in September 1908, where their caravan was dragged swiftly and dangerously and they needed protection. However, most likely, Charlotte was referring to the incident about three weeks later (October 1908) in Maidstone. Charlotte was struck in the head by a stone and the caravan pulled apart.

In September 1928 Kent newspapers published information about the three months' qualifying period for adults over 21 to enrol on the voting register ready for publication on 24 January 1929. One newspaper said that it had been officially estimated that 'the number of electors in Kent will be increased from the present figure of 575,377 to 708,977.'[29]

Some of these additional voters in Kent would have been those whose stories have been touched on in this book. An interview with each of them about their feelings, thoughts and ongoing hopes and ambitions in 1928 would have been fantastic. While there will be fragments in varying forms of historical archives about each of them, this book does not go that far. There will surely be further studies and accounts of these Kent inhabitants, more in depth about their women's suffrage work, as well as their lives after the 1928 Equal Franchise Act. In the meantime, it seems appropriate to conclude that it was not just quiet 'spade work' that took place for women's suffrage in 'the Garden of England' but also more extensive and dramatic action that was taken by the suffragettes[30] of Kent.

Notes About the County of Kent: Setting the Scene

Kent's Geography

Kent is a county in South-East England, bordering Greater London to the north-west, the county of Surrey to the west and East Sussex to the south-west. It shares a border with Essex along the River Thames and another with France (Pas-de-Calais) along the English Channel. The county town is Maidstone.

As described in a Kent newspaper in January 1909, 'This beautiful county of England, extending from Woolwich to Rye, on the south coast, a distance of 60 miles, and taking in several important towns on the way',[1] Kent has over 350 miles of coastline including sandy beaches, shingle shores and white cliffs. The county saw rapid industrialization in places such as Swanscombe, Snodland and Greenhithe, and Dartford, Erith, Crayford and Sittingbourne expanded significantly.

Kent's Boundaries

The boundaries of Kent changed during the period 1889 to 1998. Therefore this book references some areas being in Kent which are no longer.

In 1889 the County of London was created and became responsible for parts of North-West Kent including Deptford, Greenwich, Woolwich, Lee, Eltham, Charlton, Kidbrooke, Blackheath and Lewisham. In 1900 Penge also became part of the County of London.

In 1965 under the London Government Act 1963, the London boroughs of Bromley and Bexley were created. This meant that the following areas were no longer in Kent: Bexley, East and West Wickham, Crayford, Sidcup and North Cray, Erith, Northumberland Heath, Belvedere, parts of Barnehurst, Bexleyheath, Barnes Cray, Slade Green, SE2 postal district of Abbeywood, Beckenham, Orpington and Chislehurst.

In 1998 Rochester, Chatham, Gillingham and Rainham left the administrative county of Kent to form the Unitary Authority of Medway.

Kent's Transport Links

Tramways were in operation between Greenwich and Peckham and in many coastal towns. As illustrated by the advertisement in the 26 July 1884 *Thanet Advertiser*, the seaside resorts of Ramsgate and Margate were reachable from London (London Bridge Wharf) by 'The General Steam Navigation Company's Fast and Favourite Steamship *Eagle*.'[1]

The introduction of the railways throughout the county ensured that it became better connected both within the county itself and to other counties and London. In 1908, for example, it is known that a fast service from London Victoria to Dover in East Kent took just over two hours. Meanwhile, from London Charing Cross, the Ashford and Margate Line ran to Margate Sands as a fast service, taking just over three hours.[2] There were many other local branches connecting the different parts of Kent to each other, including some with only two stations.[3] By 1914 very few places in Kent were more than 3 miles from a railway station.

In 1889, traction engines were increasingly being used in Kent for road haulage. In the early 1900s, the increase in motor car traffic added to this, culminating in significant and continuous damage to the Kent road surfaces. From 1905, not only were the car registrations in Kent rising,[4] but more cars were coming into Kent from London.

Kent's Population

Census returns show Kent's population was 548,177 in 1841, 848,294 in 1871, 1,348,841 in 1901 and 1,511,806 in 1911.

Between 1801 and 1861 many large towns, including Rochester and Canterbury, doubled or trebled in size. During the same period, most Kent seaside towns saw their populations double and Folkestone and Ramsgate were noted for trebling in size. The industrial towns such as Dartford, Gillingham, Gravesend, Sheerness and Sittingbourne trebled or quadrupled, while residential towns such as Beckenham and Sevenoaks are shown to have far less significant increases.

Approximately two-thirds of the Kent parishes had more people in 1850 than in 1900. One-third had fewer people, particularly those in East Kent. This was predominantly due to movement from rural to urban areas, overseas emigration and movement further north in England to find work.

> It appears from the full census returns recently published that in regard to Kent the population has increased 8.8 per cent since 1901. The rural districts show a slower rate of increase than that of the urban, the former working out at 6.2 and the latter 9.9 per cent. Females predominate to the extent of 63 per thousand to the male population. Canterbury has the largest disposition in the sexes of any town in the county, there being 1,102 females to every thousand males.[1]

Health Care in Kent

In 1908, Dr. W.J. Howarth was appointed as the first Medical Officer of Health for Kent. By 1910 his department in Maidstone consisted of four doctors, two women inspectors of midwives and three clerks.

The main public health matters in Kent at the time were discharge of sewerage and provision of water, particularly in the rural areas. Between 1908 and 1910 there were also problems with refuse from London being dumped in Kent. This again is an indication of the proximity of Kent to London.

Much work occurred on the prevention and treatment of tuberculosis from 1911, following the enactment of the Insurance Act. A county sanatorium was built in Lenham near Maidstone. Other sanitoriums were also built, including the one in Tonbridge, West Kent, where Ethel Violet Baldock died (see Chapter One).

In 1913 Dr. Greenwood succeeded Dr. Howarth and by 1914 he had a much larger department: thirty-four full-time and twenty-four part-time staff.

Education in Kent

In the mid-1800s not many girls got an education. Some wealthy girls had governesses, others went to secondary school, but they learned 'feminine subjects' such as needlework, art and, if lucky, French. Pioneering educationalist Emily Davies led a successful campaign to include serious subjects and examinations for girls like those included for boys. In 1869 Emily set up Britain's first residential college for women at Hitchin in Cambridgeshire. Some 20 miles from Cambridge, this was the first women's university. Five students were there initially, taught by lecturers from Cambridge University; any willing to cycle the 40-mile round trip and to risk their reputation by teaching women. The college moved to Girton, just 2 miles from Cambridge University, in 1896. The women completed the same courses as the men, but did not graduate or receive any certification. Under the new headmistress Elizabeth Welsh, the women began to rebel and campaign against this. Many of these women campaigned for women's suffrage, some campaigning in Kent.

Public education was in its infancy. In 1870 the Education Act was passed, allowing voluntary schools (often run by religious societies) to continue, while establishing a system of 'school boards' to build and manage schools in areas not yet provided for. At this time in Kent, the majority (approximately three-quarters) of elementary schools were charity or church-managed. By 1900 Kent had a good spread of elementary schools and had made significant advances in technical and higher education.

Kent County Council was established in 1889. The provision and facilitating of technical education became one of the responsibilities of the newly-established council. Kent County Council delegated this responsibility in the urban areas by awarding each urban authority a portion of the government grant correlated to the population of the district. The proviso was that the urban authority had to use the money in a way approved by the Technical Education Committee established by the County Council. At this time, many urban areas had technical institutes and so the main objective of the urban authorities was to expand these. In the rural areas there were no institutes, but lectures and demonstrations had been taking place on a range of scientific subjects. The County Council's Technical Education Committee tapped into these existing lectures and increased and subsidized them. Examples of technical education then increased in rural areas were woodcarving, dairying, principles of agriculture, bee-keeping, horseshoeing, cookery, needlework, laundry, nursing, poultry-keeping, egg-production, cottage gardening and cultivation of allotments.

> In 1891, County Councils were permitted by legislation to give financial assistance to any local authority willing to develop technical education. The Tonbridge Board immediately took a lease of No. 1 Salford Terrace for one year to experiment with it as a Technical Institute. The first term began with 112 students, the second had 142. From then on there was no doubt as to its success: its books remained full until technical education became more organised with the 1902 Education Act. At the Institute young people over 14 could attend classes, day or evening, in Science, Art, Technical Drawing, Woodcarving, Dressmaking, Typing, Shorthand, Carpentry, Cooking and Book-keeping. The 'Annual Lists' of passes, prizes and National Awards which were reported to the local press for many years would indicate a thriving establishment.[1]

In 1892 to 1893, attendance at the rural lectures and demonstrations was reportedly good, in some locations over 100.

Feedback seemingly revealed, however, that they were not attended by many working-class people. This initial good level of interest of attendance started to dwindle. Over time, with lessons learned, less emphasis and money were placed on this rural technical education and efforts were concentrated on making permanent technical institutes in the urban areas. Additional grants were made available to urban technical institutes and grammar schools for such provision in return for places being found for pupils from rural areas. The Technical Education Committee then gave scholarships to these pupils from rural areas.

In 1897 the Technical Education Committee began awarding scholarships to women to attend higher education. Prior to this, girls had been financed to receive further education in cookery and nursing. At the same time, men had received scholarships for horticultural and agricultural studies. A few years after 1897 it is understood that a Horticultural College in Swanley became a technical college for women only.

In 1894, the South Eastern Agricultural School and College at Wye near Canterbury (Wye College) opened. A nearby farm was also leased and used as a dairy school for women. Wye College was affiliated to London University as a School of Agriculture and soon established a high reputation.

In 1902 the Education Act made Kent County Council responsible for elementary education (with some areas of exception) and higher education (excluding Canterbury). The County Council established an Education Committee and delegated its powers under this Act to it. Two women were members of this Education Committee, the first women to serve on any County Council Committee. One was Miss Eleanor Wigan who 'was to remain a member of the Kent Education Committee until 1945, being vice-chairman 1928 to 1930. She also became the first woman member of the County Council in 1922 and the first woman alderman in 1929.'[2]

In 1902 there were 432 elementary schools, now all managed by Kent County Council. Secondary schooling was uneven geographically and girls were hardly catered for. There were only three secondary schools for girls, providing for 376 pupils in all of Kent. By 1905 this had improved, with eight further secondary schools being opened, seven for girls only. This increase is understood to have compared favourably with other counties at the time. Girls' grammar schools were established in Ashford, Bromley, Chatham, Dartford, Dover, Folkestone, Gravesend, Ramsgate, Sittingbourne, Tonbridge and Tunbridge Wells. This expansion continued and by 1913 there were sixteen secondary schools and scholarships being funded by the Kent Education Committee to other old endowed grammar schools.

Improvements were also made to the standard of teacher training and attraction of women students. Kent was a stakeholder in the development of Goldsmith's Teacher Training College at New Cross and in 1907 opened a hostel for women students from Kent.

In 1906, the Kent press reported that the new Education Code meant that organized games for both girls and boys in elementary schools would form part of the curriculum. They proclaimed that 'one afternoon in every week is to be spent on the playing fields. It is suggested that cricket, football, hockey and rounders should be adopted for boys, and "similar appropriate games for girls", a term which allows managers of schools a pleasantly wide choice of feminine exercises.'[3]

Sadly, examples of these 'feminine exercises' were not listed. Three years later in East Kent, the Folkestone Education Committee were reporting successes in their compulsory curriculum study of housewifery. Entitled 'Juvenile Housewives', the article reported that 'Much is said and written in these days of the necessity of training school girls more in what is to be expected of them in after life,[4] rather than enforcing upon them scientific and brain-racking subjects for which, perhaps, they have neither the aptitude nor desire.'[5]

The housewifery skills taught included cookery and laundry. One of the local councillors judging the work being shown by the school reportedly said

> He was thankful that the Education Committee had taken the matter up as they had done, because, in his

humble opinion, it was a work which should be thought of before a good many things in elementary schools. It was a matter of great importance that children should learn everything which made them fit for the duties of after life, when they left school. A great many things would be remedied if girls were taught how to keep house properly, for they would be able to keep their big brothers, and later their husbands at home, instead of having them go elsewhere.[6]

Another councillor present at this exhibition of girls' work went further, proclaiming that while girls could, if they liked, learn a little Latin, Greek, Hebrew or algebra as extras, it was really important for them to be proficient in sewing, cooking and laundry. This, he said, would 'ensure good and comfortable homes in later years'. He concluded that 'With a thorough knowledge of them [sewing, cooking, laundry] they [girls] would have nothing to fear. They would be little Dreadnoughts,[7] and need not trouble about votes for women, for they would be a real power at home.'[8]

Communications in Kent

Described by Kent inhabitant and South-Eastern Railway employee Charles Walker as 'the magic wire',[1] the telegram worked by converting written messages letter by letter using electrical impulses. The first installation of the electrical telegram in the south-east was along the Tonbridge to Maidstone branch of the South-Eastern Railway in 1844. By 1850, the South-Eastern Railway had 180 miles of telegraph line and 47 telegraph stations.

From 1870 the telegram operation was run by the nationalized Post Office. By 1884 the cost of sending a telegram had dropped from 5s for a twenty-word message to 6d for twelve words. This allowed more people to make use of the system.

The *Free Press* on 24 November 1877 reported to its Tonbridge readers that 'A great change has come over the condition of humanity. Suddenly and quietly, the whole human race is brought within speaking and hearing distance.'[2] This referred to the introduction of the telephone. However, it was another ten years before the telephone reached Kent as a regular service. In January 1887 there were seventeen exchanges with the one in Maidstone having sixteen lines. By February 1895 further progress had been made with, for example, Tunbridge Wells, Tonbridge, Hadlow, Wateringbury and Yalding being telephonically connected to Maidstone. There were few households with private lines owing to the cost. However, call offices were set up to allow anyone to make use of a telephone, yet even by the 1920s, the post and occasional telegrams were the most used means of social communication.

Communication at the time was very different to nowadays. It was not the age of social media, but of letters, postcards and later telegrams, of magazines, newspapers, posters, bills (leaflets), of word of mouth via acquaintances and friendships, marches, demonstrations and tours. Imagine how sophisticated the 'votes for women' campaign would be today among all the varied women's suffrage groups with the use of our many social media options. Remember also how the laws so greatly restricted women's choices and rights including with regard to marriage, children, property ownership, jobs and careers, health and representation. Consider the social climate at the time; one of women being responsible for all things domestic in and about the home. Add to this the fact that the government was making it difficult for the suffrage campaigners to spread their word, gain and keep support, and one can only start to imagine the enormity of the challenges faced by these women. The part played by men involved in campaigning for women's suffrage must also not be forgotten, for they too would have faced significant challenges.

Now consider this in the context of the county of Kent, the most south-easterly county in England with its many borders with other Home Counties and London and indeed France via the English Channel. It also had a larger geographical area at the time of the women's suffrage movement. With such a vast geographical spread and difference, the stories that have emerged about those in Kent involved in the suffrage movement are likewise different and varied. This book tells such stories, but also strives to show a web of communication and cross-fertilization of ideas and strategies between groups within Kent and those in bordering counties and indeed London. As described, the London Press permeated Kent and the activities of Kent suffragettes featured in newspapers and publications in other areas of the country.

The pilgrimage from Kent to Central London via South-East London in 1913 is an example of note and therefore covered in detail in this book. Thousands of women's suffrage supporters converged on Hyde Park with strong support from all parts of Kent, following the orchestration of three routes through the county. However, on a less obvious and far more discreet level there are many more such examples. At the time these smaller tokens of collaboration and information-sharing may not have been as fruitful as hoped, but in conjunction with all the other small-scale exchanges would have cumulatively contributed to 'the cause'. Think of the county of Kent and the sellers of women's suffrage publications; the speakers unable to finish their speeches due to hostility; those providing lodgings and food, and even loaning horses to touring suffragettes; those not joining as full suffrage society members but as a more flexible, less onerous 'friend'; those opening up their homes and gardens for meetings; those making banners, decorating venues and selling tickets; those making jam for imprisoned suffragettes; and all the other ways in which contributions were made. They all supported 'the cause', enabling the message to be spread widely and reach many; the extent of which it is difficult to quantify in the modern day.

Endnotes

Preface

1. Millicent Garrett Fawcett speaking at Bromley NUWSS meeting, *Bromley Record*, March 1907.

Introduction

1. Crawford, Elizabeth, *The Women's Suffrage Movement: A Reference Guide 1866–1928* (Routledge, 2001), p.xii

Glossary

1. *Folkestone, Hythe, Sandgate & Cheriton Herald*, 19 July 1913, p.6.
2. Term coined by *The Globe* newspaper, March 1912.
3. Included in a published article in the *Sevenoaks Chronicle and Kentish Advertiser*, 29 June 1906.
4. Used in the *Sevenoaks Chronicle and Kentish Advertiser*, 13 July 1906.
5. Referred to in a national prize-winning limerick written by a Kent man and included in the *Dover Express and East Kent News*, 7 February 1908.
6. *Daily Chronicle* 1909 and referenced in *Votes for Women*, 1909.
7. Referred to in the *Weekly Dispatch*, 13 April 1913.

Chapter 1

1. Following the March 1912 hammer attacks, *Votes for Women* reported that the *Globe* newspaper had coined a new word

by describing the suffragettes who were smashing windows as 'vitrifragists' or 'glass-breakers'.

2. Crawford, Elizabeth, *The Women's Suffrage Movement: A Reference Guide 1866–1928* (Routledge, 2001), p.xii.

3. Interview with Ethel Violet Baldock's great-niece Margaret Ayres, July 2017. Margaret Ayres' grandmother was Ethel's older sister, Frances Baldock. Margaret has many family albums, stories that she has been told and even stories that were written down by one of Ethel's other older sisters, Emma.

4. *The Times*, Wednesday, 6 March 1912.

5. Cited in HO0140 piece no. 298, Home Office Calendar of Prisoners tried at Sessions of Peace in Newington Court for the year 1912.

6. Cited in HO0140 piece no. 298, Home Office Calendar of Prisoners tried at Sessions of Peace in Newington Court for the year 1912.

7. Home Office File HO/144/1195/220196 from 1912.

8. Taken from same, James Scott, 3 March 1912 report as previously referenced (from Home Office file HO/144/1195/220196).

9. HO/144/1193/220196 and HO/144/1195/220196.

10. HO0140 piece no. 298, Home Office Calendar of Prisoners tried at Sessions of Peace in Newington Court for the year 1912.

11. *Votes for Women*, 15 March 1912, p.361.

12. *Votes for Women*, 15 March 1912, p.381.

13. *Shields Daily News*, 6 November 1912.

14. The National Archives 7LGA/1/2. Record of Louisa Garrett Anderson's trial on 5 March 1912.

15. *Votes for Women*, 2 February 1912, p.279.

16. *Votes for Women*, 16 February 1912, p.305.

17. *Votes for Women*, 16 February 1912, p.305.

18. Friday, 15 March 1912, the *Lichfield Mercury*.

19. *Western Daily Mercury*, Monday, 11 March 1912, quotation from Lord Haldane speaking at Oxford on night of Saturday, 9 March 1912.

20. *Birmingham Gazette and Express*, Monday, 11 March 1912.

21. *The Vote*, Saturday, 23 March 1912, p.265.
22. *Literature of the Women's Suffrage Campaign in England*, edited by Carolyn Christensen Nelson (Broadview Press, 2004), p.158.
23. 'D x' refers to the block in Holloway Prison where suffragettes were often placed.
24. *Literature of the Women's Suffrage Campaign in England*, edited by Carolyn Christensen Nelson (Broadview Press, 2004), pp.163–4.
25. Ibid., pp.167–8.
26. Ibid., p.165.
27. Ibid., pp.166–7.
28. Violet Ann Bland was recorded in the court papers as both 37 and 34 but was actually born in 1863, so would have been approximately 49 years old at the time of her arrest.
29. On 18 November 1910, 300 WSPU members marched to the Houses of Parliament to demonstrate against the government's refusal to take the Conciliation Bill further. A wall of police greeted them. When they attempted to pass, the women and men were assaulted and arrested. It is recorded that 117 women and 2 men were arrested that day.
30. *The Vote*, Saturday, 9 March 1912, pp.230–31.
31. Ibid., p.232.
32. Ibid., pp.232–33.
33. Ibid., pp.232–33.
34. Ibid., pp.232–33.
35. Violet Ann Bland, *Votes for Women*, 5 July 1912.

Chapter 2

1. *Documenting History: Women's Suffrage*, Peter Hicks (Wayland, 2009), p.8.
2. Spelled in this way on the petition.
3. Spelled in this way on the petition.
4. Parliamentary Archives, HC/CL/JO/6/416.
5. Blackheath became part of the county of London in 1889. Prior to that it was in the county of Kent.

6. Above this text the total number of signatures was recorded as '1521'.

7. Parliamentary Archives, HC/CL/JO/6/416.

8. Crawford, Elizabeth, *The Women's Suffrage Movement: A Reference Guide 1866–1928* (Routledge, 2001), p.69.

9. Possible additions in the third edition published in 1869.

10. *A Brief Summary in Plain Language of the Most Important Law of England Concerning Women*, Barbara Leigh Smith, Third Edition, Revised with Additions (Trubner & Co., 60 Paternoster Row, 1869), p.18.

11. London School of Economics, Mill Taylor Papers, vol. XII, 144, 29 May [1866]. Draft letter Helen Taylor to Marion Chadwick.

12. Reported in Ann Dingsdale thesis, 'Generous and lofty sympathies': The Kensington Society, The 1866 Women's Suffrage Petition and the development of mid-Victorian Feminism, December 1995, University of Greenwich Library. Source: London School of Economics, Mill Taylor Papers, vol. XX, 169, 5 June 1866. Rachel Chadwick to Helen Taylor.

13. London School of Economics, Mill Taylor Papers, vol. XIII, 197, 29 May 1866. Mary Ellis to Helen Taylor.

14. London School of Economics, Mill Taylor Papers, vol. XXII, 429. Caroline Lindley to Helen Taylor.

15. The initial list of names has been taken from UK Parliament document created for Vote 100 celebrations, dated June 2016.

16. Blackheath became part of the county of London in 1889. Prior to that it was in the county of Kent.

17. London School of Economics, Mill Taylor Papers, vol. XXII, 429. Caroline Lindley to Helen Taylor.

18. Description of the reverend taken from the Electoral Register of 1866. From the British Library Archive SPR. Mic.P.4/BL.K.18/2.

19. The Miss Garrett mentioned here is Elizabeth Garrett Anderson (1836–1917), née Garrett. She was a Kensington Society member.

20. Girton College, Emily Davies, Family Chronicle.

21. Greenwich became part of the county of London in 1889. Prior to that it was in the county of Kent.

22. Ann Dingsdale thesis, 'Generous and lofty sympathies': The Kensington Society, the 1866 Women's Suffrage Petition and the development of mid-Victorian Feminism, December 1995, University of Greenwich Library, p.43.

23. Lee became part of the county of London in 1889. Prior to that it was in the county of Kent.

24. *Thanet Advertiser*, 24 December 1864.

25. Ann Dingsdale thesis, 'Generous and lofty sympathies': The Kensington Society, the 1866 Women's Suffrage Petition and the development of mid-Victorian Feminism, December 1995, University of Greenwich Library, p.10.

26. *Maidstone Journal and Kentish Advertiser*, 17 October 1864.

27. *Thanet Advertiser*, 6 December 1862.

28. *The Women's Suffrage Movement in Britain and Ireland: A Regional Survey*, Elizabeth Crawford (Routledge, 2006), p.189.

29. Reported in Ann Dingsdale thesis, 'Generous and lofty sympathies': The Kensington Society, the 1866 Women's Suffrage Petition and the development of mid-Victorian Feminism, December 1995, University of Greenwich Library. Source: E.W. French to Helen Taylor, 28 March 1868. London School of Economics, Mill Taylor Papers, vol. XIII, 198.

30. Gravesend Reporter, *North Kent and South Essex Advertiser*, 23 May 1868, p.3.

31. 'Generous and lofty sympathies': The Kensington Society, the 1866 Women's Suffrage Petition and the development of mid-Victorian Feminism, December 1995, University of Greenwich Library, p.128. Source: London School of Economics, Mill Taylor Papers, vol. XIII, 198 and 199.

32. Address cited in 1851, 1861 and 1871 censuses.

33. According to the 1861 census.

34. According to the 1871 census.

35. According to the 1851 census.

36. Crawford, Elizabeth, *The Women's Suffrage Movement: A Reference Guide 1866–1928* (Routledge, 2001), p.53.

37. According to the 1851 census.
38. Compliments.
39. Reported in Ann Dingsdale thesis, 'Generous and lofty sympathies': The Kensington Society, the 1866 Women's Suffrage Petition and the development of mid-Victorian Feminism, December 1995, University of Greenwich Library, p.132. Source: London School of Economics, Mill Taylor Papers, vol. XXII, 429. Caroline Lindley to Helen Taylor.
40. By independent researcher and author Elizabeth Crawford in *The Women's Suffrage Movement: A Reference Guide 1866–1928* (Routledge, 2001).

Chapter 3

1. *Kent and Sussex Courier*, 14 May 1909.
2. *Sevenoaks Chronicle and Kentish Advertiser*, 19 June 1908, p.4.
3. *Kent and Sussex Courier*, 12 June 1908.
4. Ibid.
5. *Sevenoaks Chronicle and Kentish Advertiser*, 26 June 1908.
6. *Kentish Mercury*, 26 June 1908, p.4.
7. *Kent and Sussex Courier*, 26 June 1908, p.2.
8. Ibid.
9. Ibid.
10. Ibid.
11. Ibid.
12. Ibid.
13. Ibid.
14. Ibid.
15. *Sevenoaks Chronicle and Kentish Advertiser*, 26 June 1908.
16. *Kent and Sussex Courier*, 26 June 1908, p.2.
17. Ibid.

Chapter 4

1. *Women's Franchise*, 21 May 1908, p. 556.
2. Ibid.
3. Ibid.

4. *Miss Muriel Matters: The Fearless Suffragist who fought for Equality*, Robert Wainwright (Allen & Unwin, 2017), p.123.
5. Violet Tillard, unpublished obituary by Muriel Matters, 22 February 1930. Also cited in *Miss Muriel Matters: The Fearless Suffragist who fought for Equality*, Robert Wainwright (Allen & Unwin, 2017), pp.127–8.
6. *Western Times*, 30 October 1908, p.16.
7. *Kent and Sussex Courier*, 3 July 1908, p.7.
8. From headline of article in *Kent and Sussex Courier*, 3 July 1908, p.7. Headline read: 'Disgraceful scene on the common. Ladies hustled.'
9. *Kent and Sussex Courier*, 3 July 1908, p.7.
10. Ibid.
11. Ibid.
12. Ibid.
13. Ibid.
14. Ibid.
15. *Women's Franchise*, 23 July 1908, p.44.
16. *Kent and Sussex Courier*, 3 July 1908, p.10.
17. *Women's Franchise*, 23 July 1908, p.44.
18. *Women's Franchise*, 16 July 1908, p.33.
19. Ibid.
20. Ibid.
21. Ibid.
22. *Women's Franchise*, 13 August 1908, p.77.
23. *Women's Franchise*, 27 August 1908, p.93.
24. Ibid.
25. Ibid.
26. Ibid.
27. *Women's Franchise*, 20 August 1908, p.85.
28. *Folkestone, Hythe, Sandgate and Cheriton Herald*, 22 August 1908, p.7.
29. Ibid.
30. *Women's Franchise*, 20 August 1908, p.85.
31. Ibid.
32. Ibid.
33. *Women's Franchise*, 3 September 1908, p.104.
34. Ibid.

35. Ibid.
36. Ibid.
37. Ibid.
38. Ibid.
39. Ibid.
40. Ibid.
41. The owners of the garden in which the garden party was held was the brother and sister-in-law of their colleague, Dr Knight. This was reported by Charlotte Despard in *Women's Franchise*, 3 September 1908, p.104.
42. *Women's Franchise*, 27 August 1908, p.93.
43. *Women's Franchise*, 3 September 1908, p.104.
44. Ibid.
45. Ibid.
46. *Folkestone, Hythe, Sandgate and Cheriton Herald*, 22 August 1908, p.7.
47. Ibid.
48. *Dover Express and East Kent News*, Friday, 28 August 1908.
49. *Women's Franchise*, 3 September 1908, p.104.
50. It is understood that Miss Henderson left the tour and the Tillard sisters, Violet and Irene, joined. As reported in the *Women's Franchise*, 3 September 1908, p.104.
51. *Dover Express and East Kent News*, Friday, 28 August 1908.
52. Ibid.
53. Ibid.
54. Ibid.
55. *Women's Franchise*, 3 September 1908, p.104.
56. *Women's Franchise*, 10 September 1908, p.115.
57. *Dover Express and East Kent News*, Friday, 28 August 1908.
58. Ibid.
59. Ibid.
60. *Western Times*, 31 January 1908, p.16.
61. Ibid.
62. *Women's Franchise*, 10 September 1908, p.115.
63. Ibid.
64. Ibid.
65. Ibid.
66. *Women's Franchise*, 17 September 1908, p.127.

67. Ibid.
68. Ibid.
69. Ibid.
70. A Mr Rose of Sandwich is reported as piloting Mrs Despard around Sandwich so that she could call on sympathizers. This was reported in *Women's Franchise*, 17 September 1908, p.127.
71. *Women's Franchise*, 17 September 1908, p.127.
72. Ibid.
73. Ibid.
74. Ibid.
75. Ibid.
76. *Women's Franchise*, 24 September 1908, p.139.
77. *Canterbury Journal and Farmers Gazette*, Saturday, 19 September 1908, p.3.
78. Ibid.
79. *Women's Franchise*, 24 September 1908, p.139.
80. Ibid.
81. Ibid.
82. *Whitstable Times and Herne Bay Herald*, Saturday, 26 September 1908.
83. Spelling taken from *Western Times*, 31 October 1908, p.16.
84. *Whitstable Times and Herne Bay Herald*, Saturday, 26 September 1908.
85. *Votes for Women*, 15 March 1912, p.380.
86. Ibid.
87. *Whitstable Times and Herne Bay Herald*, Saturday, 26 September 1908.
88. *Women's Franchise*, 8 October 1908, p.163.
89. Ibid.
90. Ibid.
91. Ibid.
92. *Whitstable Times and Herne Bay Herald*, 10 October 1908, p.3.
93. *Women's Franchise*, 8 October 1908, p.163.
94. *Whitstable Times and Herne Bay Herald*, 10 October 1908, p.3.
95. *Women's Franchise*, 8 October 1908, p.163.
96. *Gloucestershire Echo*, 2 October 1908, p.4.

97. Ibid.
98. *Women's Franchise*, 8 October 1908, p.163.
99. Ibid.
100. *Sevenoaks Chronicle and Kentish Advertiser*, 9 October 1908, p.5.
101. Ibid.
102. *Women's Franchise*, 22 October 1908, p.188.

Chapter 5

1. Found in many sources. One was the *Kent & Sussex Courier*, 19 March 1909, p.5.
2. *The Women's Suffrage Movement: A Reference Guide 1866– 1928*, Elizabeth Crawford (Routledge, 2001), p.179.
3. HO 220196/658.
4. Ibid.
5. Member of West of England branch of the WSPU Mrs Lillian Mary Dove Wilcox (1875–1963) and Leeds-born Theresa [Frances] Garnett (1888–1966) who went on to be force-fed while hunger-striking during another term of imprisonment in Horfield Gaol.
6. HO 220196/658.
7. Ibid.
8. *The Vote*, 8 October 1909, p.4.
9. One of these 'others' was Laura Ainsworth. Hilda Burkitt was another; she was the niece of the Misses Burkitts, and Kate Parry Frey (paid organizer for the National Constitutional Society) stayed with the Misses Burkitts in Dover in 1912.
10. HO 220196/658.
11. *Votes for Women*, 15 March 1912, p.381.
12. *Kent and Sussex Courier*, 19 April 1912, p.2.
13. Says 'instituted' but assume meant 'initiated'.
14. Idem.
15. *Kent and Sussex Courier*, 19 April 1912, p.2.
16. *Kent and Sussex Courier*, 19 April 1912, p.9.
17. Home Secretary.
18. Miss Evelyn Billing, cited Rule 243a.

19. *Kent and Sussex Courier*, 19 April 1912, p.9.
20. *Kent and Sussex Courier*, 2 August 1912, p.7.
21. Ibid.
22. *Whitstable Times and Herne Bay Herald*, 16 March 1912.
23. *Votes for Women*, 24 May 1912.
24. HO 220196/575.
25. HO 220196. The quotation is from the typed memorandum from the Prison Commission in the Home Office requesting the numbers forcibly fed during 1912 from the governor of Holloway Prison. The memorandum was dated 20 March 1913 and the governor's handwritten reply was dated 22 March 1913.
26. *Votes for Women*, 24 May 1912, p.549.
27. HO 220196/630.
28. *Votes for Women*, 26 April 1912, p.479.
29. *Votes for Women*, 3 May 1912, p.494.
30. *Votes for Women*, 10 May 1912, p.510.
31. *Votes for Women*, 31 May 1912, p.575.
32. *Votes for Women*, 14 June 1912, p.606.
33. *Votes for Women*, 21 June 1912, p.617.
34. HO 220196/575.
35. HO 220196/575. From report by Dr Charles Edward Hoar, dated 5 July 1912.
36. *Sunderland Daily Echo and Shipping Gazette*, 28 March 1912.
37. HO 220196/630.
38. *Votes for Women*, 24 May 1912, p.547.
39. *Votes for Women*, 2 July 1909, p.878.
40. *The Globe*, 30 June 1909, p.10.
41. *Votes for Women*, 2 July 1909, p.879.
42. *London Daily News*, 22 November 1911, p.5.
43. Ibid.
44. *Votes for Women*, 28 June 1912, p.632.
45. *Votes for Women*, 24 November 1911, p.125.
46. *Votes for Women*, 12 July 1912, p.664.
47. Ibid.
48. *Daily Herald*, 8 February 1913, p.2.

49. *The Women's Suffrage Movement: A Reference Guide 1866– 1928*, Elizabeth Crawford (Routledge, 2001), p.311.
50. *Kent and Sussex Courier*, 3 May 1912, p.2.
51. It appears the reporting here is not entirely accurate as Maud Joachim was the niece of a famous musician, Joseph Joachim (violinist and composer).
52. *Kent and Sussex Courier*, 3 May 1912, p.2.
53. *Votes for Women*, 24 May 1912, p.551.
54. *Votes for Women*, 15 March 1912, p.383.
55. *Western Daily Mercury*, 28 March 1912.
56. *Votes for Women*, 15 March 1912, p.381.
57. HO 220196/630.
58. HO 45/11057, File 234294.
59. Page 3.
60. *Western Times*, 29 April 1919, p.3.
61. *Dover Express*, 2 May 1919, p.2.
62. Meaning a physician who works in the place of the regular physician when they are absent.
63. HO 220196/575.
64. *Votes for Women*, 28 June 1912, p.632.
65. The *Observer*, Sunday, 3 October 1909.
66. In the 1911 census, Iain Mackinnon Jefferiss was aged 32 (b.1879), with occupation of 'medical practitioner'. Born in Perthshire. Married (for two years) to Mary (23) who was born in Northampton. In 1911, had a 1-year-old son, Frederick James Gordon, and a female servant.
67. This last part of the sentence has been added in with 'without experience' crossed through. It appears to be in the same handwriting so presumably was sent to the Home Office in this way.
68. HO 220196/575.
69. Preliminary Report on the Forcible Feeding of Suffrage Prisoners, Agnes Savill, M.D., C. Mansell Moullin, F.R.C.S., and Sir Victor Horsley, F.R.S., F.R.C.S., published in the *British Medical Journal*, 31 August 1912, p.505.
70. Ibid.
71. Ibid.

72. *What Forcible Feeding Means*, Frank Moxon, M.B., R.S. (The Women's Press, London, 1914), p.15.
73. *Sunderland Daily Echo and Shipping Gazette*, 27 June 1912.
74. The Cover of the Act, dated 25 April 1913.
75. *The Suffragette*, 27 June 1913, p.618.
76. *Nottingham Journal*, 23 June 1913, p.5.
77. Ibid.
78. *The Vote*, 27 June 1913, p.142.
79. *The Suffragette*, 4 July 1913, p.638.
80. *The Suffragette*, 27 June 1913, p.618.
81. Ibid.
82. Ibid.
83. *The Suffragette*, 4 July 1913, p.638.
84. Ibid.
85. Ibid.
86. Ibid.

Chapter 6

1. *London Daily News*, 18 November 1905.
2. *London Daily News*, 9 March 1903, p.8.
3. *Votes for Women*, 5 March 1909, p.402.
4. *Votes for Women*, 26 November 1909, p.138.
5. Ibid.
6. *Votes for Women*, 21 January 1910, p.270.
7. Ibid.
8. *Votes for Women*, 25 March 1910, p.406.
9. Ibid.
10. *Votes for Women*, 21 January 1910, p.270.
11. *Votes for Women*, 25 March 1910, p.406.
12. Ibid.
13. *Votes for Women*, 13 May 1910, p.538.
14. *Votes for Women*, 10 May 1910, p.138.
15. Ibid.
16. Ibid.
17. *Votes for Women*, 13 March 1914, p.370.

Chapter 7

1. *Votes for Women*, 10 September 1909, p.1158, quoting the *Daily Mail*.
2. From London as not based in Kent ordinarily. Note that in her account of this event in *Votes for Women*, 10 September 1909, Jessie Kenny refers to the three women arriving safely at their lodgings.
3. *Votes for Women*, 10 September 1909, p.1157.
4. Suffragettes approached Mr Asquith on Clovelly Golf Course in Devon in June 1909.
5. *Votes for Women*, 10 September 1909, p.1157.
6. Referred to in Kent newspaper *Folkestone, Hythe, Sandgate & Cheriton Herald*, 11 September 1909, p.2.
7. Emmeline Pethick-Lawrence joined the WSPU after conversing with Annie Kenney. She and her husband would later split from the WSPU and Christabel Pankhurst and join the WFL.
8. *Western Daily Mercury*, 30 March 1912, p.10.
9. Ibid.
10. *The Women's Suffrage Movement: A Reference Guide 1866–1928*, Elizabeth Crawford (Routledge, 2001), p.297.
11. *Votes for Women*, 10 September 1909, p.1157.
12. *Folkestone, Hythe, Sandgate & Cheriton Herald*, 11 September 1909, p.2.
13. Ibid.
14. This official version released for the prime minister was included in newspapers throughout the country including the *London Evening Standard* on 8 September 1909.
15. *London Evening Standard*, 8 September 1909.
16. *Folkestone, Hythe, Sandgate & Cheriton Herald*, 11 September 1909, p.2.
17. It is known from the account given by Jessie Kenny in *Votes for Women* on 10 September 1909 that this was Vera Wentworth.
18. *London Evening Standard*, 8 September 1909.
19. *Folkestone, Hythe, Sandgate and Cheriton Herald*, 11 September 1909, p.2.
20. *Votes for Women*, 10 September 1909, p.1157.

21. Ibid.
22. Ibid.
23. *Folkestone, Hythe, Sandgate and Cheriton Herald*, 11 September 1909, p.2.
24. It is known from the account given by Jessie Kenny in *Votes for Women* on 19 September 1909 that this was Elsie Howie.
25. *London Evening Standard*, 8 September 1909.
26. *Folkestone, Hythe, Sandgate and Cheriton Herald*, 11 September 1909, p.2.
27. *Wells Journal*, 9 September 1909, p.6.
28. *Votes for Women*, 10 September 1909, p.1158.
29. *Speaking for themselves, The Personal Letters of Winston and Clementine Churchill*, edited by their daughter Mary Soames (Black Swan, 1999), p.27.
30. *Votes for Women*, 10 September 1909, p.1158, quoting the *Daily Chronicle*.
31. *Votes for Women*, 10 September 1909, p.1158.
32. *The Women's Suffrage Movement: A Reference Guide 1866–1928* (Routledge, 2001), p.297.
33. *Votes for Women*, 10 September 1909, p.1157.

Chapter 8

1. This extract was from *The Methuen Drama Book of Suffrage Plays* edited by Naomi Paxton (Methuen Drama, 2013), Introduction, x.
2. *Dover Express and East Kent News*, Friday, 16 July 1909.
3. In the printed version of this play, Winifred is Ethel's sister. In the article reported by the *Dover Express and East Kent News* on Friday, 16 July 1909, it states 'his sister'.
4. The colours of the Women's Social and Political Union were purple, white and green. This extract was from *The Methuen Drama Book of Suffrage Plays* edited by Naomi Paxton (Methuen Drama, 2013).
5. *Sevenoaks Chronicle and Kentish Advertiser*, Friday, 21 January 1910, p.5.

6. This was the AFL's first fund-raising matinee in conjunction with the Women Writers' Suffrage League. For this Edith Craig produced Cicely Hamilton's 'Pageant of Great Women'.

7. A book published nearly every year, listing the peerage (titled aristocracy) of Great Britain and Northern Ireland.

8. This extract was from *The Methuen Drama Book of Suffrage Plays* edited by Naomi Paxton (Methuen Drama, 2013), p.51.

9. Line for Mrs Brewster from *The Methuen Drama Book of Suffrage Plays* edited by Naomi Paxton (Methuen Drama, 2013), p.52.

10. Line for Ernest Hobb from *The Methuen Drama Book of Suffrage Plays* edited by Naomi Paxton (Methuen Drama, 2013), p.53.

11. Line for Nell Roberts, a suffragette from *The Methuen Drama Book of Suffrage Plays* edited by Naomi Paxton (Methuen Drama, 2013), p.53.

12. This extract was from *The Methuen Drama Book of Suffrage Plays* edited by Naomi Paxton (Methuen Drama, 2013), Introduction, xii.

13. Lines for Marjorie Brewster from *The Methuen Drama Book of Suffrage Plays* edited by Naomi Paxton (Methuen Drama, 2013), p.59.

14. Line for Nell Roberts, a suffragette from *The Methuen Drama Book of Suffrage Plays* edited by Naomi Paxton (Methuen Drama, 2013), p.59.

15. Line for Mr Brewster from *The Methuen Drama Book of Suffrage Plays* edited by Naomi Paxton (Methuen Drama, 2013), p.63.

16. This extract was from *The Methuen Drama Book of Suffrage Plays* edited by Naomi Paxton (Methuen Drama, 2013), Introduction, xiii.

17. Meaning Marjorie Brewster.

18. Line for Nell Roberts, a suffragette from *The Methuen Drama Book of Suffrage Plays* edited by Naomi Paxton (Methuen Drama, 2013), p.65.

19. This extract was from *The Methuen Drama Book of Suffrage Plays* edited by Naomi Paxton (Methuen Drama, 2013),

Introduction, xiii, in which is quoted the programme for the play's Scala Theatre, London performance on 12 November 1909.
20. The *London Illustrated News*, 1907.
21. *Vote for Women and Other Plays*, edited and introduced by Susan Croft.
22. Ibid.
23. *Sevenoaks Chronicle and Kentish Advertiser*, 24 January 1913.
24. *Sevenoaks Chronicle and Kentish Advertiser*, 31 January 1913, p.4.
25. Ibid.
26. Ibid.
27. Ibid.

Chapter 9

1. Liddington, Jill, *Vanishing for the Vote* (Manchester University Press, 2014), p.305.
2. *Votes for Women*, 31 March 1911, p.431.
3. Census entry, 1911.
4. *Votes for Women*, 5 August 1910, p.746.
5. *Votes for Women*, 26 August 1910, p.782.
6. *Votes for Women*, 2 September 1910, p.794.
7. *Canterbury Journal, Kentish Times and Farmers' Gazette*, 29 March 1902, p.902.
8. Cycling UK website.
9. *Canterbury Journal, Kentish Times and Farmers' Gazette*, 4 September 1909, p.5.
10. Census entry, 1911.
11. *Votes for Women*, 19 May 1911.

Chapter 10

1. *Sheffield Daily Telegraph*, 26 June 1912, p.8.
2. Ibid.
3. At a meeting in Dundee reported in *The Times*, 4 February 1909.

4. *Clementine Churchill* by her daughter Mary Soames (Cassell, London, 1979), p.59.

5. *Manchester Courier and Lancashire General Advertiser*, 21 August 1908, p.13.

6. Letter dated 18 October 1909 from Winston Churchill to his wife Clementine. From *Speaking for Themselves: The Personal Letters of Winston and Clementine Churchill* (Black Swan, 1999), p.33.

7. *Clementine Churchill* by her daughter Mary Soames (Cassell, London, 1979), p.59.

8. She became the first woman to take her seat in the House of Commons.

9. *London Gazette*, August 1912, referred to in *Votes for Women*, 16 August 1912, p.12.

10. *Sheffield Daily Telegraph*, 14 August 1912, p.7.

11. *The Daily Chronicle*, August 1912, referred to in *Votes for Women*, 16 August 1912, p.12.

12. The *Standard*, August 1912, referred to in *Votes for Women*, 16 August 1912, p.12.

13. *Sevenoaks Chronicle and Kentish Advertiser*, 16 August 1912, p.2.

14. *Votes for Women*, 16 August 1912, p.12.

15. *Western Daily Press*, 14 August 1912, p.5.

16. *Framlingham Weekly News*, 17 August 1912, p.4.

17. *Leeds Mercury*, 17 August 1912, p.6.

18. *Dundee Courier*, 17 August 1912, p.5.

19. *The Scotsman*, 17 August 1912, p.7.

20. Ibid.

21. *Nottingham Journal*, 17 August 1912, p.5.

22. *Whitstable Times and Herne Bay Herald*, 17 August 1912, p.2.

23. *Kent & Sussex Courier*, 22 November 1912, p.2.

24. *Folkestone, Hythe, Sandgate & Cheriton Herald*, 30 November 1912, p.5.

25. *Sevenoaks Chronicle and Kentish Advertiser*, 13 December 1912, p.2.

26. *Sevenoaks Chronicle and Kentish Advertiser*, 27 December 1912, p.5.

27. Ibid.

Chapter 11

1. *Taunton Courier and Western Advertiser*, 26 February 1913, p.1
2. *Women of Kent Rally to the Cause: A Study of Women's Suffrage in East Kent 1909–1918* by Laura Probert (Millicent Press), p.97.
3. *Folkestone, Hythe, Sandgate & Cheriton Herald*, 8 February 1913.
4. *Folkestone Baptist Magazine*, February 1913.
5. *Folkestone, Hythe, Sandgate & Cheriton Herald*, 29 March 1913.
6. Reported in *The Common Cause*, 26 December 1913, p.717.
7. *Kent and Sussex Courier*, 21 March 1913, p.7.
8. *Kent and Sussex Courier*, 2 May 1913, p.5.
9. *Whitstable Times and Herne Bay Herald*, 22 March 1913.
10. *Kent and Sussex Courier*, 21 March 1913, p.8.
11. *Kent and Sussex Courier*, 28 March 1913, p.5.
12. Ibid.
13. *Folkestone, Hythe, Sandgate & Cheriton Herald*, 29 March 1913, p.10.
14. *The Suffragette*, 18 April 1913, p.452.
15. *Northampton Chronicle and Echo*, 11 April 1913.
16. *Sheffield Evening Telegraph*, 11 April 1913, p.5.
17. P.415.
18. *Whitstable Times and Herne Bay Herald*, 19 April 1913, p.3.
19. *Kent and Sussex Courier*, 2 May 1913, p.5.
20. *The Suffragette*, 18 April 1913, p.452.
21. *Diss Express*, 2 May 1913.
22. Ibid.
23. *Kent and Sussex Courier*, 2 May 1913, p.5.
24. Ibid.
25. Ibid.
26. Ibid.
27. *Kent and Sussex Courier*, 18 July 1913, p.3.
28. *Weekly Dispatch*, 13 April 1913.
29. *Kent & Sussex Courier*, 19 September 1913, p.2.
30. *Bucks Herald*, Saturday, 10 May 1913, p.7.

31. *Bromley Record*, July 1913, p.135.
32. *The Vote*, 18 July 1913, p.202.
33. Ibid.
34. *Kent & Sussex Courier*, 19 September 1913, p.2.
35. Ibid.
36. *The Suffragette*, 2 January 1914, p.271

Chapter 12

1. Sister of Charlotte Despard. She was a poor law guardian and honorary treasurer of the Midland Region of the National Union of Women's Suffrage Societies in 1910 and by 1913 the president of the NUWSS and chairman of the West Midland Federation.
2. President of Tunbridge Wells branch of the NUWSS.
3. *Kent & Sussex Courier*, 25 July 1913, p.11.
4. The NUWSS used its journal, *The Common Cause*, to give notes to new readers about the objects and methods of the union. Included in many and found in the 25 July 1913 edition (p.280) was reference to their official colours being red, white and green.
5. *The Common Cause*, 6 June 1913, front page.
6. *The Common Cause*, 6 June 1913, p.142.
7. *The Common Cause*, 20 June 1913, p.176.
8. *The Common Cause*, 4 July 1913, p.213.
9. 25 July 1913, p.11.
10. *The Common Cause*, 4 July 1913, p.213.
11. *The Common Cause*, 4 July 1913, p.215.
12. *The Common Cause*, 4 July 1913, p.211.
13. *Folkestone, Hythe, Sandgate & Cheriton Herald*, 19 July 1913, p.6.
14. *The Common Cause*, 20 June 1913, p.176.
15. *The Spectacle of Women: Imagery of the Suffrage Campaign, 1907–14*, Lisa Tickner (Chatto & Windus, 1987), pp.142–3. Source: Editions of *The Common Cause*, 1913.
16. *The Common Cause*, 27 June 1913.
17. *Dover Express*, 4 July 1913.
18. *The Common Cause*, 4 July 1913, p.211.
19. *The Common Cause*, 20 June 1913, p.175.

20. *The Common Cause*, 27 June, p.186.
21. *Dover Express*, 4 July 1913.
22. *Hastings and St Leonard's Observer*, 5 July 1913.
23. The author has found contradictions between reported dates. The accuracy of all these dates cannot therefore be verified at this stage.
24. *The Common Cause*, 25 July 1913, p.280.
25. *Votes for Women*, 25 July 1913, p.628.
26. *The Common Cause*, 25 July 1913, p.274. Used in a report of active hostility in Letchworth, Hertfordshire.
27. Open four-wheeled horse-drawn carriages.
28. *The Common Cause*, 11 July 1913, pp.235 & 236.
29. *The Common Cause*, 18 July 1913, p.256.
30. Unknown.
31. *Whitstable Times and Herne Bay Herald*, Saturday, 12 July 1913, p.8.
32. *The Common Cause*, 18 July 1913, p.256.
33. *The Common Cause*, 25 July 1913, p.281.
34. *The Common Cause*, 25 July 1913, p.278.
35. *The Common Cause*, 18 July 1913, p.258.
36. Ibid.
37. *The Common Cause*, 25 July 1913, p.278.
38. Cited in *The Common Cause*, 25 July 1913, p.281. Possible typo intended as 'Katherine' which is used everywhere else when referring to Miss Ward, or could be a different Miss Ward.
39. *The Common Cause*, 25 July 1913, p.281.
40. *The Common Cause*, 25 July 1913, p.278.
41. *Kent & Sussex Courier*, 18 July 1913, p.7.
42. *The Common Cause*, 18 July 1913, p.247.
43. *The Common Cause*, 18 July 1913, p.249.
44. *The Common Cause*, 18 July 1913, p.256.
45. *Folkestone, Hythe, Sandgate & Cheriton Herald*, 19 July 1913, p.9.
46. *The Common Cause*, 18 July 1913, p.256.
47. *Dover Express*, 11 July 1913, p.2.
48. *The Common Cause*, 18 July 1913, p.256.
49. Ibid.

50. *Folkestone, Hythe, Sandgate & Cheriton Herald*, 12 July 1913, p.5.
51. *The Common Cause*, 18 July 1913, p.256.
52. Ibid.
53. *The Dover Express*, 11 July 1913.
54. *The Dover Express*, 11 July 1913, p.2.
55. *The Common Cause*, 18 July 1913, p.256.
56. *Dover Express*, 18 July 1913, p.8.
57. Ibid.
58. Ibid.
59. *Dover Express*, 18 July 1913.
60. *The Common Cause*, 18 July 1913, p.278.
61. *Folkestone, Hythe, Sandgate & Cheriton Herald*, 19 July 1913, p.9.
62. Information found in letter to *Folkestone, Hythe, Sandgate & Cheriton Herald*, 26 July 1913, p.10.
63. *Folkestone, Hythe, Sandgate & Cheriton Herald*, 19 July 1913, p.9.
64. Ibid.
65. *The Common Cause*, 25 July 1913, p.278.
66. *Folkestone, Hythe, Sandgate & Cheriton Herald*, 26 July 1913, p.10.
67. Ibid.
68. *The Common Cause*, 25 July 1913, p.278.
69. *Folkestone, Hythe, Sandgate & Cheriton Herald*, 19 July 1913, p.9.
70. Ibid.
71. Ibid.
72. *The Common Cause*, 25 July 1913, p.278.
73. *Folkestone, Hythe, Sandgate & Cheriton Herald*, 19 July 1913, p.9.
74. Ibid.
75. Ibid.
76. *The Common Cause*, 25 July 1913, p.278.
77. Whilst it is reported in the *Folkestone, Hythe, Sandgate & Cheriton Herald*, 19 July 1913, page 9, that *Mrs* Cooke was present, it seems most likely that this was actually a misquote and was in fact *Miss* Geraldine Cooke.

78. *Folkestone, Hythe, Sandgate & Cheriton Herald*, 19 July 1913.
79. Whilst it is reported in the *Folkestone, Hythe, Sandgate & Cheriton Herald*, 19 July 1913, page 9, that *Mrs* Cooke was present, it seems most likely that this was actually a misquote and was in fact *Miss* Geraldine Cooke.
80. Ibid.
81. *The Common Cause*, 25 July 1913, p.278.
82. *Hastings and St Leonard's Observer*, 5 July 1913.
83. *Sevenoaks Chronicle and Kentish Advertiser*, 4 July 1913.
84. *The Common Cause*, 25 July 1913, p.281.
85. *Kent & Sussex Courier*, 11 July 1913, p.10.
86. Ibid.
87. *The Common Cause*, 25 July 1913, p.281.
88. *The Common Cause*, 4 July 1913, p.223 and *The Common Cause*, 25 July 1913, p.281.
89. *Kent & Sussex Courier*, 11 July 1913, p.9.
90. *Kent & Sussex Courier*, 25 July 1913, p.11.
91. Ibid.
92. Ibid.
93. Ibid.
94. Ibid.
95. Ibid.
96. Ibid.
97. Ibid.
98. Ibid.
99. Ibid.
100. Ibid.
101. Ibid.
102. Ibid.
103. *Kent & Sussex Courier*, Friday, 18 July 1913, p.2.
104. This specific time was included in the *Sevenoaks Chronicle and Kentish Advertiser* of Friday, 18 July 1913.
105. *Sevenoaks Chronicle and Kentish Advertiser*, Friday, 25 July 1913.
106. *Kent & Sussex Courier*, 25 July 1913, p.10.
107. *Sevenoaks Chronicle and Kentish Advertiser*, Friday, 25 July 1913.

108. Likely to have included some of the twelve new members enrolled at a meeting in Sevenoaks on 11 June 1913 when Fru Anker spoke. Cited in *The Common Cause*, 25 July 1913, p.281.
109. *Sevenoaks Chronicle and Kentish Advertiser*, Friday, 25 July 1913.
110. *Sevenoaks Chronicle and Kentish Advertiser*, 4 July 1913.
111. *Sevenoaks Chronicle and Kentish Advertiser*, Friday, 25 July 1913.
112. Ibid.
113. *Bromley Record*, September 1913, p.167.
114. *Borough News*, 1 August 1913.
115. Ibid.
116. *Bromley Record*, September 1913, p.167.
117. *Borough News*, 1 August 1913.
118. Ibid.
119. *Sevenoaks Chronicle and Kentish Advertiser*, Friday, 25 July 1913.
120. *The Common Cause*, 25 July 1913, p.279.
121. *The Common Cause*, 8 August 1913, p.315.
122. *The Common Cause*, 25 July 1913, p.282.
123. *The Globe*, 26 July 1913, front page.
124. *The Common Cause*, 1 August 1913, p.293, author cited as Wilma Meikle.
125. Letters exchanged between Mrs Fawcett and Asquith are in Box 89 of Fawcett Archives.
126. Letter sent 'To the Suffragist Ministers who received the deputation from the National Union of Women's Suffrage Societies' on 8 August 1913 (Fawcett Archives, Box 89).
127. *The Common Cause*, 13 June 1913.

Chapter 13

1. *The Vote*, 13 July 1913, p.107.
2. *The Vote*, 18 July 1913, p.202.
3. *The Vote*, Friday, 25 July 1913, p.218.
4. *The Vote*, 1 August 1913, p.232.

5. *The Vote*, 13 July 1913, p.107.
6. *The Vote*, 4 July 1913, p.159.
7. *Sheffield Daily Telegraph*, 10 June 1913, p.7.
8. *The Vote*, 4 July 1913, p.168.
9. Ibid.
10. Ibid.
11. *The Common Cause*, 28 March 1913, pp.873–74.
12. *Pall Mall Gazette*, 11 February 1914, p.5.
13. *Huddersfield Daily Examiner*, 11 February 1914.
14. *Newcastle Journal*, 12 February 1914, p.10.
15. *The Vote*, 11 July 1913, p.186.
16. *The Vote*, 28 August 1914, p.298.
17. *The Vote*, 18 July 1913, p.201.
18. *The Vote*, 1 August 1913, p.232.
19. *The Vote*, 8 August 1913, p.249.
20. Ibid.
21. *The Vote*, 18 July 1913, p.202.
22. *The Vote*, 8 August 1913, p.249.
23. Ibid.
24. Ibid.
25. Ibid.

Chapter 14

1. *The Suffragette*, 1 August 1913, p.715.
2. Ibid.
3. *The Suffragette*, 25 July 1913, p.706.
4. Ibid.
5. Ibid.
6. *Kent & Sussex Courier*, 1 August 1913, p.7.
7. *The Suffragette*, 1 August 1913, p.719.
8. Ibid.
9. Ibid.
10. *The Suffragette*, 25 July 1913, p.706.
11. Named in *The Suffragette*, 8 August 1913, p.739.
12. *Pall Mall Gazette*, 7 August 1913, p.4.
13. Ibid.

14. *Kent and Sussex Courier*, 15 August 1913, p.2.
15. *The Suffragette*, 15 August 1913, p.771.
16. *Hastings and St Leonard's Observer*, 30 August 1913.
17. *The Suffragette*, 29 August 1913, p.804.
18. *The Suffragette*, 15 August 1913, p.771.
19. Ibid.
20. *Kent and Sussex Courier*, 15 August 1913, p.2.
21. Ibid.
22. *The Suffragette*, 15 August 1913, p.771.
23. Ibid.
24. Ibid.
25. Ibid.
26. *Kent and Sussex Courier*, 15 August 1913, p.2.
27. *The Suffragette*, 22 August 1913, p.780.
28. *The Suffragette*, 22 August 1913, p.788.
29. Via *The Suffragette*, 29 August, p.807.
30. *The Suffragette*, 29 August 1913, p.805.

Chapter 15

1. *Sevenoaks Chronicle and Kentish Advertiser*, 8 March 1918, p.4.
2. *On Her Their Lives Depend: Munitions Workers in the Great War*, Angela Woollacott (University of California Press, 1994), p.193.
3. *Kent and Sussex Courier*, 14 August 1914, p.2.
4. *Kent and Sussex Courier*, 10 December 1915, p.5.
5. Ibid.
6. Quoted in *One Hand Tied Behind Us: The Rise of the Women's Suffrage Movement*, Jill Liddington and Jill Norris (Rivers Oram Press, 2000), but footnoted in there from Fawcett, M.G., *The Women's Victory and After*, p.133.
7. *Kent and Sussex Courier*, 21 June 1918, p.4.
8. *Kent and Sussex Courier*, 21 June 1918.
9. *Dover Express*, 20 December 1918, p.6.
10. *Kent and Sussex Courier*, 17 May 1918, p.6.
11. *Sussex Courier*, 20 December 1918, p.6.

12. Ibid.
13. *Kent & Sussex Courier*, 4 April 1919, p.7.
14. Ibid.
15. *Folkestone, Hythe, Sandgate & Cheriton Herald*, 21 December 1918, p.3.
16. Ibid.
17. Ibid.
18. *Sevenoaks Chronicle and Kentish Advertiser*, 8 March 1918, p.4.
19. *The Common Cause*, 18 July 1919, p.182.
20. Ibid.
21. Ibid.
22. *The Vote*, 2 May 1924, p.143.
23. *The Vote*, 29 June 1928, p.207.
24. *Folkestone, Hythe, Sandgate & Cheriton Herald*, 25 February 1928, p.2.
25. *The Vote*, 13 July 1928, p.222.
26. *The Vote*, 13 July 1928, p.223.
27. Ibid.
28. *The Vote*, 13 July 1928, pp.223–24.
29. *Kent & Sussex Courier*, 7 September 1928.
30. This term is used here to refer to all those involved in the campaign for women's suffrage.

Kent's Geography

1. *The Courier*, 1 January 1909.

Kent's Transport Links

1. *Thanet Advertiser*, 26 July 1884, p.2.
2. Timetable included in the *Whitstable Times and Herne Bay Herald*, 15 August 1908, p.6.
3. Canterbury and Whitstable Branch, connecting Canterbury with Blean Halt.
4. Doubling from 1905 to 1906 from 1,305 to 2,456 respectively; then rising by 400 to 800 every year to 5,133 in 1910 and by

1,000 to 2,000 a year to 11,738 in 1914. Taken from *History of the Kent County Council, 1889–1974*, prepared by Elizabeth Melling, B.A., Assistant County Archivist (Printed by Kent County Council, 1975).

Kent's Population

1. *Whitstable Times and Herne Bay Herald*, 17 August 1912, p.2.

Education in Kent

1. *Mid-Victorian Tonbridge*, edited by C.W. Chalklin, Kent County Council (no date), p.7.
2. *History of the Kent County Council, 1889–1974*, prepared by Elizabeth Melling, B.A., Assistant County Archivist (Printed by Kent County Council, 1975), p.21.
3. *Sevenoaks Chronicle and Kentish Advertiser*, 13 July 1906.
4. From this it appears that the author meant 'life after school', i.e. skills for life.
5. *Folkestone, Hythe, Sandgate & Cheriton Herald*, 12 June 1909, p.5.
6. Ibid.
7. Meaning 'fearless persons'.
8. *Folkestone, Hythe, Sandgate & Cheriton Herald*, 12 June 1909, p.5.

Communications in Kent

1. *Late Victorian & Edwardian Tonbridge*, edited by C.W. Chalkin (Kent County Council, 1988), p.17.
2. The *Free Press* (Tonbridge), 24 November 1877.

Index